LOST IN TRANSMISSION

LOST IN TRANSMISSION

Studies of Trauma Across Generations

Edited by

M. Gerard Fromm

KARNAC

First published in 2012 by
Karnac Books Ltd
118 Finchley Road, London NW3 5HT

British Library Cataloguing in Publication Data

A C.I.P. for this book is available from the British Library

ISBN 978 1 85575 864 3

Edited, designed and produced by The Studio Publishing Services Ltd
www.publishingservicesuk.co.uk
e-mail: studio@publishingservicesuk.co.uk

www.karnacbooks.com

CONTENTS

To Trey, Kai, Leo, and Eliza

In the hope that all transmissions are wonderful
And those that aren't, become meaningful

ACKNOWLEDGEMENTS AND PERMISSIONS

A few of the chapters that follow have been previously published elsewhere. I am grateful to the publishers for their permission to include them in this volume.

Wiley-Blackwell Publishing has authorized the republication of Ilany Kogan's chapter, which was originally titled "Working with psychotic and non-psychotic patients in situations of terror and military dictatorships: Report of Panel held at the 43rd Congress of the IPA, New Orleans", first published in the *International Journal of Psychoanalysis*, 2004, *85*: 1247–1249. It was then collected in the author's 2007 book, *The Struggle Against Mourning*, under the title, "Working with sons and daughters of Holocaust survivors in the shadow of terror", published by Jason Aronson.

Dori Laub's chapter was originally published under the same title in *Contemporary Psychoanalysis*, 2005, *41*: 307–326. My chapter (Chapter Seven) was originally published in 2006 in the *Journal of the American Academy of Psychoanalysis and Dynamic Psychiatry*, *34*: 445–458, under the title, "A view from Riggs: Treatment resistance and patient authority—II. Transmission of trauma and treatment resistance". I am grateful to the editor, Dr Douglas Ingram for his permission to republish this article, which will also be included in the forthcoming volume,

Treatment Resistance and Patient Authority: The Austen Riggs Reader, edited by Dr Eric Plakun, published by Norton, who also grants permission for it to appear in this volume.

Material from Vera Muller-Paisner's chapter was expanded into the volume, *Broken Chain*, published by Pitchstone Publishing in 2005. I am grateful to Kurt Volkan, Pitchstone's founder and editor, for his permission to include related material in the present volume.

I am greatly indebted to Vamik Volkan, MD, Senior Erikson Scholar at Austen Riggs, for suggesting, inspiring, and contributing in so many ways to this book. I am also very grateful to Lee Watroba, Executive Assistant of the Erikson Institute, for her patience, deadlines, diligence, and endless good humour. Finally, I owe special thanks to Maryjane Fromm, whose encouragement, counsel, and deep support are an ongoing gift.

Permissions summary

M. *Gerard Fromm*
"A view from Riggs: Treatment resistance and patient authority—II Transmission of trauma and treatment resistance"
Guilford Press

Ilany Kogan
"Working with psychotic and non-psychotic patients in situations of terror and military dictatorships. Report of panel held at forty-third congress of the IPA New Orleans
Wiley Publishing

"Working with sons and daughters of Holocaust survivors in the shadow of terror"
Jason Aronson Press

Dori Laub
"Traumatic shutdown of narrative and symbolization: A death instinct derivative"
Contemporary Psychoanalysis

Barri Belnap, MD, is a psychiatrist and psychotherapist on the medical staff of the Austen Riggs Center, where she oversees psychopharmacology, and, with David Mintz, MD, defined the discipline of psychodynamic psychopharmacology in various writings and presentations. Her interest in the treatment of psychotic conditions has led to presentations at the Lacanian Clinical Forum and the Casus Belli conferences.

Françoise Davoine, PhD, and her husband, Jean-Max Gaudilliere, PhD, are psychoanalysts practising in Paris, where they have worked for many years with traumatized and psychotic patients. On the faculty of the Ecole des Hautes Etudes en Sciences Sociales, where they lead a yearly interdisciplinary seminar on "Madness and the social link," they are the authors of *History Beyond Trauma*.

Virginia Demos, EdD, is a staff psychologist at the Austen Riggs Center. Editor of a volume on Silvan Tomkins entitled *Exploring Affect*, she has authored many articles on affective development in infancy and is currently working on a book integrating her clinical work with her work on infancy, affect, and motivational theory.

M. Gerard Fromm, PhD, is the Evelyn Stefansson Nef Director of the Erikson Institute for Education and Research at the Austen Riggs Center. On the faculties of the Massachusetts Institute for Psychoanalysis, the Berkshire Psychoanalytic Institute, Harvard Medical School, and the Yale Child Study Center, he is co-editor, with Bruce L. Smith, PhD, of *The Facilitating Environment: Clinical Applications of Winnicott's Theory*.

Kevin Kelly, MD, is a practising psychoanalyst in New York City, as well as Clinical Associate Professor of Psychiatry and Director of the Communication Skills Curriculum at Weill Cornell Medical College, and Lecturer in Psychoanalysis at Columbia University. He is also a Medical Officer in the Fire Department of New York and past President of the NY Celtic Medical Society.

Ilany Kogan, MA, is a training analyst at the Israel Psychoanalytic Society. She is a clinical supervisor, teacher, and adviser in training institutions throughout Germany as well as in Romania and Turkey. She has worked with, and written extensively about, Holocaust survivors' offspring, as well as those of perpetrators. She received the Elise M. Hayman Award for the study of the Holocaust and Genocide. Her books include *The Cry of Mute Children, The Struggle Against Mourning*, and *Escape from Selfhood*.

Dori Laub, MD, is a practising psychoanalyst in New Haven, Connecticut; Clinical Professor of Psychiatry at the Yale University School of Medicine; Co-Founder of the Fortunoff Video Archive for Holocaust Testimonies; and Deputy Director for Trauma Studies for Yale's Genocide Studies Program. He has published on the topic of psychic trauma in a variety of psychoanalytic journals and has co-authored, with Shoshana Felman, *Testimony: Crises of Witnessing in Literature, Psychoanalysis, and History*.

Peter Loewenberg, PhD, is a training and supervising analyst and former Dean of the New Center for Psychoanalysis in Los Angeles. He is Professor of History and Political Psychology at UCLA and author of many articles and books, including *Decoding the Past: The Psychohistorical Approach* and *Fantasy and Reality in History*. He received the Nevitt Sanford Award for his professional contributions to the field of

Political Psychology in 2010, chairs the International Psychoanalytical Association's China Committee and is the editor (with Nellie Thompson) of *100 Years of the IPA*.

Vera Muller-Paisner is a psychoanalyst and former research consultant for the International Study Group for Trauma, Violence and Genocide at Yale University, where she had an appointment in the Department of Psychiatry. From 1997 to 1999, her long-standing interest in the transmission of trauma across generations and cultures led to her work as Director of Training and Principal Investigator of a project in Warsaw, Poland, called "Broken Chain".

Howard Stein, PhD, a psychoanalytic, medical and organizational anthropologist, is Professor and Special Assistant to the Chair in the Department of Family and Preventive Medicine, University of Oklahoma Health Sciences Center in Oklahoma City, where he has taught since 1978. He is author or editor of twenty-six books, including *Nothing Personal, Just Business* (2001) and, more recently, *Insight and Imagination* (2007), and the author of over 250 articles and chapters, many of which deal with organizational trauma.

Vamik Volkan, MD, is an Emeritus Professor of Psychiatry at the University of Virginia, Senior Erikson Scholar at the Erikson Institute, and Emeritus Training and Supervising Analyst at the Washington Psychoanalytic Institute. He received the Sigmund Freud Award from the city of Vienna and is the author or co-author of forty books and the editor or co-editor of ten more. Dr Volkan was nominated for the Nobel Peace Prize for examining conflicts between opposing large groups, carrying out projects in various troubled spots in the world for thirty years, and developing psychopolitical theories arising from his fieldwork and observations.

Introduction

M. Gerard Fromm

For two consecutive autumns, the Erikson Institute organized its Fall Conferences around the theme, "Lost in transmission: a study of trauma across generations". The Institute is the education and research arm of the Austen Riggs Center, a small psychiatric hospital in Stockbridge, Massachusetts, where quite troubled patients are treated with intensive psychotherapy in an open therapeutic community setting. This unusual programme allows us access to many aspects of our patients' lives, including the opportunity to hear, in some depth, about their parents and grandparents. Thus, we come to feel the unfolding generational narrative our patients are intimately, and generally unconsciously, a part of.

It was not lost on us that Halloween followed soon after our Fall Conferences: All Hallow's Eve, the night before All Saints Day and the Day of the Dead. The ancient Celtic origins of Halloween hold that on this last night of their year, witches and evil spirits roam the world, ghosts not yet contained by death, mourning, and sanctification, or by mother earth and inscription on a tombstone. Americans spend an enormous amount of money on Halloween, second only to that spent on Christmas and far more than on any other holiday. But what are we doing on Halloween? Might we be enacting, unconsciously and collectively, a ritual in the service of protecting society, a ritual in which we dress our children up in frightening masks and invite them to play "trick or treat" with us. In other words, are we costuming the next generation in the dangerous, split-off, and unburied images of a preceding generation and having them say to us: "Treat us well or *they* will come back through us." The drama of Halloween might have always cautioned us about the intergenerational transmission of trauma, and the presentations in these two conferences suggested that we would do well to heed its warning.

Some of those presentations are collected in this volume along with other invited papers on this topic. They build upon the idea that what human beings cannot contain of their experience—what has been traumatically overwhelming, unbearable, unthinkable—falls out of social discourse, but very often on to and into the next generation as an affective sensitivity or a chaotic urgency. The word "symptom" comes from the Greek and means "to fall together", and the fallout of trauma from one generation to the next is one aspect of our study. But the Greek root of the word "symbol" means "to throw together" and carries a more active connotation (Balmary, 1979). As Freud suggested, what appears at first to be a person's symptom might turn out to be a symbol; in the context of this book, a symbol of an unconscious mission assigned by the preceding generation. The transmission of trauma can be the transmission of a task: for example, the task of repairing a parent or avenging a humiliation.

A number of years ago on a visit to my mother, I recognized the melody she was absentmindedly humming to herself. It was a Joan Baez song that I had played many times during a summer when I was in college. I doubt that she had heard it in the intervening twenty-five years. The name of the song was "I Still Miss Someone", and a central, recurrent line was "I never got over those blue eyes". My mother's first baby was the only one of her children with blue eyes. She died at two weeks of age. When I was born eighteen months later, my mother gave me her obstetrician's name, which was also that of an important saint—St Gerard, the patron saint of pregnant women.

In retrospect, it seems to me that I was given a mission born of trauma: my pre-natal identity, so to speak. That I could cure my mother simply by thriving contributed to an easy confidence that, for example, the Muse will show up in time for me to meet my writing deadlines, but it has also made me vulnerable to the range of feelings involved in realizing that all cures are not so easy. And, of course, even after my arrival, my mother "still missed someone". I found myself at that musical and analytic moment with two feelings: (1) that lightning had struck and had suddenly illuminated my entire life, and (2) that I was sorry for her loss, glad that she could sing it, glad that I had given this song to her, and moved that she and I could now both let it be.

The kind of task I am describing can be more or less idiosyncratic to a given family suffering its own personal trauma, or it can be collective in response to societal trauma. In December 2001, three months after 9/11, *The New York Times* reported the following comment by Maurice De Witt, a sidewalk Santa at Rockefeller Center on Fifth Avenue, about a change in attitude he noticed that holiday season.

"The normality is not there. The parents will not let the hands of their children go. The kids sense that. It's like water seeping down, and the kids can feel it. Their reactions to Santa are not natural. There is an anxiety, but the kids can't make the connections." [Leduff, 2001]

This astute man was noticing a powerful double message in the parent's action. Consciously and verbally, the message was "Here's Santa. Love him." Unconsciously and physically, it was "Here's Santa. Fear him." The unnamed trauma of 9/11 was communicated to the next generation by the squeeze of a hand, and it took someone outside the twosome, perhaps someone in the position of the Third (Muller, 1996), like this Santa, to see and name the trouble. Erik Erikson (1959) noticed similar phenomena. He wrote about "the subtler methods by which children are induced to accept . . . prototypes of good and evil" (p. 27); the way that "minute displays of emotion", including "minute socioeconomic and cultural panics", "transmit to the human child the outlines of what really counts" (p. 28). "Every neurosis," he says, is "somatic tension, isolated anxiety, and *shared* panic, all at once" (p. 28).

The story of the sidewalk Santa is a story about anxiety falling from one generation to the next, but it would not be too great a step to consider the possibility of a given child's being nominated to carry and represent an anxiety on the parents' behalf. To the degree that the child does so, the rest of the family might feel more free to let difficult feelings sink below their own consciousness. The task of transmission might sometimes have to do with one generation's cultivating a sensitivity in the next, so that it can warn about, or perhaps even take on the responsibility for, the ways in which the present is shaping itself into a nightmare from the past.

An Eriksonian example of a more poignant sort comes from Sue Erikson Bloland's book, *In The Shadow of Fame* (2005). After describing her parents' first meeting at a glamorous masked ball in Vienna, she writes:

> It was almost uncanny the way my parents' early experiences had prepared them to connect with each other as adults: Dad had never known his biological father. Mother had hardly known hers. They had both experienced crushing parental disapproval and had felt estranged from families and peers. Both had felt like misfits in the social worlds in which they had grown up. Yet each of my parents had also been admired and championed by one all-important adult: Dad by his mother, Karla; and Mother by her grandmother, Nama . . . [p. 67]

> (E)ach of my parents fulfilled the denied ambitions of their mothers . . . [P]rior to Karla's marriage to Theodor, she had chosen for herself a bohemian lifestyle . . . Although she chose social conformity over the pursuit of youthful interests, she clearly invested Dad with the task of fulfilling her own secret longings as an intellectual . . . [p. 69]

> Mom's mother, Mary, seems to have been thwarted in all her efforts to find fulfillment in life—inhibited, it seems, by both a need for conformity and a pervasive fearfulness. Mary fought hard against Mother's rebellious spirit, but Mother always suspected that behind that disapproval was a secret envy of Mother's willingness to flout convention and to explore the world so fearlessly . . .

> Mother's mission to inspire and heal others seems to have had its origins in her response to the fearful and depressive Mary, whom Mother cared for when she was injured or ill . . . [pp. 69–70]

> My parents both had troubled mothers whom they longed to heal, which surely had some bearing on their mutual commitment to the healing arts. They both felt oppressed by their parents' anxious conformity to social convention and needed to affirm themselves by defying that convention. And, just as important, I believe, they had both relied heavily on a sense of being special . . . (T)heir mission as healers was infused with a rebellious spirit and with an undeniable sense of grandiosity. [p. 70]

Sue Bloland then describes how this remarkably successful and productive effort to transform childhood trauma was tragically challenged in adult life. When Sue was five years old, a son was born to the Eriksons. His name was Neil, and he suffered from Down's Syndrome. The doctors gave him only a year or two to live and, consistent with the medical opinion of the time, recommended his immediate institutionalization in order that he receive the care he would need. With his wife anesthetized for post-childbirth surgery, Erik felt forced to make a critical decision alone, something he never felt able to do without his wife. The advice of close colleagues was to accept the doctors' recommendation and to do so immediately, before Joan could bond with the baby. He followed this guidance, telling his children that Neil had died at birth. Thus began a family tragedy of depression, suppressed rage, guilt, and shame co-existing uneasily with great accomplishment and public adulation. Bloland writes:

> My brothers and I had been told that Neil had died. But there was no burial, no ritual, no ceremony to mark his existence or his passing from our lives. Our parents didn't seem to grieve so much as they threw themselves into frenetic activity in an attempt to assuage their pain. . . . Worst of all for their relationship and for the family, they never talked about Neil—with each other or with us. [p. 25]

There seems to be an almost inevitable outcome to traumatic experience cut out of social discourse; the next generation must deal with it and sometimes even represent it. Bloland reflects on her own experience as a child:

> I embarrassed them all. . . . In an odd way, it seems I took on the role of Neil. I was the child who was somehow unable to function normally in a family in which the appearance of normality was of the utmost importance. I did not conceal the anguish that pervaded our family life. [p. 30]

There is such painful irony in the transmission of trauma. Erik Erikson, the illegitimate son of an abandoning father, fathers a defective, in a sense illegitimate, son whom he abandons. He suffers all his life from the secret of his own paternity and creates a secret paternity for his children. Joan, the daughter of a mother who breaks down into a depression so severe that she sends her children to be cared for by relatives in California, becomes deeply depressed and uncharacteristically passive after Neil's birth, and leaves him—and perhaps this part of herself—in care in California. Such is the deep resonance of generational trauma.

But, perhaps, there is another kind of irony in this story as well. Sue felt the dissociating forces in her family whenever emotional painful topics were approached. And she often complied with this dynamic, as though sparing her parents *her* transmitting the traumatic affects back to them.

> It left me with a pervasive fear of opening my parents' wounds and seeing the anguish on their faces that any reference to a painful issue might suddenly evoke. I dreaded the abrupt sense of disconnection from them that inevitably followed. [p. 37]

But she also, without fully realizing it, kept Neil alive. Years later, in analysis, she had a dream in which she had the facial features of a Mongolian. In a sense, through a deep identification with her brother, part of Sue Bloland had been "lost in the transmission" of her family's tragedy, until her analyst hears the dream reference to Neil. Reclaiming herself, Sue Bloland also reclaimed the full story of her family, including of the brother she actually buried, upon his death at age twenty-one, without ever knowing him.

For clinicians attuned to the transmission of trauma, one sees its operation and its effects with great frequency. In a recent clinical case conference, a young male patient told the staff that the hospital "is haunted by the forces of the dead. They are here as much as there are helping people here." The great Spanish film director, Luis Bunuel, once commented that the artist provides for society "an essential margin of alertness." Perhaps, people whose sensitivities eventually develop into serious vulnerability, leading them toward breakdown and patienthood, are sometimes doing something similar, that is, providing a chaotic and often bizarre alertness to affects and events from the past that are nevertheless part of the here and now. To the degree that this process must remain at an unconscious level, a crucial part of a person's subjectivity is "lost in transmission". As with Sue Bloland for the Erikson family, this experience of being lost, of being haunted and of haunting, might, if things go well, be transformed into deep discovery for oneself and for others.

The frame of reference in these chapters has to do with the truly traumatic, that which cannot be contained by one generation, and necessarily, and largely unconsciously, plays itself out through the next generation. We are, therefore, not talking about "blaming the parents". Sometimes today, advances in the genetic and biological study of mental illness seem reflexively used in our culture as a social defence against parental guilt. And the economic imperatives of current American life might actually make for enormous guilt in parents about what they can or cannot do for and with their children. But the topic of this volume is not "bad parenting". We are talking about something more complicated, more forgiving, and also more frightening: trauma, and a family's effort over time—in a way out of their awareness and out of their control—to deal with it. Freud spoke about the family's "archaic heritage" (1939a, p. 98); one task of trans-mission might be to resist the dissociation of that heritage and to bring its full, tragic story into social discourse.

The chapters that follow attempt to address the heritage of trauma, and to do so from both clinical and societal perspectives. The first chapters consider aspects of the legacy of the Holocaust, the study of which, through the experience of the children of those who survived it, broke ground for the new field of transmission studies. The next chapters look inside the consulting room and examine the transmis-sion of trauma in more ordinary clinical practice, trauma that is some-times personal to a family and sometimes a reverberation of what some theorists have called "the big history" (Davoine & Gaudilliere, 2004). The final chapters offer reflections on the theme of transmission from the angle of more recent, large-scale traumatic experiences within American society.

References

Balmary, M. (1979). *Psychoanalyzing Psychoanalysis*. Baltimore, MD: Johns Hopkins University Press.

Davoine, F., & Gaudilliere, J-M. (2004). *History Beyond Trauma*. New York: Other Press.

Freud, S. (1939a). *Moses and Monotheism. S.E., 23*: 3–137. London: Hogarth.

Leduff, C. (2001). A bleaker Santa's-eye view: bell-ringer sees more anxi-ety and less giving. *The New York Times*, 5 December.

PART I
SHADOWS OF THE HOLOCAUST

Introduction

The field of transmission studies, within the larger category of trauma studies, exploded in the 1970s with attention to the suffering and family dynamics of second-generation Holocaust survivors, those who had grown up with, and taken in psychically, the parental generation that encountered what Lacan calls the Real and Ilany Kogan calls "the cataclysmic event which changed the shape of human history forever".

Kogan's chapter lays out the emotional scenario for those children who identify deeply with their parents' damage as well as those who seem to have had their parents' images of people, events, and the world deposited forcefully within them. She asks what happens when these children face traumatic events in their current lives and illustrates her answer with two moving clinical vignettes. Powerful themes of joining with the damaged other, healing them, or assuaging the guilt for not doing so, and for surviving when they have not, come through clearly, as does the profound confusion between past and present, and inner and outer, with which such people struggle when they face present-day trauma.

Profound confusion—the sense of being completely lost—is also a theme in Vera Muller-Paisner's chapter: confusion as a consequence of trauma to the sense of identity one has grown up with. She tells the story—many stories really—of Polish Jews who did not know they were Jewish and spent their lives growing up as Catholics, one of them even becoming a priest. The impact on their sense of themselves and the relationship dilemmas that follow are described poignantly. But side by side with the sudden shock of this deeply unsettling information is the theme of secrets and the sense that something was being held back all along. This double awareness—the simultaneous sense of knowing and not knowing—is another aspect of the experience of trauma transmission.

Dori Laub's chapter returns us to the impact of past trauma on current events, but this time in the coincidence of trauma, within the clinical setting, for patient, analyst, and supervisor. Building especially on Green's work, he offers a rich description, both theoretical and clinical, of the way in which trauma destroys the capacity to cognize, symbolize, and remember, creating a "hole" in the psyche, which is responded to by others, particularly in the next generation. His discussion of the death instinct—a controversial and ill-defined concept within psychoanalysis—is linked compellingly to the effects of trauma in both victims and perpetrators and to the destruction of the internalized good object, what Laub tenderly calls the "inner thou", the ongoing dialogue with whom is the wellspring of our functioning and humanity.

Peter Loewenberg closes this section of the book by returning us to Freud's original description of psychic trauma, a discovery made in the face of the emotional casualties of the First World War. In experience-near terms, Loewenberg lists several clinical characteristics, which specify the suffering, but also the adaptation, of the next generation, and shows us how the unspeakable of history erupts as pure anxiety. He then takes us to the story of his own family, bringing both empathy and wisdom to these reminiscences. His reflections warn us strongly about the terrible irony in the transmission of trauma: that the victimized often reverse their traumatic helplessness by becoming victimizers, thus continuing the cycle of trauma. But he also holds out hope for the breaking of the cycle, as one generation could get hold of the legacy it has received, translate that transmission into narrative, grieve its effects, and open a reparative future.

CHAPTER ONE

The second generation in the shadow of terror

Ilany Kogan

Introduction

I n his book *Persistent Shadows of the Holocaust: the Meaning to Those Not Directly Affected*, Moses (1993) describes the Holocaust as an unprecedented, systematic attempt to achieve "racial purity" through the extermination of innocent people. Reduced in the eyes of their persecutors to the lowest form of life, entire peoples—as well as homosexuals and the physically and mentally deformed—were regarded as a threat to the "Aryan race"; as invaders of the "Aryan body," they were to be totally and completely annihilated in order to purge the German genetic pool of their taint. Thus, the Nazi's "Final Solution" represented an utter and total debasement and dehumanization of some groups of people by another group, a cataclysmic event which changed the shape of human history forever.

The trauma of the Holocaust is often transmitted to, and absorbed by, the children of survivors. The psychoanalytic literature on the offspring of Holocaust survivors states that the Holocaust is transmitted to them through early, unconscious identifications which carry in their wake the parents' perception of an everlasting, life-threatening inner and outer reality (Axelrod, Schnipper, & Rau, 1978; Barocas &

Barocas, 1973; Kestenberg, 1972; Klein, 1971; Laufer, 1973; Lipkowitz, 1973; Rakoff, 1966; Sonnenberg, 1974). These children, whose minds have been impregnated with mental representations of the atrocities of the Holocaust deposited by their parents, carry within themselves powerful feelings of loss and humiliation, guilt and aggression. They often feel compelled to enact the parents' suppressed traumas, thereby echoing their parents' inner world (Auerhahn & Laub, 1984).

"Enactment", putting into action, is a non-verbal behaviour, which reflects what occurs between patient and therapist in the analytic situation, with the emphasis on the way the analyst participates in the process. This might be compared to "acting out" and "acting in". "Acting out" is the attempt to avoid painful knowledge in treatment by means of acting instead of remembering and communicating. "Acting in" is defined as acting in the transference; it might be the only way available to the patient to relive an experience and to convey it to the therapist.

In the context of the Holocaust, I view "enactment" as a general term that includes some of the attributes of both "acting out" and "acting in". In this sense, "enactment" can serve the purpose of avoiding painful knowledge and memory (similar to the objective of "acting out") while, at the same time, it is the only way available to the patient to relive an inner experience (as in the process of "acting in"). This use of "enactment" differs from that of analysts who primarily stress its interactive aspects. These analysts believe that enactment (or "actualization," as it is termed by Sandler and Sandler, 1978) reflects what occurs in the relationship between patient and analyst and the analyst's part in the process (Chused, 1991; Jacobs, 1986, 2000; McLaughlin, 1992; Renik, 1993; Schafer, 1982). I define "enactment" as the compulsion of Holocaust survivors' offspring to recreate their parents' experiences in their own lives through concrete acts. Thus, "enactment" is the externalization of traumatic themes from the past, and not what occurs in the relationship between patient and analyst in the analytic situation (Kogan, 2002).

I will describe in brief the two mechanisms by which the transgenerational transmission of historical trauma occurs: "primitive identification" (Freyberg, 1980; Grubrich-Simitis, 1984a,b; Kogan, 1995, 1998, 2002, 2007a,b; Kogan & Schneider, 2002) and "deposited representation" (Volkan, 1987a, p. 73). "Primitive identification" refers to the child's unconscious introjection and assimilation of the damaged parent's self-images through interactions with that parent. This process is an attempt to heal the parent and help him recover. This identification leads to a loss of the child's separate sense of self and to an inability to differentiate between the self and the damaged parent. (I find this phenomenon similar to the identification which takes place in pathological mourning, which Freud (1917e) describes as a process whereby the mourner attempts to possess the object by becoming the object itself, rather than bearing a resemblance to it. This occurs when the mourner renounces the object, at the same time preserving it in a cannibalistic manner (Green, 1986; Grinberg & Grinberg, 1974). It is this type of identification that is at the core of the offspring's inability to achieve self-differentiation and build a life of his or her own.)

"Deposited representation" is a concept that emphasizes the role of the parent, who unconsciously, and sometimes even consciously, forces aspects of himself on to the child. By doing so, the parent affects the child's sense of identity and gives the child certain specific tasks to perform. In these cases, the children become the reservoirs for deposited images connected to the trauma, which often initiate unconscious fantasies linked to it. The children are compelled to deal with the shame, rage, helplessness, and guilt that the parents have been unable to work through for themselves (Volkan, 2002).

The question I wish to address here is what happens when children whose Holocaust-survivor parents have undergone victimization, actual abuse, and humiliation encounter traumatic reality in the present? What is the impact of this external reality on their inner life, their perception of reality and their defences?

Life-threatening reality does not reactivate only a simple recollection of traumatic events, but it also reactivates in the children the mental representation of the Holocaust that they share with their parents. These include real events of a traumatic nature, conscious and unconscious fantasies regarding these events, intense feelings of mourning and guilt, and defences against unacceptable feelings such as shame, guilt, or aggression (Kogan, 2003; Moses, 1993; Roth, 1993).

I will now present clinical vignettes from two cases in which the life-threatening situation of the *Intifada* in Israel reactivated mental representations of the Holocaust and had an impact on their perception of reality, reinforcing their manic defences.

The case of Daphna

Daphna, a forty-six-year-old high-school teacher, married and the mother of a sixteen-year-old boy, was a member of a small group of extreme leftists who strongly advocated the pro-Palestinian position. Not only did she participate in the big peace demonstrations organized by Israel's left-wing parties, but she also stood at crossroads together with several other women, holding up signs that promoted their pro-Palestinian views. These signs often evoked furious reactions from passersby, many of whom responded by shouting angrily at the demonstrators. These angry reactions never deterred Daphna from what she was doing. On the contrary, they increased her emotional excitement and the importance of these demonstrations for her.

Daphna was the daughter of a Holocaust survivor father and a mother who arrived in Israel with her parents before the Second World War. Her father's parents and siblings were taken to Auschwitz, where they were gassed and their bodies cremated in the ovens. Daphna's mother had suffered from depression throughout her life, which worsened with age. Her psychic situation deteriorated after the birth of Daphna, the younger of two children.

Daphna remembered her mother as a sad, passive, very silent woman, who had difficulties in coping with the simple chores of life. "I grew up with a shadow," said Daphna about her mother. Daphna's parents lived in a little village. From the time she was a baby, Daphna lived in a children's home, together with the other children. She was told that after her birth her mother had become so depressed that she would sometimes forget to feed her. When this was discovered, other women took charge of her.

When Daphna was nine years old, the family moved to the USA for a period of three years. Her mother had a very bad reaction to leaving Israel, where she had led a sheltered life and where her children had been cared for. Daphna remembered that during this period her mother would lie in bed for days on end, unable to buy food or cook for her family, never responding to teachers' requests to discuss the problems the child was having in school. Father took care of these matters, and Daphna learned to live with a depressed, psychically dead mother.

Upon their return to Israel, Daphna was placed in a boarding school, where she began to thrive. She was a good student, had many friends, and led the life of a normal adolescent.

When Daphna was thirteen, her mother committed suicide. Father was the one who found her burnt corpse near the oven, and an empty bottle of pills which she had apparently swallowed before putting her head inside the oven (it was an old-fashioned gas oven with an open flame). It was never clear whether the mother had died from gas inhalation or from the flames that consumed her body after she had poured gasoline over herself. Daphna was shocked and horrified by this terrible event.

Nobody talked with Daphna about what happened; her father never mourned his wife. Daphna knew that the shocking death of her mother must have reminded him of his lost relatives who died in the gas chambers. After about two years, he was hospitalized because of a psychotic depression. Daphna visited him regularly in the hospital and was terribly ashamed of the way he looked and behaved.

After the initial shock, Daphna made a conscious decision to get on with her life. She studied and worked, and married a man she did not love, out of fear that she would remain an old maid. She gave birth to her first child, a boy. Throughout her life, Daphna was plagued by terrible headaches and periodic depressions. She encountered great difficulties in raising her son, and, in spite of giving him love and care, she sometimes lost her temper and became violent, a fact which tormented her deeply and aroused feelings of guilt. Daphna was in therapy for a period of ten years, at the end of which her therapist developed a terminal illness.

Daphna sought analysis two years ago, when her older brother, at the age of fifty-one, became ill and was hospitalized in a mental institution because of a mental breakdown. Concerned that she, like her older brother, might suffer a psychotic breakdown at the fatal age of fifty-one (the age at which her mother had committed suicide), Daphna decided to seek analytic treatment.

I will not describe our painful analytic journey over the last three years. Instead, I will examine Daphna's reaction to the life-threatening situation in Israel over the last few years as revealed in analysis. I will illustrate this with a vignette from one of our sessions:

D (Daphna): There are so many terrorist attacks. I am so angry about it. I feel like another Holocaust is descending on us.

We were silent for some moments.

D (continuing): There is a story about a frog. A frog is insensitive to differences in temperature. So, if you slowly warm up water to boil the frog, it will not jump out of it, because it does not feel the danger. This happened to the Jewish people in the past. Those who did not run away from the Holocaust, look what happened to them, they all got cooked in the oven. It's the same with us now. We don't pay attention to what's going on until the situation gets really bad.

I was frightened by Daphna's words. Perhaps she is right, I thought to myself. Nobody knows what the future will bring upon us. Then, my thoughts turned to Daphna's tragic mother, who had put her head in an oven, possibly choosing to concretely follow the fate of her relatives who had been gassed and cremated in Auschwitz. Was the mother the "frog who was insensitive to pain", I asked myself, or was her psychic pain so overwhelming that she destroyed herself in order to get rid of it?

Further on, we delved into Daphna's fantasies regarding the political demonstrations that she participated in at crossroads. We discovered that Daphna was not reacting to external reality only out of political conviction and striving for peace, but she was also reacting to an internal world full of fear and feelings of guilt.

D: You know, yesterday I was demonstrating together with other women against the occupation of the territories. When I took part in these demonstrations in the past, people threw tomatoes at us or cursed us. I heard that women who demonstrated were beaten and needed hospitalization. I thought, with the level of violence being so high, there are people who might shoot us. I feel like the Jews at the beginning of the Nazi era, when they were persecuted in the streets.

What a mixture of past and present, I thought to myself. Apparently, Daphna felt that she lived back at the beginning of the Nazi era and that her persecutors were after her.

D (after some moments of silence): I feel I do not have the right to live a life of my own, that I have to be punished. Like religious people, I also say to God: "I am paying my dues, I demonstrate against the war every Friday at noon, every Saturday night, you should have mercy on me."

I (Ilany): What do you feel you should be punished for?

D: I don't know. It has to do with my mother. How could I never have noticed what was going to happen to her? I was so preoccupied with the stupid things of adolescence. I wasn't really concerned with her well-being. You know, when I came home for visits from the boarding school before she killed herself, she always wanted to hug me and kiss me. I didn't want her to do that; I rejected her. I wasn't a baby any more, and she never did that when I was a child. Suddenly she wanted to hug me all the time; is it possible that she needed my embrace and I wasn't aware of it? And what about my father? I knew that all his relatives perished in the ovens, and now mother perished in the same way. He could not survive that. I knew it, but I could not save him. How can I allow myself to live a normal life in Israel when life is so crazy!

From this short vignette we can see that, by participating in demonstrations, Daphna on a conscious level was fighting for pacifist ideas, while unconsciously she was trying to mitigate the tremendous burden of guilt she felt toward her parents.

Daphna transferred the guilt-ridden relationship with her mother and father to her son and this relationship became another source of torment for her. Daphna perceived herself as a hungry, needy person who destroyed all those who became close to her—her parents, her son, her former therapist, as well as myself in analysis. I will illustrate this by the following excerpt from a session:

D: Sometimes I think I don't want Benny to go to the army. I am forty-eight and he is eighteen; it is the end of my life. Sometimes I think about my ambivalence toward him, maybe I want him to die. When he was little, I was sometimes so aggressive toward him, almost violent. I went to work once a week, and then my husband gave him a bottle. Benny hated it. I felt I was forcing him to do something he didn't want to do, that I was traumatizing him. I know that my mother was very depressed after my birth and that she sometimes forgot to feed me. When this was discovered, neighbours came in and fed me the bottle.

I: Perhaps you are afraid that in the relationship with your son you were unconsciously repeating some of your own experiences with your mother.

D: Yes, definitely. I feel terribly destructive, especially towards people who are close to me. I have very powerful needs.

I: Are you perhaps afraid that you will destroy me with your powerful needs and that I will break down like your mother, or become ill like your former therapist, and will not be able to give you the caring and support you need from me in analysis?

D: Exactly so. I'm afraid that nobody can really withstand my own needy self, nobody can survive my needs and my destructiveness. And I am also afraid that Israel is a short episode in the history of the Jewish people, this *Intifada* can become our next Holocaust.

The above material illustrates how the shadow of the Holocaust affected Daphna's life. Daphna identified with her mother's victim/ aggressor aspects. In the role of victim, she was the baby of a persecutory mother who could have murdered her by starving her to death. In the role of aggressor, not only did she feel guilty for not saving her mother (and indirectly also her father) from death and destruction, but she also accused herself of destroying her mother because of her needy, ravenous self. This polarized attitude, in which love and hatred were split apart, was projected on to her son, and she felt that she was simultaneously his potential saviour and his murderer.

The case of Isaac

Isaac, a thirty-year-old scientist, married and the father of a three-year-old child, sought analysis because of uncontrolled outbursts of anger toward his family and his subsequent feelings of guilt and unhappiness. Isaac came to analysis during a time of crisis in his life: his father, aged seventy-two, had committed suicide several weeks previously. The father had suffered from pain in his testicles for over a year before being diagnosed with prostate cancer. He underwent an operation and radiation therapy, after which tests showed that the cancerous cells had completely disappeared. Only the pain persisted, increasingly affecting his psychic state.

Isaac's father was a simple man who had worked as a technician his entire life, devoting most of his free time to sports and athletics. Recently, these activities were greatly hindered by the constant pain that had begun tormenting him, and which gradually led to overwhelming depression. Despite his recovery and the good prognosis, despite all the love and support he received from his family, Father decided to end his life. It was Isaac's mother who found his body dangling from a rope in the shower. Father left a note for his family: "My dear family, please forgive me, I cannot stand it any more."

Isaac came to me during the first month after his father's death. His appearance was striking: he had delicate features and long hair, which gave him a feminine appearance. He observed the Jewish custom of not shaving during the period of mourning, and the beard adorning his face lent him a most bizarre look. He had great difficulty talking and stuttered terribly during the first session. His strange appearance and fragmented speech made me regard him as more emotionally ill than he really was, a fact that I realized later on in analysis.

During this stage of treatment we reconstructed his parents' story: Isaac was the son of a Holocaust survivor father and a mother whose family had been living in Israel for several generations. His father had been in a concentration camp between the ages of fourteen and nineteen. Isaac knew very little of his father's life during that period, except for the fact that only his father and his father's brother had survived.

Isaac's own history revealed a very intelligent and talented young man. During high school he was already taking courses at university, and at the age of twenty he had completed a first degree in science. He was then drafted into the army, working there in his field of expertise, and at the same time was sent by the army to study for a PhD. Now, at the age of thirty, he had a family whom he loved, he had close friends, and was conducting research at a prominent scientific institute. He complained that in spite of all this, he would sometimes feel depressed. During these periods, he had little energy for work. Nowadays, he was especially upset by his angry outbursts toward his wife and child.

Isaac described the atmosphere in his parents' home as coercive. He was the only son of a couple who had been childless for many years, and was very much loved and over-protected by his mother. The relationship with his father was more complex and ambivalent. Although proud of the boy's intellectual achievements, the father was never ever satisfied with him. In contrast to his mother, who spoiled him, his father wanted him to be totally independent, physically and emotionally. The sensitive young boy learned that he had to "become a man". He was urged to look out for himself and to engage in sports in order to develop his body. He was expected to learn a profession that would earn him a great deal of money, with no regard for his real interests.

The boy found himself under great pressure to fulfil his father's ego-ideal, but also felt very antagonistic about it. He felt a great deal of anger toward his father, but, afraid to hurt him, he learnt to keep his feelings in check and behaved in a passive–aggressive manner. He adopted the mechanism of turning his aggressive feelings against himself, which caused him to become periodically depressed.

Certain changes occurred in Isaac's appearance and behaviour during therapy. He stopped stuttering, and his speech became clearer. At the end of the first month after his father's death, he shaved off his beard (it is a Jewish custom not to shave during the first month after a parent's death). His long hair still adorned his feminine features, but without the beard, he no longer looked so bizarre.

Enquiring about his hair, I discovered that Isaac had not always worn his hair long. (Hair length has symbolic value. The unconscious meaning of hair length in children of Nazi persecutors has been the subject of research (Kogan & Schneider, 2002)). There was a period in school and during his army service when he said that he had looked like a "normal" guy. In the attempt to understand how he defined "normal" or "abnormal", Isaac mentioned a homosexual encounter that almost occurred at the age of nineteen, during his army service. Immediately after breaking up with a girlfriend, he became very close to a young man several years older. He and this man were supposed to meet and spend the night together, but at the last moment Isaac got cold feet and did not turn up. The man was very offended and the relationship ended.

In analysis, we tried to understand this episode in light of information about his father's life that was revealed to Isaac during the first month after his father's death. A cousin told Isaac about some of the dreadful events in his father's life during the Holocaust. One terrible episode was about his father and the uncle who had survived: the brothers peeped through a fence and saw their mother and sister being marched off to the gas chambers. Another terrifying story was that Father, who was a handsome boy at the time, had been sexually exploited by men in the concentration camps. The cousin remembered one of the things Father had said: "Men were always after me, the younger ones during the day, the older ones at night." Isaac remembered his father warning him in this regard: "You are such a handsome boy, you are the type for men, they will be after you!"

We tried to understand Isaac's behaviour in light of his father's powerful message to "behave like a man". Isaac now realized that having long hair and looking feminine was the most rebellious action he could have taken against his father. Consciously, Isaac was rebelling against the masculinity that he felt was expected of him. Unconsciously, Isaac almost repeated his father's fate when he came close to a homosexual encounter, but fled from it at the last moment.

After elaborating this episode in analysis, Isaac cut his hair. Having to a certain extent worked through his love and anger towards his father, this rebellion was no longer necessary.

Describing his feelings about the life-threatening situation in Israel, Isaac revealed that he had years ago acquired a revolver, which he kept in a locked drawer. He said, "I have to have a revolver; it can be very useful in case we are attacked by terrorists; in case they break into my house, I will not be completely impotent." After further enquiry, Isaac connected his feelings of impotence to the past sexual exploitation of his father by the Nazis.

Working through his father's suicide, we connected the father's traumatic history to his illness and its outcome. Apparently his illness, the surgery, and the radiation therapy had left his father impotent. The unbearable pain he complained of might have been an unbearable combination of physical as well as psychic pain. This trauma, superimposed upon his father's earlier trauma, possibly led to his final act of self-destruction.

The life-threatening situation in Israel reactivated in Isaac traces of his father's concern over his masculinity, which he had transmitted to Isaac in ways that went beyond words. In acquiring the revolver, Isaac was attempting to defend not only himself and his family from Palestinian terrorists, but he was also trying to ensure that his manhood would not be damaged, living his father's past in his own present life.

Discussion

I will now discuss the impact of traumatic external reality on the perception of reality and on the defences of Holocaust survivors' offspring, as shown by the above cases. In the two cases described above, the patients' psychic realities were, in large part, structured by unconscious fantasies and guilt feelings related to their parents' traumatic past. Life-threatening external reality and terror reinforced their internal fears and made it more difficult for them to differentiate between internal and external reality, and this had an impact on their defences. It caused them to react to their external world with behaviour dominated by fantasies and unconscious fears evoked by their parents' Holocaust past. The reality of the Holocaust often penetrated the current reality through real or imagined enactments (Bergmann, 1982; Kogan, 2002).

In the case of Daphna, the threatening external situation increased her feelings of omnipotence, leading her to recreate, through her pro-Palestinian demonstrations, a past world in which she was exposed to death and destruction. She experienced these demonstrations as life-threatening situations that "transposed" (Kestenberg, 1972) her into the Holocaust past of her father. The tragic repetition of the Holocaust trauma by her mother reinforced the mental representations of the Holocaust. This brought a distortion of reality, and she regarded the angry Jews as her Nazi persecutors. In addition, by demonstrating for peace and exposing herself to an imagined danger, she fulfilled her conscious wish of acting as a saviour to Jews (by omnipotently trying to prevent another Holocaust) as well as to Palestinians (by helping the underdog). On an unconscious level, Daphna was attempting to alleviate the guilt stemming from the trauma of her mother's suicide, followed by her father's illness and death, while at the same time coming close to death in order to overcome it.

In the case of Isaac, external reality was experienced not only as an existential threat, but also as a potential threat to his manhood. Fearing his father's fate, Isaac acquired a revolver to defend himself against a possible attack on his manhood, which had been his father's misfortune. Perhaps, in his unconscious fantasies, Isaac perceived the Palestinian terrorists who might break into his house as Nazi aggressors raping his body. The threatening external reality reactivated the lack of differentiation between Isaac and his father, causing him to relive his father's traumatic past in his own present. In this mixed reality, the revolver represented the phallus (thus fulfilling his father's message to become a man) as well as the weapon that enabled Isaac to defend his manhood against those who wished to destroy it.

Both cases are marked by great confusion between past and present, fantasy and reality, internal and external. External life-threatening situations led to a distorted perception of reality, and reinforced the patients' need to enact the traumatic themes from their parents' lives in their own present.

I wish to conclude by saying that we can conceive of Daphna's and Isaac's parents as typical of many Jewish mothers and fathers who were damaged by the Holocaust. In writing about the reaction to the Gulf War among second generation Holocaust survivors living in Israel, I observed that

> a large segment of the Israeli population linked the threat of the Gulf War to the Holocaust history of the Jewish people. It is therefore possible that the collective memory of past traumas, in a certain sense, turned us all into the second generation. [Kogan, 1995, p. 145]

Thus, I would dare say that the current ongoing threatening and terrifying situation in Israel has reactivated the traumatic Holocaust past, with all its devastating affects and implications, not only among those who were directly affected by the Holocaust and their offspring, but among an entire population.

References

Auerhahn, N. C., & Laub, D. (1984). Annihilation and restoration: post-traumatic memory as pathway and obstacle to recovery. *The International Journal of Psychoanalysis, 11*(3): 327–344.

Axelrod, S., Schnipper, O., & Rau, J. (1978). Hospitalized offspring of Holocaust survivors: problems and dynamics. Paper presented to the Annual Meeting of the American Psychiatric Association, May.

Barocas, H. A., & Barocas, C. B. (1973). Manifestations of concentration camp effects on the second generation. *American Journal of Psychiatry, 30*: 820–821.

Bergmann, M. V. (1982). Thoughts on superego pathology of survivors and their children. In: M. Bergmann & M. Jucovy (Eds.), *Generations of the Holocaust* (pp. 287–311). New York: Basic Books.

Chused, J. (1991). The evocative power of enactments. *Journal of the American Psychoanalytic Association, 39*: 615–638.

Freud, S. (1917e). Mourning and melancholia. *S.E., 14*: 239–258. London: Hogarth.

Freyberg, J. T. (1980). Difficulties in separation-individuation as experienced by offspring of Nazi Holocaust survivors. *American Journal of Orthopsychiatry, 50*(1): 87–95.

Green, A. (1986). *On Private Madness*. London: Hogarth.

Grinberg, L., & Grinberg, R. (1974). The problem of identity and the psychoanalytical process. *International Review of Psycho-Analysis, 1*: 499–507.

Grubrich-Simitis, I. (1984a). From concretism to metaphor: thoughts on some theoretical and technical aspects of the psychoanalytic work with children of holocaust survivors. *The Psychoanalytic Study of the Child, 39*: 301–319.

Grubrich-Simitis, I. (1984b). Vom konkretismus zur metaphorik. *Psyche, 38*: 1–28.

Jacobs, T. (1986). On countertransference enactments. *Journal of the American Psychoanalytic Association, 34*: 289–307.

Jacobs, T. (2000). Unbewusste kommunikation und verdeckte enactments in analytischen setting. In: U. Streeck Errinern (Ed.), *Agieren und Inszenieren* (pp. 97–127). Gottingen: Vanderhoeck & Ruprecht.

Kestenberg, J. S. (1972). How children remember and parents forget. *International Journal of Psychoanalytic Psychotherapy, 1–2*: 103–123.

Klein, H. (1971). Families of Holocaust survivors in the kibbutz: psychological studies. In: *Psychic Traumatization: After-effects in Individuals and Communities*. Boston: Little & Brown.

Kogan, I. (1995). *The Cry of Mute Children: A Psychoanalytic Perspective of the Second Generation of the Holocaust*. London: Free Association Books.

Kogan, I. (1998). Working with Holocaust survivors' offspring: from trauma to history through clinical intervention. *Psycho-analytic Psychotherapy in South Africa, 6*(1): 30–41.

Kogan, I. (2002). Enactment in the lives and treatment of Holocaust survivors' offspring. *Psychoanalytic Quarterly, 71*(2): 251–272.

Kogan, I. (2003). On being a dead, beloved child. *Psychoanalytic Quarterly, 72*: 727–767.

Kogan, I. (2007a). *The Struggle Against Mourning*. New York: Jason Aronson.

Kogan, I. (2007b). *Escape from Selfhood*. London: IPA Publications.

Kogan, I., & Schneider, C. (2002). The Nazi heritage and gender identity. *Journal of Applied Psychoanalytic Studies, 4*(1): 49–62.

Laufer, M. (1973). The analysis of a child of survivors. In: E. J. Anthony & C. Koupernik (Eds.), *The Child in His Family: The Impact of Disease and Death* (363–373). New York: John Wiley.

Lipkowitz, M. (1973). The child of two survivors: the report of an unsuccessful therapy. *Israeli Annals of Psychiatry and Related Disciplines, 11*: 141–155.

McLaughlin, J. (1992). Nonverbal behavior in the analytic situation: the search for meaning in nonverbal cues. In: S. Kramer & S. Akhtar (Eds.), *When the Body Speaks: Psychological Meanings in Kinetic Cues* (pp. 131–161). Northvale, NJ: Jason Aronson.

Moses, R. (1993). *Persistent Shadows of the Holocaust: The Meaning to Those Not Directly Affected*. Madison, CT: International Universities Press.

Rakoff, V. (1966). Long-term effects of the concentration camp experience. *Viewpoints, 1*: 17–21.

Renik, O. (1993). Analytic interactions: conceptualizing technique in light of the analyst's irreducible subjectivity. *Psychoanalytic Quarterly, 62*: 553–571.

Sandler, J., & Sandler, A.-M. (1978). On the development of object-relations and affects. *International Journal of Psychoanalysis, 59*: 285–293.

Schafer, R. (1982). *Retelling a Life*. New York: Basic Books.

Sonnenberg, S. (1974). Children of survivors: workshop report. *Journal of the American Psychoanalytic Association, 22*: 200–204.

Volkan, V. (1987a). *Six Steps in the Treatment of Borderline Personality Organization*. Northvale, NJ: Jason Aronson.

Volkan, V. (2002). September 11 and societal regression. *Group Analysis, 35*(4): 456–483.

CHAPTER TWO

The broken chain:
legacies of trauma and war

Vera Muller-Paisner

T he legacy of trauma needs only one moment in time, one moment in history to re-emerge with a different meaning. New associations can reframe the task of transmission to the next generation. Events such as the Holocaust continue to bring to our doorstep new ways of examining trauma, across generations, in different parts of the world, over a span of more than sixty years.

After the Second World War, many Holocaust survivors who stayed in Poland replaced their Jewish identity with the safety of a national identity as a Pole and Christian. Today, after more than sixty years, in a society that was Communist and anti-Semitic, Christian families have been discovering the secret of Jewish roots. Many elder family members, on their deathbeds, alter family history by declaring that they are Jews, and often ask to be buried in Jewish cemeteries.

Poles, raised to find their place in society as Catholics, are suddenly facing the dilemma of discovering parents who are Jews. Educated as Christians, they are trying to redefine religious identity. They are left with the task of trying to grasp the fear and horror of their family's Holocaust narrative, to understand their relationship to it, and to attempt to form a new identification that would integrate and include this experience. In 1990, there were approximately 4,000 Jews in Poland. By 1996, there were between 10,000–20,000, and the number is rising, without immigration adding to it.

The shock of discovering a family connection to an event like the Holocaust creates an empty hole. Not knowing fills the hole with fantasies of what took place, with feelings of dread that it was unthinkable and unspeakable. The horrors remain unspeakable, even in countries such as the USA, in places like Massachusetts and Washington DC. The former Democratic presidential candidate John Kerry, a practising Catholic, discovered only fifteen years ago that his grandfather, Frederick Kerry, born as Fritz Kohn, was Jewish. Madeline Albright, the secretary of state in the Clinton administration, learnt in 1997 that three of her four grandparents were Jewish. Both found the discovery to be a revelation of their family history. It has also *become* the family history of their children, the next generation, inevitably changing their sense of identity.

Erikson (1959) argues that the key problem of identity is the capacity of the ego to sustain sameness and continuity in the face of changing fate. Internal changes, which are the result of living, and changes in the milieu affect the direction and power of trauma's transmission. Family stories help us with our sense of identity and give us a narrative to hold on to, add to, and pass on to the next generation. We know our family history and can tell the story of how we came to be. Family characteristics of the past and present become familiar to us. We become connected to the way past generations have acted.

History, culture, and religion form a large part of an identity to which one feels related. Although it is enriching to feel part of more than one history, it becomes almost untenable to regard oneself as part of these two religions, as Catholic and Jew simultaneously, suddenly, in the midst of a life cycle and in Poland, where these religions have traditionally been defined in exclusive terms. One entity has been considered part of the "national" character and the socially accepted majority, while the other has historically been a hated, distrusted member of a minority and the victim of trauma.

Most Jews who remained after the 1968 purge went underground, along with their tradition. The following generations, unaware of their legacy and the unconscious survival strategies of their parents, became part of the majority, only slightly aware of the "others": those ethnic out-groups and minorities that make up the unconscious evil identity, which every ego is afraid to resemble. They experienced their identities as solid, characterized by the social likeness to others, rooted in the perception of sameness as well as being recognized as such. Shaped by the social and political circumstances of the particular moment in time, their identities made sense of the world. They understood their past and their place in the present; it seemed that future generations would internalize a legacy that was continuous.

The following stories are about the forces of time, society, and war, where, for survival, the roots of family religious identity have been kept secret from spouses and children, breaking the chain of legacy and continuity. I will share with you fragments of interviews as well as group process that took place in Poland between 1998 and 2000, after a year of research, fundraising, and training. My vision was to create support groups for those who needed a "holding environment" while they were struggling with who they found themselves to be. Working closely with staff in Poland, we named the groups "Broken Chain". Members of Broken Chain had not grown up knowing and relating to Holocaust trauma and did not seek to be recognized as Jews, necessarily. Each had to find their own way out of their crisis of identity. Each story was complicated and multi-dimensional.

A farmer approached one of his three sons telling him that, although he loved him like a son, the farm, the land, belonged only to blood, to Catholic blood, and he was a Jewish child whom they had saved from certain death. In his fifties, the son of the farmer, dressed in farm clothes, leading the only life he knew, discovered that he was not who he thought he was, and began the search through archives in Warsaw for his "true" family.

A priest, ordained in 1966, had always searched the mirror for a resemblance to his parents and had wondered why his father had implored him not to enter the priesthood. The priest (*New York Times*, International, Sunday October 10, 1999) told the only mother he knew that he sensed a secret. In 1978, when his mother was hospitalized, he asked her again about "that secret". At last, she admitted that there was one. He had been born in 1943 to a Jewish couple. He was told that his birth mother begged for his life and said to the only mother he knew, "You are a devout Catholic. You believe in Jesus, who was a Jew. So try to save this Jewish baby for the Jew in whom you believe, and one day he will grow up to be a priest." Father Romuald Waskinel was astonished, for he had fulfilled the prophecy of his mother, a woman he had never knowingly met. Not knowing what to do with his future, he wrote a letter to Pope John Paul II, asking for guidance. He received a response supporting his work as a priest and teacher, at Lublin's Catholic University. His Jewish name is Jakub Weksler.

I found myself working with a population that was just beginning to suffer the transmitted traumas of the Second World War, without having witnessed the horrors and without having emigrated. Holes in developmental time were being unearthed, creating identity crises that were internal, societal, and transcending two or more generations. For those who were anti-Semitic, it was like finding the enemy next door or actually within. For others, it was shame and the need to hide, or the need to tell and be accepted, or to find a way to forget. Yet, there were some who never felt like the others, and who were interested in the possibility of finding spirituality in Judaism. As individuals and as a society, Catholic Poles felt betrayed, either by self-discovery of their Jewish roots or that discovery in those close to them, such as spouses, parents, friends, and priests.

The interviews I conducted were with people of different generations; they illuminated the various conflicts and struggles newly discovered Jewish Poles felt in trying to tolerate oneself and to be tolerated. Each life cycle had levels of anxiety that were age-specific. Youth retained some idealism, but family dynamics were often overpowering. Anxiety also was heightened with thoughts of a marriage partner. Discovery after marriage added the fear of spousal rejection and possible job dismissal. When children were involved, decisions when or whether to tell the children needed to be anticipated. Religious instruction continued to be part of the school curriculum. Children who did not go to religious classes were thought to be Jews or Gypsies, and often treated as outcasts.

Agnieszka was seventeen years old when she discovered that she was Jewish. This had happened in the past year. She paused in her conversation with me, telling me that the circumstances had been difficult. She was staying with her grandmother while her parents were travelling abroad. Her grandmother was killed in a car accident. Unable to reach her parents, Agnieszka was in a panic and called her mother's sister who lived in a neighbouring country. Her aunt came immediately to help with funeral arrangements. Agnieszka was puzzled and shocked by the surname on the death certificate. It sounded Jewish. She asked her aunt, and was told that indeed the surname was Jewish, and that she and her mother were Jews. However, it was a secret from her father and brother. "So that's the family secret", she said, "My mother keeps it and my aunt doesn't." Agnieszka had asked her aunt to tell her any family history that she knew. She was told that her grandmother survived the war by hiding under garden tools in a small shed on the Aryan side of town. She foraged for food only at night.

Agnieszka wanted to know more but, when she asked for the truth upon her mother's return, her mother denied the story, saying that many families had changed their names during those times and that the family was not Jewish. Agnieszka remained persistent until her mother acquiesced and told her the truth, but made her promise not to tell her father or brother. I asked Agnieszka how this secret affected her. Holding on to the cross that she wore on a chain around her neck, she said: "I am Catholic, well, now I don't know what to think about it. I'm lost." She said that the secret was a strain on her relationship with her father and brother. There were times when unpleasant things were said about Jews in her home. She did not want to keep this secret but her mother insisted. She thought that surely her father would understand.

Agnieszka attended Catholic school, where she had heard anti-Semitic remarks. When she heard "Jewish people to the gas," she wanted to say something, but was conflicted and afraid. She did not know whether she would remain a Catholic or become Jewish in an ethnic way. The only certainty was her allegiance and identity as a Pole. Maintaining a sense of "sameness" with one parent whose Jewish identity had been discovered meant a partial splitting. It brought new considerations of the self as the despised "other", as well as losing her identification with the Catholic majority. It was as if Agnieszka had lost her map of family history and future tradition all at once.

Regina told me that her life changed on an ordinary day when she was sixteen years old and peeling potatoes with her mother. She was speaking to her mother about ambivalent feelings regarding religion. Regina had been baptized and remembered her strong connection with her father as they shared going to church together when she was young. It was an argument about the Holy Trinity with her priest when she was thirteen that had turned her away from religion. There was a long silence. Still peeling potatoes, in a low voice her mother chose that moment to tell her that she—the mother—had been born a

Jew. Her mother had told no one, including her husband, about this secret.

For months Regina felt uncomfortable. She said, "I had problems trying to understand who I was, having a Jewish mother." However, books about what it meant to be a Jew and their relationship to Polish history and culture had become available in the late 1980s. An American rabbi had come to Warsaw in 1990 and was available to help those interested in gathering information about Jewish roots. Regina openly pursued her understanding of Judaism for the next several years and decided to try to live a "Jewish life". Regina's mother accepted her choice, although she was saddened by her daughter's desire to move out of her house in order to lead a more observant Jewish life. She was also afraid for her daughter's future as a Jew in Poland.

Her father, however, stopped talking to her when she shared her discoveries with her younger brother. He became enraged that she would talk to his Christian son about "Jewish things". She responded by saying that his son was also her brother, and she was sharing with him part of his heritage. Her father became estranged from both his daughter and his wife, telling them both that had his wife acted the way Regina had, he would never have married her. Regina expressed heartbreak with the way her family was splitting. Separation from her father was excruciating. She attempted to write letters to him explaining her reasons for wanting to explore Jewish tradition and stated that she had not tried to separate her brother from him. She only wanted her brother to be able to explore both traditions, since he was also the son of a Jewish mother. Her father replied that he would never forgive her. He wanted Christian tradition to be followed by his children and their children. He felt robbed of his future progeny and claimed that she had become a stranger and that he would never accept her choice.

Ula, at twenty-three, was horrified when her mother revealed that they were Jewish. She did not think that she would be able to consider marriage until she sorted out her religious identity. She wondered, as a Jew, if she would be considered an acceptable marriage partner. She felt her biological clock ticking but wondered about the future of raising children as Jewish in Poland. She thought that time had worked against her and wished she had known earlier in order to have had more time to integrate her sense of self.

Adult conflicts were even more complicated. Adults thought more about family history, its place in society and the responsibility for the direction of family tradition. Stefan was forty-five years old and the father of two teenage children. He told me that he had become aware of being Jewish during a political situation in Poland. It was the beginning of a wave of anti-Semitism during the 1968 nationwide purge of Jews. He was seventeen and his parents, who were professors, had problems at the university. He said that he felt robbed at having learnt so late, but had not felt harmed by being Jewish, because he had not known that he was. He had known that his grandmother on his mother's side was married to a German. The information omitted was that she was a Jew who needed her German husband to save her from harm. He said, "Not being told was a mistake, yet not knowing gave me additional safety, which was lost once I knew. I feel that being a Jew in Poland is not easy. One is never considered a real Pole. It is like having a double identity, which is stressful and difficult."

I asked him how many children he had and whether they knew about their Jewish heritage. Stefan had felt conflicted about telling them, because knowing would remove a net of safety, but said that a situation had presented itself that gave him no choice. At fifteen, his daughter came home from school with anti-Semitic jokes. He seized the moment to tell her and then also told his son. He would have liked to be able to pass on more of the family's history and said, "I would like to learn more about being Jewish. It made quite a strong impression on me to find out, but I was never anti-Semitic so I didn't have that problem. I should have known much earlier that I was a Jew. It is important to know family history and tradition. I somehow lost time by not knowing myself. I knew myself superficially."

Members of the support groups had been aware of anti-Semitism and might have felt anti-Semitic themselves, but they had never felt the hatred directed at them because they had not considered themselves to be Jews. Feelings of persecution were shocking for people raised as Catholics, in a country with a Catholic majority. They now had to consider themselves as part of the hated minority, and feared anti-Semitism. Several reluctantly admitted to circling the building where we were going to meet several times, and entering only when they were sure not to have been seen. Most were afraid to tell their spouses and children. Many no longer felt legitimate in church, nor did Judaism feel legitimate. They felt a complete loss of identity.

The world and people around them had not changed, yet having their Jewish roots unearthed had changed their lives, including their history, without a visible trace of alteration. Anti-Semitic friends unknowingly created an atmosphere where open discussion became impossible. It was hard to talk or not talk about anti-Semitism on the outside. It was especially important to keep the secret at work, if one was dependent on others for job security. Several members felt badly about being Jewish and wished they could forget their discovery or put it aside. Not liking Jews made it very difficult to be one.

There were conflicts about telling children and asking them not to tell schoolmates. One woman started to cry and asked the group how you can expect a child to be proud of a heritage that needed to be kept a secret for self-protection and the safety of the family. A member who had told her son that he was Jewish said that she was at a loss to help her son find meaning as a Jew, since she felt that her Jewish part had no content. "It feels empty," she said, "I don't know what to transmit to my son." Several members had told only one member of the family their secret, entangling that person in a web of complicated loyalties.

Conversation about history and the positive values of Jewish family roots began to come forward in the support groups. However, the voices would flip from positive to negative quite easily. There were dialogues about Jews behaving like victims by submitting to the ghetto, as well as Jews being the perpetrators and killers of Christ. One member reported the atmosphere at home as always being prepared for the worst. She said that she had not understood it until the missing piece of her Jewish roots fell into place. She felt much better knowing, and felt closer to her family when she understood their past. It was more important to feel integrated, even if the circumstances were difficult. Another member reported that his family did not seem to plan for anything in life, including the future. Life was seen as precarious, with everything being potentially lost, regardless of effort. He soon realized that depression and the Holocaust were the background for that world-view.

One woman had felt stifled by her father and had not understood the reason for this. He would hardly allow her to leave the house. She had not understood what her mother meant when she often said to him in disgust, "What do you know about the war? You spent it under floorboards!" She now understood that overprotecting children was a Jewish trait brought on by trauma. She also thought that she had spent her life metaphorically "under floorboards" and now needed to free herself.

The group spoke about the Holocaust, which gave them a new historical marker with which to understand their families. It allowed them to gain a real existence emotionally. Discussions furthered their understanding of how the legacy crept surreptitiously, unnoticed, into the next generation. Empathy and sadness for the traumas endured by each family surfaced.

After several weeks, a man brought in his frustration about not having found an approach to telling his wife that he was Jewish. A woman responded by saying that she had been able to tell her two children, but had not been able to tell her husband. Another woman reflected that she was able to tell her husband but felt afraid to tell her in-laws. Her husband told her that he did not like Jews and thought his family felt the same way. There was considerable fear about what would happen to relationships after family members learned about the discovery of Jewish roots. The conversation turned to marriages built on lies, the continuation of lying, its consequences, and the consequences of exposing the truth. There were a few members who were able to tell their spouses and felt greatly relieved by their spouse's unbiased acceptance.

Today, the political context and societal prohibitions in Poland have lifted enough for history to present a moment, a window of opportunity, for the exploration and healing of its latest victims of trauma's transmission. What meaning and task will be transmitted? We can say that this condition was started by, and bound to, the Holocaust. Is it possible to begin a partial Jewish identity as a *victim* of the Holocaust? Bound to a trauma previously seen as an externalized "bad" image? Group members of Broken Chain would need to be able to feel linked with the Jewish identity of victimization and loss before being able to proceed toward integration. Time is needed for the possible redirection of ego and libidinal investment as well as psychic organizational change. Internalized shifts between opposing group identities in individuals need to be worked through.

When I asked members of the struggling Jewish community the reason why they remain in Poland, several responded by saying that Poland's soil was rich with Jewish blood and leaving would be the same as abandonment. The metaphor of blood and soil bears a resemblance to Nazi ideology in the fantasy of forming a single body and a common blood of a nation in order to unite with the object. The use of the same symbol of blood might represent identification with the aggressor or a revenge–repair fantasy. By staying in Poland and reviving a Jewish community, the rebirth of a Jewish nation and new Jewish blood would be a triumph for the lost Jewish blood of the past. Or, the trauma of the Holocaust might change its function to one of integration.

The need to treat societal traumas is great, even more so with the trauma brought to the doorstep of America on 9/11. We face the likelihood of the continuation of a paradox: the unconscious transmission of highly charged, trauma-related tasks to the next generation, but the loss of their meaning in the silence that surrounds them. It behoves us to continue to do research, to interpret, and to illuminate the cycles of trauma so that future generations may be able to understand the meaning and consequences of their legacies.

Reference

Erikson, E. H. (1959). Identity and the life cycle. In: *Psychological Issues, Part 1* (pp. 1–171). New York: International Universities Press.

CHAPTER THREE

Traumatic shutdown of narrative and symbolization: a death instinct derivative?

Dori Laub

Through a detailed clinical vignette and a review of the relevant literature, this chapter attempts to illustrate the failures in narrative formation, symbolization, and even in the process of psychoanalytic listening and comprehension, which occur in the wake of events of massive psychic trauma. Inexplicable gaps and absences occur in what should be all too evident and readily known, and the processes of exploratory curiosity come to a halt. The author attempts to explain this phenomenon through the cessation of the inner dialogue with the internalized good object, the "inner thou" that is annihilated in massive trauma. He tries to demonstrate the role the death instinct derivatives play in this presumed shutdown of processes of association, symbolization, and narrative formation. Such death instinct derivatives are unleashed once the binding libidinal forces of object cathexis are abolished and identification with the aggressor (the only object left in the internal world representation) takes place. Implications for psychoanalytic psychotherapy with severely traumatized patients are discussed and illustrated by another case vignette.

A case of countertransference blindness

The analyst was a candidate in psychoanalytic training and this was his first control patient. The analyst was a child survivor who had spent two years between the ages of five and seven in a concentration camp during the Second World War. Before he started working with this patient, his immigration status in the USA was in question and threatened to interrupt his psychoanalytic training. He was advised by the Institute that if he could not assure his stay in the USA for a sufficient length of time, he could neither start his first control case nor could he proceed with his classes. He felt he was about to be deported again, exiled from the country he lived and worked in, and banished, or at least not protected, by the Institute in which he was training. An unexpected change in US immigration law allowed for a resolution of this crisis, and he was referred his first control patient.

The supervisor of the case was a very eminent psychoanalyst, also a refugee from Nazi-occupied Europe. He was known and admired for his flexibility and tolerance and for his original writings on the new object relation experience psychoanalysis offered, which would allow re-examination of damaging object relationships in early childhood, thus setting a healing process in motion.

The candidate's control case was a woman in her late twenties, single, and working as a teacher. She was the elder of two children, having a brother five years younger, of whom she was intensely jealous, because she regarded him as the parents' favourite. Aside from working, her life was pretty empty. She had very few friends and no social life to speak of. She had never had a relationship with a man, and had never fallen in love. Her symptoms were episodes of depression, hopelessness, and panic attacks, one of which landed her in the emergency room.

Once on the couch, she became very suspicious of the analyst, reading all kinds of feelings into his abstinence. She felt that from the moment she came into his office, he treated her with contempt, put her down, was cold, and always critical. She likened him to her mother, whom she thought of as distant and very harsh. Transference interpretations, however, did not change the situation. She had frequent angry outbursts, yelling in such a loud voice that the analyst next door, a colleague, humorously asked the candidate what he was doing to this patient. Was he torturing her? Upon reflection years later, the analyst thought that the question might have been relevant.

From past history, it emerged that the patient was born shortly before the Second World War and that her father was drafted soon thereafter. He served in the Pacific theatre. As early as 1942, he disappeared and his fate was unknown. He was considered Missing in Action. The mother regarded him as dead. The analyst could imagine a little girl with a depressed, grieving mother, who was perhaps unavailable to her. Reconstructions of this kind, however, made no difference, either.

It is interesting to note that during a three-month window, when the supervision was interrupted and the analyst presented the case in a seminar to his colleagues, his patient's situation did change. Everyone in the seminar was intensely curious about the patient, her fantasy love life, her dreams, and her possibilities for meeting a man. The analyst, himself, felt freer while presenting his case to his colleagues in training and not to his supervisor. It was during this window that the patient had her one and only date with a man.

Many of the feelings the analyst harboured in the supervisory setting and towards the Institute that nearly interrupted his training were permeated by his childhood persecution experiences and inhibited his creativity and his analytic freedom to explore. Therefore, when supervision resumed, the analytic situation reverted to what it had been before. As things were not going well in the analysis, the supervisor suggested that the candidate sit the patient up and speak to her face to face. The candidate was afraid that he was going to lose the credit he needed for the completion of his analytic training if he followed this advice. He was also afraid that he would be asked to leave his training, as almost half of his class had been, because of unsatisfactory progress. The threat of near deportation that had preceded the work with his patient was also very much on his mind.

Further details from the history of the patient showed that the father miraculously returned at the end of the war and was decorated with the Silver Star, one of the highest military decorations in the USA. There was still no information as to the whereabouts of the father during his several years' absence, nor were there any questions asked about this by the analyst or by the supervisor. Neither registered surprise that would have led to enquiries. The analytic process was stalemated. There were only her angry outbursts, which occurred again and again. After nearly four years of rather barren work, the analyst told the patient that he could not see how he could further help her and that another therapist might.

All this happened between 1969 and 1973. Shortly after the interruption of the analysis because of the stalemate it reached, the analyst served as a psychiatrist with the IDF forces in the Yom Kippur October War in 1973. He was stationed in a treatment facility in Northern Israel, which received casualties from the Syrian front. To everybody's surprise, the proportion of psychiatric casualties was staggering. Reservists had been called up from synagogues, thrown into makeshift units and sent into the battlefield to stem the Syrian advance. The abruptness of the transition into combat, the absence of a familiar social support network which the comrades in arms from their regular unit, with whom they trained and served, provided, the enormity of losses, dead and wounded, and above all the level of violence they were exposed to, lead to the psychological decompensation of many.

What the analyst observed was that the most severe and least treatable casualties were children of Holocaust survivors. One such case arrived in a deep depressive stupor. He had no name, no family, no memory. On spending hours upon hours in a dimly lit tent with him and gently prodding him, the analyst gradually learnt that he had been a radio operator on the front line, who saw tank crews stop on their way to the battlefield and then listened to their voices on the radio. He heard their last messages before they went silent. They were out of ammunition and surrounded by Syrian tanks. To him, it strongly resonated with the images of many family members who had been murdered in the Holocaust and whose names were mentioned but little more was said about them. They were, nevertheless, ubiquitously present to him in their very absence and in their silence. Gradually, as he was making this connection, he emerged from his stupor, remembered his name, and recognized his wife, who was about to give birth to a baby. The baby, a son, was named after one of the fallen tank commanders.

Another example is a soldier who was brought in suffering a state of psychotic agitation. His utterances made no sense; his affect and his behaviour were severely out of control. He was a military policeman whose duty it was to prevent civilians from reaching the front line. He had failed to stop a car with two men in it, only to find it later destroyed with two mangled bodies inside. He proceeded to boot a

Syrian POW officer in the head. In his ramblings, he told of his father's stories of SS men smashing the heads of Jewish children into a wall. The front line brutalities triggered the memory of the tales of brutalities he grew up with and was more then he could contain. His mental state did not improve in spite of robust pharmaco- and psychotherapeutic interventions, and he had to be transferred to a chronic facility.

The familial exposure to Holocaust violence in these two men increased their vulnerability to the violence of the battlefield. Whereas other soldiers could better insulate themselves from it by using the customary defences against traumatic experiences, such as dissociation, derealization, depersonalization, and others, for these two, such defences no longer worked. Extremes of violence had for them a personal–historical context that was continuously present and, therefore, could not remain unnoticed and be pushed aside.

In the years that followed these experiences, the analyst became very much involved with clinical work with PTSD and with the transgenerational transmission of trauma. On reflecting about his analytic case described earlier, he began to piece things together in a new and different way. It dawned on him that a very likely explanation for the father's absence for several years was that he had been detained in a Japanese POW camp. The analyst had read of the severe treatment of American POWs by the Japanese and could better understand now why the father had been awarded the Silver Star. Did he possibly undergo torture and did that experience intrude itself into the analytic space?

The analyst realized that after father's return, the joyful couple celebrated the occasion by having a new baby. The patient, perhaps appropriately, was excluded from this celebration. It was imaginable that the father, after years spent in a POW camp, could have been suffering from PTSD symptoms, and some of his traumatic experiences might have been transmitted to his daughter. The analyst suddenly felt that he understood the patient's terror, helplessness, and resultant rage, but unfortunately it had not occurred to him to ask the question that would have enlightened him about the father's whereabouts during the war, or his symptomatology after he came back. Belatedly, he could only guess that the father might have suffered from nightmares for years and was perhaps emotionally withdrawn from his little daughter.

In retrospect, what is striking here is the absence of such curiosity, the lack of creative speculation, and the question of whether the analyst's own childhood camp experience had blinded him to the possibility that the patient might have experienced her own camp-related trauma in her childhood. It was as though the analyst himself experienced a shutdown of reflection and self-reflection that led to a lack of curiosity about something that was very close to the surface, if not obvious. *He just did not notice* that he did not know the reason for the father's absence and his whereabouts during that absence. What is also striking is that even the supervisor, who was known for his extraordinary clinical sensitivity, had not asked this question either. Was he, too, perhaps, unaware of the effect of his own traumatic experience? Did the suppressed memory of his own persecution exert a force that blinded him to the possibility that a similar event might have happened in the patient's family? Years later, the analyst wondered whether this was a case of double countertransference blindness, his own, and that of his supervisor.

The unfortunate outcome was a depressed, suspicious patient screaming on the couch. Her depression was interpreted as a deprivation of maternal care because of her mother's own sense of bereavement and depression when the father disappeared. What was not heard, however, was what might have been the *true* nature of the patient's scream. It might have had more to do with the father's severe and prolonged traumatic experiences in a Japanese POW camp during the Second World War.

What is striking in this vignette is the inexplicable absence, or rather shutdown, in both analyst and supervisor, of the processes of analytic hearing, associating, integrating, and, ultimately, comprehending through the processes of symbolization exactly what the patient experienced and re-enacted in the analytic setting. The missing father and the implications of his return, material that lay clearly in front of their eyes, had not been acknowledged or explored. How can we explain this? Is it possible that the patient's transgenerationally received traumatic experience reverberated with echoes of the massive life trauma that both analyst and analytic supervisor had experienced? Is that what stopped the analytic process in its tracks, allowing for no empathic enquiry, for no associative linkages to be formed, thus keeping the three traumata discrete and frozen in their place? And is this an example of the particularity of the traumatic experience that is not limited to a specific place or time and plays itself out over the course of several generations?

Before offering my own answers to these questions, I wish to review the work of others related to this problem. Wilson and Lindy (1994), who deal with the phenomenon of empathic strain in their book, *Countertransference in the Treatment of PTSD*, have coined the term "empathic withdrawal" (p. 16) to explain such moments in the analytic process. This concept might be partially relevant, yet the totality of the empathic shutdown, the absolute quality of the blindness in professionals otherwise attuned to the subtlest hints points, in my opinion, at forces more powerful and deeper than defensive ego operations. The origin of these powerful forces will be explored later in this presentation.

The nature of traumatic experience

Let us now turn to discussions of the traumatic experience itself in an attempt to comprehend this phenomenon. Clinicians and scholars (Auerhahn, Laub and Peskin, 1993; Caruth, 1996; Oliner, 1996), describe trauma as occurring "out there", not as an event related to an experiencing subject, the "I". It is likened to an external event dissociated from the narrator who has gone through it. Often, survivors emphasize that they indeed live in two separate worlds, that of their traumatic memories (which is self-contained, ongoing, and ever-present) and that of the present. Very often they do not wish, or are completely unable, to reconcile these two different worlds. The memory is, thus, timeless; the experience is frozen. It is automatic and purposeless, bereft of meaning. Caruth (1996, pp. 91–92) states, "Traumatic experience . . . suggests a certain paradox: that the most direct seeing of a violent event may occur as an absolute inability to know it". "It is not simply, that is, the literal threatening of bodily life," Caruth tells us, "but the fact that the threat is recognized as such by the mind *one moment* too late. The shock of the mind's relation to the threat of death is thus not the direct experience of the threat, but precisely the *missing* of this experience, the fact that, not being experienced *in time*, it has not yet been fully known" (p. 62).

Yet, in spite of, and perhaps because of, their separateness, of their having a life of their own, the power the memories of trauma exert on the continuance of life is immeasurable. Van der Kolk, McFarlane, and Weisaeth state, "Terrifying events may be remembered with extreme vividness or maybe totally resist integration . . . trauma can lead to extremes of retention and forgetting" (1996, p. 282) In any case, these memories remain intense, yet frozen, immutable, and unaltered by the passage of time. They are not subject to assimilation or to evolutionary change through integration in the associative network. They remain discrete, retaining their magnetic power in their contradictory detailed and persistent clarity and in the concomitant dense yet absorbing opaqueness that enshrouds them. They are qualitatively different from ordinary memories.

According to Van der Kolk and colleagues,

> Traumatic experiences are initially imprinted sensations and feeling states and are not collated and transcribed into personal narratives. Our interviews with traumatized people as well as our brain imaging studies with them seem to confirm that traumatic memories come back as emotional and sensory states with little capacity for verbal representation . . . they may be encoded differently from memories for ordinary events . . . perhaps because extreme emotional arousal interferes with hippocampal memory functions. . . . This failure to process information on a symbolic level, which is essential for proper categorization and integration with other experiences, is at the very core of the pathology of PTSD. [ibid., pp. 296, 282]

Kafka, in an article from a series of commentaries on September 11th, states,

> Patients' comments about witnessing either the event or the live television footage of September 11th, such as 'I cannot believe this is happening. This must be a film, fiction, or science fiction,' illustrate the sense of unreality concerning the reality of the terrorizing event. [2002, p. 32]

This continues to be the case with material obtained from interviews of lieutenants of Osama bin Laden.

> The interviewees spoke of bin Laden as if he were a kind of rock star. They spoke of the blood of terrorist acts as if describing television shows. Just as performance, the stage, the prop often have a kind of 'hyper reality,' a plastic shine and hardness in contrast to the reality of

natural materials' characteristic 'give', the terrorists' transformation of reality is mirrored in the initial inability of the terrorized individual to accept as reality what confronts him. [*ibid.*, p. 32]

Another contributor, Elsa First, describes the reaction of the children of intermediate school 89, who had a clear view of the World Trade Center from their classroom windows, where they gathered when the second plane hit.

"At first we were laughing and joking with each other, because we thought it was a movie, like an action movie, with special effects,'" one eleven-year-old boy commented, "but then the people began jumping from the windows, on fire, and we stopped laughing because then we knew it was real." [First, 2002, p. 44]

First concludes, "Identification with the helpless falling bodies broke the defensive depersonalizations" (p. 44).

The testimony of a Japanese journalist in her thirties who works in New York, born long after Hiroshima, contains additional layers of associations and meaning. From her office in midtown, she could see the World Trade Center, and described the scene for me.

I could see the fire, the smoke. It was so thick, but I was so busy. I had to prepare for the meeting taking place that day. People were coming in, flying in. I had no time to look. Only now it dawns on me what was really happening—that the towers collapsed. Ben, my husband, could have been killed. I walked out into the street and I looked up the streets of Manhattan. I saw the brilliant sky, the sun shining; looking downtown I saw billowing clouds of smoke, people covered with ashes.

One should remember that this woman is Japanese, remembering stories of other ashes. "People were running, an unending tidal wave. A few hours later, nobody was there. New York was a ghost town." What is striking in these accounts is the inability to cognitively and emotionally grasp what was really happening, by the journalist, the school children, patients in psychotherapy, or even the terrorists themselves, and the use of a frame—the window, the television screen—to both contain and distance these events from the experiencing self.

Attempting to understand the absences

How are we to understand these "absences", these "blanks" in our experience and the framing, distancing strategies put in place when atrocities penetrate our consciousness? To come to know something is to process new information, to assimilate and integrate an experience into one's own inner world representation. It is essentially to build a new construct inside ourselves. Moore defines memories of trauma as "*new* constructions of a previously constructed reality which was originally based on some particular direct experience" (1999, p. 167, my italics). These, in fact, can even be someone else's experiences:

> That which might otherwise be constructed overwhelms the construction process and therefore the constructor. . . . We know this has occurred only when *others* are able to supply a narrative. The traumatized person lacks the ability or the opportunity, or both, to initiate, create or integrate this interaction. Potential reality overflows the capacity to construct it, and the result is not a reality created by one's experience, but the loss of one's capacity to participate in it at all. (*ibid.*, p.168, my italics]

What, specifically, overwhelms the process of construction and, therefore, the constructor himself, resulting in a total loss of one's capacity to participate in one's own reality?

To process information, to make it our own, we employ the process of symbolization. In her paper on symbol formation in ego development, Klein states, "not only does symbolism come to be the foundation of all fantasy and sublimation, but more than that, it is the basis of the subject's relation to the outside world and to reality in general" (1930, p. 238). Therefore, to perceive, grasp, or participate in reality, the process of symbolization needs to be in place. "Symbol formation," according to Segal, "governs the capacity to communicate, since all communication is made by means of symbols" (1957, p. 395). She proceeds, "Symbols are needed not only in communication with the external world, but also in internal communication" (p. 396), that is, with oneself. "The capacity to communicate with oneself by using symbols, is, I think, the basis of verbal thinking, which is the capacity to communicate with oneself by means of words" (*ibid.*)

Freud himself, in one of his earliest works, the monograph on aphasia (1953), originally published in 1891, already emphasized the importance of associations between words and of words with other (sensory) elements, in order to create meaning. He posited an aphasia of the first order, verbal aphasia, in which only the associations between the single elements of the word representations are disturbed. An aphasia of the second order is the asymbolic aphasia, in which the association between word and object representations is disturbed. Freud postulated an internal psychic event, a thing representation, which came to be linked to another psychic event, a psychological word representation. A linkage between the two psychic events created the symbol—the psychological word. "All object representations that are linked to a word are a symbol. To speak then is to symbolize in words, the representations of a bodily mind" (Rizzuto, 1993, p. 123). Rizzuto emphasizes that, for Freud, listening was an active process.

> It requires a certain inner speech to ourselves. The word we understand is the combined word of the person who spoke and the inner word we spoke to ourselves. This inner word has a psychic history already. Listening, therefore, means associating external words to inner words, and in the end, we hear ourselves internally. [*ibid.*]

In other words, Freud saw the formation of the symbol as occurring in the context of such internal communicative process. I would strongly support such an understanding of symbolization as an internal dialogic process. One comes to know one's story only by telling it to oneself, to one's internal "thou".

Reality, therefore, can be grasped only in a condition of affective attunement with oneself. Massive psychic trauma, however, is a deadly assault, both on the external and the internal "other", the "thou" of every dialogic relationship. The executioner does not heed the victim's plea for life, and relentlessly proceeds with the execution. The "other", the "thou", who is empathically in tune and responsive to one's needs, ceases to exist and faith in the possibility of communication itself dies. There is no longer a "thou", either outside or inside oneself, a thou whom one can address. An empathic dyad no longer exists in one's internal world representation. There is no one to turn to, even inside oneself. It is an utterly desolate landscape, totally void of life and of humanity, permeated by the terror of the state of objectlessness. It is this state of dread, of catastrophic object loss, that compels the victim to internalize the only object available to him, that of the perpetrator, as a malignant self object (Kohut, 1971), leading to the so-called "identification with the aggressor".

Kirschner has written in a similar vein about his definition of trauma as an interpersonal event or experience that disrupts the symbolic framework and, thereby, threatens to damage the internalized "good object". He emphasizes that "the good object—and here I refer explicitly to an internalized sense of goodness in its most symbolic sense—is essential to the capacity for emotional participation in the world of others and perhaps for psychic survival" (1994, p. 238). In summarizing the work of other psychoanalytic theoreticians, he states,

> I argue that what is fundamentally at stake across the theories of trauma of Ferenczi, Klein, Winnicott and Lacan (and the list could be expanded) is the constant threat of destruction or loss of "the good object" and that the therapeutic efficacy of psychoanalysis is, therefore, closely connected with its function of maintaining or restoring this symbolic object. [*ibid.*, p. 239]

The role of the death instinct

I would add that it is the very presence of this good object that makes possible and safeguards the communicative process of symbolization, the dialogue with the internal "thou" that names experiences, enhances meaning and creates narrative. Trauma, by abolishing the good object, precipitously (or gradually) shuts this process down.

For Ferenczi, trauma was a total experience in which the object/other failed the child by action or by failure to act (1931, p. 128). For Lacan, trauma was the real, non-assimilated experience that resists symbolization and language, experience that has not become speech and, thus, has not been historicized within the symbolic network of signification. For Klein, it is the internalized projected rage of the instinctually frustrated child that becomes traumatic, and it is the developmental accomplishment of the restoration and preservation of the good object in the (subsequent) depressive position that serves as its antidote. Winnicott's "good enough mothering" serves the same purpose.

I believe that the fragmenting effects of the traumatic experience can be better understood if we postulate the presence of unbound, unneutralized death instinct derivatives, the more powerful and deeper forces I alluded to earlier. The link between trauma and the unleashing of the death instinct derivatives can be found in Freud's reference to the negative effects of trauma leading to "an inhibition— even an inability to deal with life" (Freud, quoted in Kirschner, 1994, p. 238). Conscious memory is the first casualty of the unbound death instinct derivatives. Furthermore, erasure of traumatically lost objects and of the traumatic experience itself might lead the survivor to complete oblivion, or to doubt the veracity and authenticity of his own experiences. His sense of identity and continuity might be compromised; his ability to invest in intimate relationships might be severely impaired, leading to a life sense of doomed aloneness. I contend that it is the traumatic loss of the (internal) good object, and the libidinal ties to it, that release the hitherto libidinally neutralized forces of the death instinct and intensifies these clinical manifestations of its derivatives in the aftermath of massive trauma. In the absence of an internal responsive "thou", there is no attachment to, or cathexis of, the object.

To follow André Green's line of thought, with the loss of the good object (the dead mother complex), the primary ego, which is melded with the object, relentlessly relives its loss and becomes "as disinterested in itself as in the object, leaving only a yearning to vanish, to be drawn towards death and nothingness" (Green, 1986, p. 13). For Green, "this is the true expression of the death instinct" (p. 13). Later, Green puts it even more eloquently. In pointing out that when

> the lost object becomes an inaccessible good object, we come to deal with nothingness [the blank psychosis]. . . . Characterized by blocking of thought processes, the inhibition of the function of representation . . . The final result is paralysis of thought . . . a hole in mental activity [and an] inability to concentrate, to remember, etc. [pp. 40–41]

"This tendency towards nothingness is the real significance of the death instinct" (*ibid.*, p. 55). Green postulates a "negative narcissism which de-cathects ego-libido without returning it to the object" (*ibid.*, p. 13), which arises from "the destructive instincts, and [which] is only manifest in the tendency to reduce ego cathexes to naught" (*ibid.*, p. 12).

While I find the formulation described above both compelling and accurate, the limits the author sets on its applicability render it, in my opinion, incomplete. Green limits this phenomenon to the understanding of "failures" of favourable evolution. The infant, when growing up with an "emotionally dead" mother, instead of separating into an individual invested in himself, ends up narcissistically depleted in a "deathly deserted universe" (*ibid.*, p. 167). He buries part of his ego in the "maternal necropolis". At this point, I want to underscore how my view differs from Green's: I believe that the same dynamics and a comparable phenomenology hold true *not only* for the infantile symbolic maternal loss, but also for the *traumatic loss of the good internal object at any age*.

The analytic candidate in the vignette that opens this essay made the same mistake Green makes. He related the patient's empty life and the re-enactment of the bad object in the analytic transference to maternal deprivation—or, to put it in Green's words, to the "dead mother complex". He did not entertain (nor did his supervisor) the *possibility* that it was the father's probable severe traumatic experiences in a Japanese POW Camp (father's loss of the good object through his possible torture experience) that, through intergenerational transmission, introduced the bad object into the analytic space. The vignette that follows further illustrates this point.

An adolescent Holocaust survivor lost most of her immediate family while in hiding in an underground pit. The family that had remained behind perished when the ghetto was liquidated. Before going into her hiding place, she took temporary refuge with several relatives and friends in a nearby forest. There she witnessed the drowning of her cousin's baby son by his mother, because he was crying when a German search party was nearby in the forest. The survivor tried to get back to her mother in the ghetto, who stayed there with her other children and grandchildren, but mother rudely dismissed her and sent her away. This saved her life, but also deeply wounded her. She eventually joined the Partisans. When a German prisoner, a young boy, was turned over to her so she could take revenge, she bandaged his wounds instead and sent him over to a POW camp.

After the war, she married and had children. She was particularly attached to her son, keeping him very close to her, sometimes sleeping in the same bed. Her life was one of continuous flashbacks. When leaves were burned so as to clear up the foliage, she went into a panic, re-experiencing the burning synagogue where many members of her family died. She was living totally absorbed in another world that had absolute immediacy for her. Her children, including her son, although very close to her, were figures who came back from that other world. The son himself grew up to be an accomplished intellectual. There was an all-consuming yearning in him to recapture the history of his mother's world, its language, idioms, and poetry, in minutest details. In his real life, however, he found no grounding. He continuously lived in an in-between state, sometimes not eating, not showering, and literally being homeless. Night and day seemed to be a continuum. No relationship lasted and what he wanted most, to give a grandchild to his ill and aging mother, he could not carry out. He even considered committing suicide.

Interpretations aimed at reintegrating his mother's known and consciously unknown past into his life were of little value. The power of the concrete and literal experience left little space for them to even register. At some point in his career, he was invited to spend a period of time in another country, which was culturally much closer to the traditions of the place his mother came from. The therapist saw this as a unique opportunity for this patient to find himself, and indeed said so. The patient left, and soon enough found a partner, a woman who insisted that he settle down and have a family or else she would leave him. He was deeply in love with her and carried out her wish. Upon his return to this country, he visited his therapist with his new wife and baby to factually demonstrate to him the change that had taken place.

This patient is yet another example of the living out of the "dead mother complex", which allowed for no independent life of his own. He could only relive his mother's mostly untold history, her anguish, fragmentation, and her losses. The therapist's intervention consisted of an encouragement that he change the place he lived in to another place where he could find himself more at home and in more familiar surroundings, and, indeed, it was there that he could build a life of his own.

The other link between the traumatic experience and the unleashing of the death instinct derivatives occurs through the so-called "identification with the aggressor". Here again, Green's formulation about the fear of the disappearance of the bad object is of help. Confronted with the horrors of emptiness (objectlessness) (Green,

1986, p. 55), the most intolerable of states, the victim feels compelled to maintain the relation with the bad "internal" object at all costs. The traumatized patient, whose ego had been overwhelmed by excessive excitation, his protective shield shattered by the traumatic event and by the loss of the good object, in order to avoid the horrors of object-lessness and the dissolving of psychic structure, holds on to the only object left—the perpetrator–aggressor.

The death instinct and the perpetrator

Any examination of death instinct derivatives in the victim has to take into consideration the death instinct derivatives that operated in the perpetrator. The latter, by his very act of committing the atrocity, has irreversibly crossed a threshold; he has abolished the libidinal empathic tie to the other, who thereby ceased to exist in the aggressor's own internal world representation. It is that objectless, hermetically closed and closed-off "deathly deserted universe" that the victim internalizes, and *not* the aggressor's murderousness and destructiveness of the "other". The perpetrator, by turning the fantasy and nightmare into real life, by committing the murder of the "other", and thus cutting the human bond, no longer symbolizes or sublimates the derivatives of the urge to annihilate. He concretely carries out the annihilation itself, thus eliminating the "other" and compromising any potential outcome from a dialogue with him, including the process of symbolization itself.

When there is no other to communicate with, the context within which symbolization takes place is gone. A regression to the concrete, to the "symbolic equation" (Segal, 1957, p. 393), takes place. It is the killer's *crossing the line into* a world in which empathic human links no longer exist, into a void of human binding relatedness, an "other" universe, which literally enacts the death instinct itself and sets it into motion. This is what leads to its self-perpetuation, to its multiple derivatives. The killer himself continues to live this void and pass it on to his children. He does not "know" what really happened, because he stopped symbolizing and communicating with himself. The narrative is flat, repetitive, stereotypical, impoverished, overflowing with rationalizations and very self-centred; somatic preoccupations and obsessional rituals take the place of real life.

In Polanski's film based on Ariel Dorfman's play, *Death and the Maiden*, the only value of the rapist's confession when he is about to be executed lies in his confirmation of the actual facts. He has no clue as to what he has done to another person. He remembers how pleasant her body smelled and how beautiful she was. There is no self-reflection or wondering about the pain he inflicted. He confirms the historic event, but does not begin to grasp the experience of the victim. He has no feel for her terror, pain, humiliation, rage, and no trace of realization or regret is to be found in him. In such contexts, where the death instinct reins, asking questions is forbidden. Primo Levi's quote of the rule of Auschwitz "Hier is kein Warum" (Here there is no Why) applies not only to victims, but also to perpetrators, and is quite representative of that prohibition of discourse, of dialogue, and of asking questions. Nothing is acknowledged, so there is nothing to tell.

Testimonies of perpetrators usually contain very little experiential information, as if they had not been there or carried out their deeds. Such testimonies feel empty. Listeners to them often have remarkable experiences of that communicative silence. Heidi Moennich-Marks and Stephan Marks, a psychoanalyst and a social scientist who conducted a research project connected to the "Paedagogische Hochschule" of Freiburg in Germany, report:

> The following are some of our observations and counter-transference reactions: Most of the interviewees "took the floor" in most dominating, abusive and self-opinionated ways; in some ways, they re-enacted being members of the master race. In the course of the interviews we, the interviewers, often felt overrun, bulldozed, emptied, saddened, confused, sickened, abused or knocked down. During the nights following an interview, we were often haunted by nightmares about war or persecution. And indeed, Heidi once had a car accident right after an interview. [Personal communication, 3 February 2003]

Mechanisms of unleashing death instinct derivatives

We have identified four mechanisms by which the traumatic experience unleashes the derivatives of the death instinct. In one way or another, all four mechanisms relate to the loss of the internal object and the resultant loss of protective libidinal ties to it.

1. The ego boundary and protective shield shattering quality of the experience itself causes an "unbinding" of destructive forces leading to "primal repression", possibly a manifestation of the death instinct itself. "By binding excitations, the organism defers its own death derivative" (Ley, 2000, pp. 28–29).
2. The elimination of the internal other, the internal "thou" with whom every communication that leads to knowledge takes place (the libidinal ties that hitherto neutralized the death instinct are gone as well).
3. The negative narcissism that in all likelihood originates from the above. (See Green, 1986, p. 13.)
4. The identification with the death-like quality of the internal world of the perpetrator. It should be emphasized that such identification occurs in the context of the extreme vulnerability and helplessness of the state of victimhood. The victim has no recourse to either outer or inner resources. He is, so to speak, "hijacked" by the perpetrator and is physically as well as emotionally completely at his mercy. The paradigm of the "Stockholm Syndrome" partially applies here, wherein hostages identify themselves with their captors and even espouse their political beliefs.

Implications for therapy

How do we treat patients whose clinical manifestations are fuelled by death instinct derivatives? The death instinct operates silently, unobtrusively. As Freud said, "It must be confessed that we have much greater difficulty in grasping that instinct; we can only suspect it, as it were; as something in the background behind Eros and it escapes detection" (1930a, p. 121). Simply naming it is, therefore, of little use. How can we mobilize libidinal forces that can be put to use to counteract it?

The genuine experience of surprise in analyst and in patient at the totality of the death instinct effect (a large blind spot, not seeing the self-evident) might in itself be re-libidinizing, especially if such surprise is spontaneous, mutually shared, and enhances curiosity and interest to embark on a new venture of exploration. The therapeutic alliance makes an essential contribution to such re-libidinization.

Kohut's self–object and Winnicott's "holding environment" are useful concepts in understanding how the re-libidinization of the self and object and of the connection between the two occurs. Auerhahn, Laub and Peskin state (1993, p. 436), "It is only when survivors remember with someone, when a narrative is created *in the presence of a passionate listener*, that the connection between an 'I' and a 'you' is remade". As Moore put it,

> Recovery from trauma apparently requires an experience, probably not dissimilar from that originally shared with a parent in whose arms shared constructions were first initiated. . . . The infant in the mother's arms cannot ask if the mother believes her; it is the mootest of points. Correspondingly, for the severely traumatized person, the issue is not whether rape occurred or whether Auschwitz existed. There is no clinical point in involving theory to qualify such powerful and painfully established realities. The point is that such experiences be shared, constructed and reconstructed in a manner that mobilizes and repairs the constructive process itself, until a narrative that integrates the traumatic experience in the deepest and most unifying way, is established. [1999, pp. 169–170]

To follow Green's (1986) thinking, "The goal to strive for is to work with a patient in a double operation: To give a container to his content and a content to his container" (p. 42). It is providing what is needed to set a process in motion again. In Green's own words, "It seems to me that the only acceptable variations of classical analysis are those whose aim it is to facilitate the creation of optimal conditions for symbolization" (p. 295). Grubrich-Simitis (1984), in her recommendations for working with children of Holocaust survivors, emphasizes that the reconstruction of the concrete facts of the parents' past experiences, the emotional confirmation of the Holocaust, of the reality of the death camps, is something that needs to happen in the early phases of analysis. Such reconstruction allows them to resume the process of metaphorization.

Can we consider the possibility that in the case of severely traumatized patients, the analytic setting no longer contains the safety that is necessary for the analytic process to unfold? This is so because the analytic setting itself becomes the very locus of re-enactment and of reliving of the traumatic event, which, according to Grubrich-Simitis, has a de-symbolizing effect (1984, p. 17). When trauma is at the centre,

"The feeling is that something is happening which acts against the setting" (Green, 1986, p. 45). Both analyst and patient feel it, but more so the analyst, who has to protect the setting from something acting against it. When the analyst is able to achieve a certain degree of structure, "having succeeded in binding the inchoate and in containing it within a form" (*ibid.*, p. 46), his own internal process of symbolization has begun. "He constructs a meaning which has never been created before the analytical relationship began" (*ibid.*, p. 48). Whether such meaning is accurate, or how much of it he conveys to the patient, or how much of it the patient is able and willing to accept is a function of the ongoing clinical process in which continuous mutual attunement and future revisions of such constructions are inevitable. The important thing is that the analyst takes such initiative in the construction of fact and of meaning, and remains a step ahead of his analysand in his readiness to know what it is all about (Grubrich-Simitis 1984, p. 20).

Kirschner states,

> Analysts now realize that the establishment of a condition of relative safety which I've defined in terms of maintenance of the good object in its capacity to represent the symbolic order, is a pre-condition for a clinically useful transference repetition of trauma . . . it must be said that more active measures seem to be necessary to provide an atmosphere of safety and confidence required for analytic work to be sustained. I refer here to overt expressions of interest and concern, willingness to participate in discussions about "external reality" as experienced by the patient, and attention to empathic contact. [Kirschner, 1994, p. 240]

I shall end this chapter with a clinical vignette from the training analysis of the candidate whose blind spots I described at the beginning of this presentation. It is presented in the first person, because he himself is the reporter. It illustrates the approach of his own training analyst, who is not only a step ahead of his analysand, but offers him at a certain moment an item of historical information which is compellingly relevant to the aforementioned blind spots.

> As a child, I was deported to Transnistria, the part of Ukraine occupied by the Romanian Army, who were allies of the Germans. What I remembered for years was sitting with a little girl on the bank of the River Bug,

the demarcation line between the German and the Romanian occupation territory. It was a beautiful summer day; there were green meadows and rolling green hills and a winding blue river. It was like a summer camp. We were having a debate at age five, arguing whether you could or could not eat grass. I recounted this memory in my second week of analysis in 1969 and luckily enough, my analyst was Swedish. His response was, "I have to tell you something. It was the Swedish Red Cross that liberated Theresienstadt and took depositions from women inmates in the camp. Under oath, some of these women declared that conditions in the camp were so good that they received each morning breakfast in bed brought by SS officers." There could not have been a more powerful interpretation of my denial. I stopped talking about young girls, green meadows, and blue rivers and started remembering other things, my own experiences of trauma.

Conclusion

The inevitable conclusion of this chapter is that, in cases of massive psychic trauma, the establishment of a setting is required "which allows the birth and development of an object relationship" (Green, 1986, p. 47) in which the analyst participates in the construction of "a meaning which has never been created before the analytic relationship began . . . the analyst forms an absent meaning" (*ibid.*, p. 48). This is so because the survivor, in solitude, continuously faces the horrendously difficult task of dealing with his own death instinct-related inner voids, as well as with whatever he has fabricated or taken in to fend off the terror of these inner voids. In the last vignette, it was the fairy tale of the "summer camp" on the banks of the River Bug, a "pseudo-narrative" at best.

A considerable amount of death instinct-fuelled resistance has to be overcome to recognize and address these voids. Such resistance is illustrated in the first vignette as operating in all three persons involved—patient, analyst, and supervisor. What might even be far more difficult than overcoming resistances is to dislodge and evacuate the internalized empty world and pseudo-narrative of the perpetrator, to overcome the "need to maintain a relation with a bad internal object at all costs" (*ibid.*, p. 54). The analyst in the last vignette addresses the thinly veiled defence against the bad internal object (turning the memory of the concentration camp to that of a summer camp) by participating in the construction of "a meaning which has never been created before", through himself being an object that introduces new and illuminating historical information (probably related to his life experience as a contemporary witness to events hitherto unknown to the patient). The patient can, thereby, deconstruct his death instinct-permeated fairy tale of a summer camp, and now "in the presence of a passionate listener" (Auerhahn, Laub, & Peskin, 1993, p. 436) comes to be enabled to review his life experience anew.

The contribution of Green's concept of "The dead mother complex" to the understanding of the connection between death instinct derivatives and massive psychic trauma is of greatest value. As I mentioned earlier, his error lies in limiting its relevance to the absence of maternal care. I find that this connection applies to all cases of massive psychic trauma where the internal "good object" has been destroyed. The mistake the analyst made in the first vignette was believing what Green believes: that maternal deprivation alone was at the root of his patients' difficulties, thus not allowing for the possibility of the destruction of the good internal object through the traumatic experience that her father is assumed to have suffered. Perhaps this oversight is yet another manifestation of a death instinct derivative.

References

Auerhahn, N. C., Laub, D., & Peskin, H. (1993). Psychotherapy with Holocaust survivors. *Psychotherapy: Theory, Research, Practice, Training, 30*(3): 434–442.

Caruth, C. (1996). *Unclaimed Experience: Trauma, Narrative and History*. Baltimore, MD: Johns Hopkins University Press.

Ferenczi, S. (1931). Child-analysis in the analysis of adults. In: *Final Contributions to the Problems and Methods of Psycho-Analysis* (pp. 126–142). London: Hogarth, 1955.

First, E. (2002). The aftermath of September 11: parents and children. *International Psychoanalytic Association Newsletter, 11*: 43–45.

Freud, S. (1930a). *Civilization and Its Discontents. S.E., 21*: London: Hogarth.

Freud, S. (1953). *On Aphasia: A Critical Study*. New York: International Universities Press.

Green, A. (1986). *On Private Madness*. London: Hogarth.

Grubrich-Simitis, I. (1984). Vom konkretismus zur metaphorik. gedanken zur psychoanalytischen arbeit mit nachkommen der Holocaust-generation—anlä-slich einer neuerscheinung (From concretism to metaphor: psychoanalytic work with descendants of the Holocaust generation). *Psyche: Zeitschrift für Psychoanalyse und ihre Anwendungen, 38*(1): 1–27. [Also published in: From concretism to metaphor: thoughts on some theoretical and technical aspects of the psychoanalytic work with children of holocaust survivors. *The Psychoanalytic Study of the Child, 39*: 301–319.]

Kafka, J. S. (2002). The mind of the fundamentalist/terrorist: terrorizing and being terrorized. *International Psychoanalytic Association Newsletter, 11*: 31–33.

Kirschner, L. (1994). Trauma, the good object and the symbolic: a theoretical integration. *International Journal of Psychoanalysis, 75*: 235–242.

Klein, M. (1930). The importance of symbol-formation in the development of the ego. In: *Contributions to Psycho-Analysis 1921–1945* (pp. 236–250). London: Hogarth.

Kohut, H. (1971). *The Analysis of the Self*. New York: International Universities Press.

Ley, R. (2000). *Trauma: A Genealogy*. Chicago, IL: University of Chicago Press.

Moore, R. (1999). *The Creation of Reality in Psychoanalysis*. Hillsdale, NJ: Analytic Press.

Oliner, M. (1996). External reality: the elusive dimensions of psychoanalysis. *Psychoanalytic Quarterly, 65*: 267–300.

Rizzuto, A-M. (1993). Freud's speech apparatus and spontaneous speech. *The International Journal of Psychoanalysis, 74*(1): 113–127.

Segal, H. (1957). Notes on symbol formation. *The International Journal of Psychoanalysis, 38*: 391–397.

van der Kolk, B., McFarlane, A., & Weisaeth, L. (1996). *Traumatic Stress: The Effects of Overwhelming Experience on Mind, Body and Society*. New York: Guilford Press.

Wilson, J., & Lindy, J. (1994). *Countertransference in the Treatment of PTSD*. New York: Guilford Press.

CHAPTER FOUR

Clinical and historical perspectives on the intergenerational transmission of trauma

Peter Loewenberg

Trauma

T rauma is derived from the Greek term *traumatikos* for wound, meaning that external violence has caused an injury; this usage is still current in medicine and surgery. An axial event was the moment when the concept "trauma", which had been limited to bodily injury, was expanded to include damage perpetrated on the mind, identity, feelings, and self. In the words of Ian Hacking,

> Freud transformed Western consciousness more surely than the atomic bomb or the welfare state. His famous inventions, such as the Oedipus complex, are familiar enough, but we often ignore more fundamental aspects of his work. He cemented the idea of psychic trauma. [Hacking, 1996, p. 76]

It is no coincidence that the moment when Freud linked trauma from the physical to the psychic was in 1916, in the midst of the First World War.

Psychologically, trauma means a violent shock, a wound to the person's self-concept and stability, a sudden loss of control over external and internal reality, with consequences that affect the whole organism. We now recognize a spectrum of trauma and traumatic experiences. Trauma may be acute or cumulative. Freud defined "trauma" as "an experience which within a short period of time presents the mind with an increase of stimulus too powerful to be dealt with or worked off in the normal way" (Freud, 1916–1917). The external stimulus is too powerful to be mediated by the normal adaptive coping mechanisms; the person is overwhelmed and helpless. The self disappears and psychic survival is threatened. The affects and the ability to symbolize feeling states are damaged. Responses range from apathy, paralysis, dissociation, splitting, and withdrawal, to panic, terror, annihilation anxiety, fragmentation, and disorganized behaviour.

Krystal and his colleagues initiated post Second World War trauma studies in the important 1968 book, *Massive Psychic Trauma*. Krystal enunciated his thesis in his first sentence: "Extreme circumstances of traumatization—disasters, catastrophes, and overwhelming social situations—effect marked changes in the people subjected to them and leave them with lifelong problems" (Krystal, 1968, p. 1). Krystal sought to frame trauma as a broad social group problem and posed a research question: "We are interested in both the individual and group processes involved, and we will examine the harmful influences in a social sense, to see whether the survivors are more likely to form pathological families, groups, and communities" (*ibid.*, p. 2). His answer was a distinct yes—the "survivor syndrome": "We have learned to recognize a syndrome characterized by the persistence of symptoms of withdrawal from social life, insomnia, nightmares, chronic depressive and anxiety reactions, and far-reaching somatization" (*ibid.*, p. 327). He concluded,

> The survivors form abnormal families and communities. The families tend to be sadomasochistic and affect-lame. The communities are laden with the burden of guilt and shame, and preoccupied with the past. The imprinting of inferior status can be perpetuated by a number of generations . . . [*ibid.*, p. 346]

This view has been critiqued particularly by Ornstein, who questioned the focus on psychopathology. She argues that the fundamental pre-Holocaust building blocks of personality, the principles and values of the "core or nuclear self", constitute the resource of post trauma recovery. The individual builds a mental link of continuity from the healthy resilient pre-war person they were, bridging the extreme deprivation, chaos, and horror of the Holocaust to work with their repression and loss, integrate the trauma, establish and build new relationships and a firm cohesive self, which allows mourning to take place. The person they were before is the emotional foundation of their resilience and recovery (Ornstein, 2003; Ornstein & Goldman, 2006).

Many of these findings are true to my own clinical experience with Holocaust survivor children of the second generation. However, I would like to modify the phenomenology of trauma sequelae to assert the added perspective of learning and adaptation to a trauma, leading to a restructuring of an individual life and of the world, to ensure that the trauma not only cannot be repeated, but is compensated for and repaired by fundamentally changing reality, and this can often be in a positive, socially constructive direction.

Clinical observations

Many of us are now treating, or have treated, the children and grand-children of Holocaust survivors. We can see the anxieties and defences associated with former traumas in the here and now. I will outline some of these clinical characteristics of the children and grandchildren of survivors:

1. *The unspoken, unmentionable "Secret"*
    A great sadness sensed but never expressed. Grandparents and parents did not tell, and avoided answering questions, about their life in concentration camps. "They never spoke about it."
2. *The quest for safety, risk aversion*
    Conscious and unconscious messages: "Do not go too far from home!" This affected choices of university, residence, professional location, resulting in some lost opportunities.
3. *Generalized distrust and insecurity*
    Particularly of any state or government: "You never know!" You can only trust your immediate family. These families felt an urgency to create options and exits, such as holding multiple foreign passports, hiding cash from the till, and undeclared funds abroad.

4. *The edge of life or death*
    Choosing medical sub-specialities such as cardiology and working with heart attack victims who are all filled with fear and death anxiety (my "sample size" is eight, four of whom are physicians). Medical compliance is not an issue for cardiac cases: "Patients will do anything you tell them." Several physicians told me, "I want to be at the knife edge between life and death." One cardiac surgeon immediately associated to his Holocaust survivor father. The undoing and reversal are obvious. Now the sons and daughters are in the place where they know all the secrets. Instead of a killer SS man who decides on life or death, the adaptation is to become a healer and father–rescuer on the side of life, but with the same excruciating life/death tension. These motivations are accentuated among, but not exclusive to, Holocaust survivors. A medical student whose father died of a ruptured coronary embolism chose interventional radiology as his speciality. The subtleties of sublimation and adaptation are still to be fully articulated.

5. *Disturbances and disavowal of affect*
    There is severe damage to affective responses, which become minimal, inappropriate, or do not exist. An Emergency Room physician chose that speciality because she wishes to avoid a sustained relationship with her patients in which caring and affectionate feelings might develop.

6. *Paranoid ideation of persecution*
    All opponents instantly become Nazis, including among physician and psychoanalyst colleagues. There is a sensitivity and expectation of humiliation in group and conflict situations.

7. *Marked ambivalence toward parents and grandparents*
    The feelings toward parental Holocaust survivors is a mixture of pity and the fantasy of repairing damage *vs.* contempt and the wish to dissociate and separate.

8. *Ambivalence regarding Jewish identity*
    The desire to acquire immunity from anti-Semitism, gain the apparent social advantages that non-Jews have in American culture, and avoid potential Holocausts is in tension with shame and guilt at betraying the parent's cultural identity.

9. *Chronic depression and sadness*
    There is identification with the parents in prolonged mourning over the incredible burden of personal and familial grief, anger and group trauma, over too many irremediable personal losses.

Ben: a grandchild of the Shoah

Ben, a twenty-two-year-old college senior, was referred to me by his older brother, whom I had treated three years ago. He is large, stocky, with green eyes and a broad face, dresses very casually (tee shirt and short trousers), and wears his dishwater blond hair long, sometimes in a ponytail. Ben seems well adjusted, has a girlfriend of five years' standing, majors in music, and plays guitar and drums. He chose a university close to home, although he had other options. He travels across the country to hear his favourite rock group, "Phish". He has had a slipped lumbar disc (which runs in the family); an undescended testicle was surgically removed a year ago. His description of the surgery was quite without affect: "This was recommended, so I did it." He describes himself as with controlled emotions; his girlfriend has more affect and is more sexual. Ben describes his mother as a sweet person who would do anything for you, too much so. His father, a businessman in wholesale manufacturing, is always on an even keel, emotions in the middle, neither high nor low. In the spring of 1998, Ben was depressed. With his parents, he visited a psychiatrist for two sessions, someone who saw him for thirty minutes and offered him a prescription for Prozac, which he refused.

His grandmother is a survivor of the concentration camp Bergen-Belsen. His grandfather was fourteen when the war broke out. The story Ben has is that his great-grandfather put his grandfather on a bicycle in the Ukraine and told him to ride west. He knows that grandfather served in an army for five years and survived the war and British internment in Cyprus, meeting his grandmother in Israel after the war. I asked which army grandfather served in. Ben does not know. I enquired about "heading west". In 1939–1940, that meant Poland, Germany, and German occupied Western Europe. He is puzzled, but grandfather never talks about it. Ben fits many of the configurations of Shoah children of survivors I outlined. The grandparents never relate any stories or discuss their past. And, getting the family message of the unmentionable, Ben never asks.

His presenting complaint was three acute anxiety attacks that occurred on 27, 28, and 29 September. The previous ones had been a year ago in the fall. He was filled with dread, frozen with anxiety, sat curled in a foetal position, hyperventilated, and wept, not knowing why. I enquired closely about anniversaries, the Jewish holidays, which were coincident with the attacks, and other prodromal events.

At Rosh Hashana (Jewish New Year) lunch on Saturday, 27 September, he heard his father and his uncle talking about the condition of his grandfather. It shocked him to hear that his grandfather was delusional, fearing the Nazis coming for him. Ben's father had to go to the hospital to get the grandfather because he thought he was being held prisoner. Ben's view of his grandfather's dementia and impending death is "scientific"—death is a welcome end to life. Yet, he has feelings of regret for his father, uncle, and grandmother, who would be the mourning survivors.

I interpreted the "split" in his emotional life between the controlled, cold, Darwinian, "scientific" side and the feelings of dread, confusion, fear, and horror that come out in his anxiety attacks. He had a further attack at the weekend of 4–5 October, after we began psychotherapy, but was able to hold it in check, controlling his panic, for which he felt grateful.

The German case: my parents' trauma and the German traumas

The First World War was the original, the primary, catastrophe of the twentieth century. It was the first total war in history, involving the lives and the full energies of its peoples as no previous war had. Europe lost her dominance in the world. The war meant an end to the four empires: Germany, Austria, Russia, and Turkey, and a breakdown of the established social value systems of these traditional polities. The empires of Central Europe were replaced by socialist republics, which had to deal with defeat, demobilization, and unemployment, peacemaking, and reparations, inflation, and depression. For Central Europe, the defeat in the First World War meant that much more than a war was lost—an entire normative state, regime, and society were destroyed that had to be reconstituted under conditions of desperation and determined opposition.

The German civilian population first felt severe shortages due to the British blockade in 1916. The winter of 1916–1917 was known as the "turnip winter", due to the exclusive, non-nourishing and monotonous diet (Berghahn, 1987). Official food rations in 1917 were 1000 calories per day, while the health ministry considered 2280 calories a subsistence minimum. Three quarters of a million people died of starvation in Germany between 1914 and 1918 (Erdmann, 1963). The number of live births declined from 1,353,714 in 1915 to 926,813 in 1918. The birth rate per 1000 people went from 28.25 in 1913 to 14.73 in 1918. Deaths among the civilian population over one year old rose from 729,000 in 1914 to 1,084,000 in 1918. Specific causes of increased death during the war years were influenza, lung infections and pneumonia, tuberculosis, diseases of the circulatory system, diphtheria, typhus, dysentery, and diseases of the urinary and reproductive organs (Bumm, 1928). In the war's third year, the weight of neonates was 50–100 grams less at birth than before the war. Among neonates and infants, there was a decline in weight and size at birth, a decline in the ability of mothers to nurse, and an increase of rickets and tuberculosis (*ibid.*). By the third year of war, three-year-old children were 2.2 pounds lighter than normal body weight for their age. A study comparing 300 Berlin children in 1908–1909 with children of the same age in 1919 showed that boys were retarded in growth by 1.5 years and the girls were 1.25 years behind normal (*ibid.*). Young children were also particularly afflicted with rickets, tuberculosis, and parasites. These diseases are specific to a population whose biological ability to maintain health and counter infection was undermined in the malnutrition and deprivation of the war.

I learnt of this from my parents, not only through the stories and reminiscences they shared of the hunger and rare, precious, once-a-year treats, like an orange that was segmented and shared by the whole family, but literally in my mother's body. After the Second World War, when my mother was over sixty and living in California, her ophthalmologist asked whether she had been in a concentration camp. When she said "No," he explained that her retina was scarred by prolonged malnutrition in a manner only seen in concentration camp survivors. She immediately knew this must have been the hunger years of the First World War. A major theme in the concentration camp memoir literature is the ever-present hunger and thirst. (Klüger, 1992). I speculate how much of the concentration camp cruelty and hunger regimen was reversal and undoing, turning the passive experiences of childhood starvation into the active infliction of suffering on to innocent others three decades later.

The relationship between the moral, physical, and psychic trauma of the First World War on the civilian populations, particularly the children, of Central Europe, and the Nazi appeal to them during the crisis of the Great Depression after 1929 was causal (Loewenberg, 1983). The experience of civilian deprivation and trauma during the war conditioned a generation of central European youth to make Adolf Hitler a charismatic figure and his programme politically attractive to them in the early 1930s. These traumas were: (1) extreme hunger and physical privation; (2) national defeat accompanied by the discredit, collapse, and humiliation of political and social authority; (3) prolonged absence and unavailability of parents. The absence of fathers in the army and mothers through war work was equally significant for male and female children. An emotional theme and literary trope after both World Wars is the unknown stranger who suddenly appears to take his place in the family—the father returned from war and captivity (Ernst Glaeser, 1929).

The worst hyperinflation in history, which wiped out the middle class and made its virtues of thrift and calculation irrelevant, occurred in 1923 as a consequence of the peace treaties. A particular transgenerational effect of this hyperinflation was the strongly held conviction among all sectors of the German public in the value of a deflationary economic policy. In January 1923, the American dollar was worth 1800 marks; by November 1923, the mark had fallen to 4.2 trillion to the dollar. All people with savings or pensions, those on fixed incomes or salaries, in a primarily middle-class country, were financially wiped out.

I know this from the oral tradition of my family. My paternal grandfather was an educator, the owner and director of a private girls' school. My maternal grandfather was a *Royer*—a wine appraiser for the Hamburg harbour. Both of these family incomes were vulnerable to war and inflation. Education is not an edible commodity, and parents could not pay for it. During wartime, the great North Sea harbour of Hamburg had no commerce; in the inflation, the remuneration for the wine appraiser was often the gift of some bottles of wine from France or Spain, which were then bartered for food. This trauma was communicated in the oral tradition and folklore of German families so that it was recalled and operative in the minds of those born decades later. Because of this, the German polity today, including the trade unions, has consistently supported a solid currency and a counter-inflationary wage policy, making the German mark one of the world's most stable currencies in the last half century until it was fused into the Euro in 1999.

Gunther Grass develops the theme of intergenerational transmission of trauma in his novel, *Crabwalk*, which deals with the memory of the sinking, on 30 January 1945, in the frigid Baltic Sea, of the *Wilhelm Gustloff*, a cruise ship named after a minor Nazi functionary (Grass, 2002). The *Gustloff* was carrying over 9000 refugees and U-boat sailors, plus 370 members of the Naval Women's Auxiliary, wounded soldiers, and anti-aircraft gunners fleeing from the Red Army advance into Pomerania. Paul, the narrator, who was born on the sinking ship, had never written about the *Gustloff* and the circumstances of his birth, despite his mother's nagging and ranting. His mother, Tulla, however, develops a special relationship with Paul's son, Konrad, who runs a virulent neo-Nazi web site:

> She began to need my son. Konny was only ten or eleven when he fell into his grandmother's clutches. And after the survivor's reunion in Damp, where I was a nonentity, lurking on the edges while he became the crown prince, she pumped him full of tales: tales of the flight, of atrocities, of rapes—tales about things she hadn't experienced in person but that were being told everywhere . . . [Grass, 2002, p. 105]

Grass clearly presents the leaping of a generation from grandmother to grandson, and the rivalry between father and son in which the son has eclipsed his father in the grandmother's world, as well as in public.

The Shoah and Israel

I do not believe that what is perceived as the militancy and abrasiveness of Israeli foreign and occupation policy can be understood without the background psychodynamics of the trauma of the Shoah as a living presence. I was born in Hamburg in 1933; my parents left Germany for China when I was six weeks old, so I did not personally experience life under National Socialism. However, my first cousin Fred, also born in Hamburg, in 1925, did not leave Germany until 1938, meaning that he lived the first thirteen years of his life in Nazi Germany. Only he knows the full extent of that trauma. His mother told me that his four-year younger brother (b. 1929) came home from school quite bloodied but never complained. He had been beaten by Nazi youths but did not want to distress his parents.

Fred now lives in an Israeli West bank settlement and his children and grandchildren of both genders serve or have served in the Israeli army implementing Israeli policy. Israeli children visit the extermination camps in Poland. None of this can be comprehended without an understanding of the transgenerational transmission of trauma and the need to affirmatively adapt and undo the past trauma that is still so alive. Those who, two generations ago, were—in the classic Freudian definition of trauma—helpless, impotent, and hopeless, are now self-confident, competent to defend themselves, and able to exercise options of self protection.

All narratives are plotted and written from the inescapable subjectivity of the writer. This narrative is written from the point of view of my traumatized generation. One tragic aspect of the intergenerational transmission of trauma is that it is potentially generative of new trauma. To be symmetrical, this essay would have had to include the story of a Palestinian traumatized by having her home bulldozed or by the loss of a loved one. Israeli grandchildren of the Shoah have become the dominant military power in their surroundings (Israelis, and particularly Shoah survivors, will say: "Thank God it is so!"), and inevitably inflict, and, thereby, perpetuate, trauma. In 1969, at a Press Conference, Golda Meir poignantly captured the tragedy of this cycle, and the consequent moral challenge to Israelis, when she said, "When peace comes, we will perhaps in time be able to forgive the Arabs for killing our sons, but it will be harder for us to forgive them for having forced us to kill their sons."

The American neo-orthodox Protestant theologian, Reinhold Niebuhr, when speaking about America's emergence as a world power, made the case that there can be no "moral" exercise of the functions of power (Niebuhr, 1952). Innocent people (as in Hiroshima and Dresden) will always be hurt, and this means trauma, in the sense of the Biblical curse: "Upon the children, and upon the children's children, unto the third and unto the fourth generation" (Exodus, 34:7).

Chinese historical trauma and compensation

The traumas of foreign incursion and exploitation of China by the Western powers in the nineteenth and early twentieth centuries included the Opium War (1839), which ended with the ceding of Hong

Kong to Britain in 1841. The first American treaty with China, the Treaty of Wanghsia of 1844, signed by the Imperial Commissioner Ch'-ying and Caleb Cushing for the USA, placed American residents under extra-territorial civil and criminal jurisdiction of consular and mixed courts. The Boxer Rebellion (1899–1900), in which twelve foreign powers sent an international expedition that seized Tientsin and Peijing, ended with the national humiliation of foreign control of maritime and native customs and the salt monopoly. The American "Open Door" policy of 1900 was a US bid not to be excluded from the economic concessions and control of factories, steamships, mines, railways, and political spheres of influence that European powers and Japan were securing in China.

The contempt, brutality, and indignity that came with foreign interventions—international expeditions, treaty ports, foreign "concessions" on the Chinese coast and up the rivers, "gunboat diplomacy", control of tariffs and customs, railway and mining concessions to foreign investors—all contributed to a special Chinese sensitivity to the psychological issues of "face" and shame before the world. The programme of Doctor Sun Yat-Sen (1866–1925), *San Min Chu I, The Three Principles of the People* (1927), was a first attempt to free and raise China through the principles of nationalism, democracy, and livelihood; it was an inspiration to both the Kuomintang and the Communists.

The greatest Chinese historical trauma was undoubtedly the humiliation of the Japanese Imperial land, naval and air invasion, conquest, and occupation of all of eastern China and a large portion of northern, central, and southern China in the years 1937 to 1945. Japan held every important strategic objective in China from the industry of Manchuria to the southern ports of Canton and Hong Kong. The weak, corrupt, and incompetent Nationalist government was incapable of defending Chinese territory. China, an undeveloped pre-industrial land facing a world-class industrial power, had no air force, no navy, and an under-equipped, corrupt, demoralized, ineffective army. The Kuomintang army was like a sieve through which the Japanese moved in South China in 1944–1945. All of Eastern China was open to the Japanese at their will. White and Jacoby described the Chinese Army as:

> a pulp, a tired, dispirited, unorganized mass, despised by the enemy, alien to its own people, neglected by its government, ridiculed by its

allies. No one doubted the courage of the Chinese soldier, but the army had no mobility, no strength, no leadership. [White & Jacoby, 1946, p. 132]

When, on 1 October 1949, Chairman Mao Zedong in Beijing's Tian An Men Square proclaimed the People's Republic saying: "The Chinese people have stood up!" [*Zhong guo Renmin Zhan Qi Lai!*], he was repairing centuries of hurt and shame. Now China had arisen and stood as an equal before the peoples and nations of the world. The new Chinese national anthem was:

> Stand Up! Stand Up!
> Not willing to be a slave people.
> [*Qi Lai! Qi Lai!*
> *Bu yuan zuo nuli duh renmin.*]

There is a special imperative that no foreign incursion ever impinge on China again: "Stay away from our borders, out of our territory, our air space, and our rights. We insist on our status, parity, and will proudly defend the sovereignty of our territory and China's dignity as a great power in the world."

I have seen and heard students in China filled with virulent hatred for Japan and the Japanese. They are moved to stand up in conferences, their eyes filled with tears, as they express their outrage at Japanese depredations in the Second World War. This is inexplicable in terms of their immediate life experience, which commenced more than three decades after the Second World War. However, it is comprehensible in terms of their grandparents' trauma and the Chinese national historical legacy.

Conclusion

Physical privation and emotional suffering such as Central Europe experienced in the First World War (and its aftermath: e.g., the economic catastrophe of German hyperinflation), the Israeli–Palestinian encounter, and the Sino-Japanese War and occupation have demonstrably left lasting scars on the German, Israeli, Palestinian, and Chinese body politic and collective political mind. In some cases, the trauma is known, not by personal experience, but as communicated by the intense feeling states and painful, helpless anxiety of family memory, oral tradition, and national history, which the respective polities attempt to defend against and avoid reliving. That stalwart effort is emotional confirmation of the strength and persistence of trauma across generations. A person's and a society's effort to adapt to historical trauma and to restructure life in a compensatory, even reparative reality-changing effort might bring about positive, socially constructive change. But it might also—as I have suggested as a possibility in the above cases—simply "turn the tables" of trauma, as the passive experience of being traumatized becomes the active traumatizing of the other.

References

Berghahn, V. (1987). *Modern Germany: Society, Economy and Politics in the Twentieth Century*. Cambridge: Cambridge University Press.

Bumm, F. (Ed.) (1928). *Deutcshlands Gesundheitsverhältnisse unter dem Einfluss des Weltkrieges*. Stuttgart: Deutsche Verlags-Anstalt.

Erdmann, K. (1963). Die Zeit der Weltkriege. In: B. Gebhardt (Ed.), *Handbuch der Deutschen Geschichte* (49–77). Stuttgart: Union Verlag.

Ernst Glaeser, E. (1929). *Jahrgang 1902*. Berlin: G. Kiepenheuer.

Freud, S. (1916–1917). Fixation to traumas—the unconscious, Lecture XVIII. *Introductory Lectures on Psychoanalysis. S.E., 16*. London: Hogarth.

Grass, G. (2002). *Crabwalk*. Orlando, FL: Harcourt.

Hacking, I. (1996). Memory sciences, memory politics. In: P. Antze & M. Lambek (Eds.), *Tense Past: Cultural Essays in Trauma and Memory* (pp. 67–87). New York: Routledge.

Klüger, R. (1992). *Weiter Leben: Eine Jugend*. Göttingen: Wallenstein Verlag [translated in 2001 as *Still Alive*. New York: Feminist Press at the City University of New York.

Krystal, H. (Ed.) (1968). *Massive Psychic Trauma*. New York: International Universities Press.

Loewenberg, P. (1983). *Decoding the Past: The Psychohistorical Approach*. New York: Alfred A. Knopf.

Niebuhr, R. (1952). *The Irony of American History*. New York: Scribner.

Ornstein, A. (2003). Survival and recovery: psychoanalytic reflections. *Progress in Self Psychology, 19*: 85–105.

Ornstein, A., & Goldman, S. (2006). *My Mother's Eyes: Holocaust Memories of a Young Girl*. Cincinnati, OH: Emmis Books.

Sun, Y.-S. (1927). *San Min Chu I: The Three Principles of the People*, L. T. Chen (Ed.), F. W. Price (Trans.). Shanghai: China Committee, Institute of Pacific Relations.

White, T., & Jacoby, A. (1946). *Thunder Out of China*. New York: De Capo Press.

PART II
INSIDE THE CONSULTING ROOM

Introduction

C linical work, especially the unconscious material, relational dynamics, and emotional exchanges of an in-depth psychotherapy, offers a privileged window on to the nature, mechanisms, and consequences of the transmission of trauma: its horror, intimacy, and uncanny re-emergence in the transference. Each of the chapters in this section illustrates one or another aspect of this process. Their stories report on the intense feeling, the crises and the transference–countertransference dilemmas that are part of psychotherapeutic work in the area of trauma. Transmission *implicates* the next generation, and these chapters show how the therapist, too, becomes implicated in the trouble, in the service of coming to know it and holding for the patient the possibility of a future.

Vamik Volkan offers a set of reflections on how psychoanalysis moved toward de-emphasizing the effects of real world events on the developing psyche and the cost of that avoidance to the clinical outcomes and depth of self-knowledge of some patients. He argues that, more often than we might realize, resistance in the analyst to feelings associated with historical trauma in his own life dovetails with similar resistance in the patient—a "mutually sanctioned silence and denial". He goes on to reflect movingly on real world events in his own life and in the lives of family members from past generations to show how something quite powerful and meaningful was left unexplored in his analysis. Through this very personal example and through the detailed example of one of his patients, Volkan illustrates convincingly the "intertwining" and reciprocal relationship between external traumatic events and the internal wishes, conflicts, defences, and fantasies of the person living through them.

In my chapter, I argue that the transmission of trauma from one generation to the next constitutes both a powerful form of authorization—a mission from the parent—as well as a de-authorization to live one's own life. Through two clinical vignettes, I show how the Big History of social catastrophes intersects with the Little History of an individual's life, how the transmission of a parent's trauma intersects dynamically with the child's development, and how markers of transmission find their way into a therapy, often in the form of dreams or acting out. Freud spoke about unconscious communication between people; the transmission of trauma seems to use this unconscious channel, between parent and child and between patient and therapist.

Barri Belnap picks up the theme of communication and shows us how parents use rituals and idiosyncratic speech acts to convey their trauma to their children. In an arena outside of time and the ordinary rules of social relatedness, "life lessons" are transmitted, and a demand is made on the next generation to represent and also to survive an unnamed trauma. Children thus grow up feeling a sense of urgency and dread about something quite mysterious as well as a parental claim upon them that seems to disaffirm their own experience. In two powerful clinical vignettes, Belnap describes the crises in the transference that mobilize intense loyalty to the parents and constitute a battle for the patient's own life. Belnap argues that in these situations, the countertransference is potentially a crucial resource as is attention to the "signifiers" hiding in plain sight in the patient's material.

Virginia Demos joins this theme of loyalty and disaffirmed experience in an extended account of a patient's struggles to get past the abuse of her childhood, itself related to abuse and traumatic loss in her parents' lives. Reflecting on the unprocessed grief, deprivations, defensive entitlements, and achievement orientation in the parental generation, she considers the link between these dynamics and trauma-related emigration. She goes on to describe the child's identifications with both the defences and the vulnerabilities of her parents, the specialness of her redemptive task, and the role reversal implicit in the assignment to take care of them. Demos's account of the psychotherapy, including work with the family, highlights the patient's intense conflict between membership and authenticity.

Francoise Davoine contributes a brilliant and brilliantly quixotic chapter, which moves back and forth from the clinical situation to literature and history, showing us what powerful resources the latter can be in our work. Creative, playful, ironic, but fierce, Davoine laments the loss of the person in contemporary approaches to severe emotional disturbance and argues that trauma and psychosis go hand in hand, that, in fact, the deeply troubled patient is carrying out a mad research into family trauma cut out of the official narrative. Most striking is her pointing out the seeming coincidences that occur in the transference between patient and therapist and her showing us how these moments hold deep meaning for the patient as well as an essential affirmation upon which a trustworthy foundation for change might be built. Her advice that we take Don Quixote as our supervisor might at first both puzzle and amuse us, but she means it, and she tells us why.

CHAPTER FIVE

The intertwining of the internal and external wars

Vamik D. Volkan

T his chapter examines the influence of traumatizing world events such as wars, war-like situations, and drastic political changes on the psyche of the individual, and raises the controversial question of whether or not to focus on such external events and their mental representations during psychoanalytic treatment. The analysand's reactions to current or chronic traumatizing world events might severely interfere with the routine analysis of mental conflicts stemming from realistic and/or fantasized experiences of childhood. Sometimes, analysts themselves do not allow the impact of certain external events to be examined during the psychoanalytic treatment process because they unconsciously wish to protect themselves from their own anxiety and fear should the emotion of such events enter their offices. In this chapter, I also investigate the role historical processes play in the lives of ancestors in shaping our analysand's symptoms and character formations.

Ignoring traumatizing external world events

During the mid 1960s, when I was a candidate at the Washington Psychoanalytic Institute, "ego psychology" was the dominant theory in all psychoanalytic institutes under the sponsorship of the American Psychoanalytic Association. We were taught to understand our patients' internal worlds by applying Freud's structural theory that divides the mind into the id, the ego, and the superego. In the clinical setting, the focus was on exploring psychic reality only: an analysand's inner mental conflicts, resistances, development of a transference neurosis, and its resolution. Primarily, while conducting psychoanalysis, we did not focus on dangers from the outside world or on the influence of external world events on our internal worlds. We followed the psychoanalytic tradition that originated with Freud's giving up, in his early efforts to develop psychoanalytic theories, the idea of the sexual seduction of children coming from the external world in favour of the stimuli that come from the child's own wishes and fantasies for formation of psychopathology. Thus, less emphasis by classical psychoanalysis on actual seduction coming from the external world on a developing child's psyche was generalized to include de-emphasis on external international events in general as they impact upon the psychopathology of individuals affected by dramatic historical actions.

In those days, there were multiple psychoanalytic schools, but some were perceived to be more firmly established than others. For example, the followers of Melanie Klein had established themselves as a formidable group competing with ego psychologists. Kleinians, too—even perhaps more than the ego psychologists—bypassed the influence of traumatizing external historical events while treating their patients. After all, Melanie Klein herself provided a well-known example of ignoring influences of a war while treating one of her patients. In 1961, she reported the treatment of a ten-year-old boy named Richard, which had taken place during the Second World War. During Richard's treatment, the terror of the war under which Richard lived had not been examined. Richard's family had moved to the country during the war. He was upset by moving and we can easily assume that he was well aware of the external situations which had increased his anxiety.

Was Klein's ignoring of the dangerous external circumstances simply due to her theoretical stance? By not paying attention to it while treating little Richard, was she denying her own fear of the external danger? We will, of course, never know for sure why Klein did not focus on the influence of a fear-inducing war situation and why she did not explore the intertwining of an external war with an internal one while treating Richard.

There are other occasions, however, when analysts' failure to pay attention to dangerous current or chronic historical events (also to past dangerous external world events) was clearly connected with their own resistance to recalling and/or re-experiencing troublesome affects. An analyst's own resistance may dovetail with the analysand's resistance and the examination of the dangerous external world, past or present, is ignored. In the USA, Blum's (1985) description of a Jewish patient who came to him for re-analysis illustrates the extent to which mutual resistances can prevail when both analyst and the analysand belong to the same large group which was massively traumatized by an external historical event. Blum's patient's first analyst, who was also Jewish, failed to "hear" their large group's shared trauma at the hands of the Nazis in his analysand's material; as a consequence, mutually sanctioned silence and denial pervaded the entire analytic experience, leaving unanalysed residues of the Holocaust in the analysand's symptoms. Blum writes,

> Although the patient and his last analyst were both born in Europe and were both Jewish, neither one discussed the experience of debasing bigotry, the war, emigration, being a refugee, social-cultural upheaval, separation from family and friends, and cultural shock. For years, they spoke to each other without mention of each other's accent or why they were meeting in an American rather than a European office. [*ibid.*, p. 898]

Blum continues to state that there was

> a double standard in analysis. Freedom of thought and expression were compromised by tacit cues that some areas were off limits and should remain shrouded in silence. This repetition of the "conspiracy of silence" (and the suffering in silence of the family) was maintained by depriving memory of emotional meaning, and skillful displacement of discussion. [*ibid.*, p. 899]

We can only wonder how many Jewish analysts in the USA after the Second World War were like Blum's patient's former analyst and how many of them, without being aware of it, influenced the application of the psychoanalytic treatment in a way that ignored the

Holocaust-related external reality. We can only imagine that some of them exaggerated their bias toward a theoretical position called "classical psychoanalysis" that is focused only on the patient's internal world during the analytic treatment.

We now know clearly that in post-Second World War Germany as well, there has been both German and German–Jewish analyst-supported resistance to exploring the intertwining of the internal and external wars and the influence of the Nazi era traumas on analysands' psyches. In the early 1960s, while treating an ethnic German analysand and a Jewish analysand, German–Jewish analyst Anna Maria Jokl left for Israel without completing the two patients' analytic work, and it was not until the mid-1990s that she was able to piece together and report the complex influences of their large-group identities on the scene of analysis (Jokl, 1997).

German-speaking psychoanalysts, such as Grubrich-Simitis (1979), Eckstaedt (1989) and Streeck-Fischer (1999) have explored the difficulties of "hearing" and having empathy with Nazi-related influences in their German and Jewish patients. Eckstaedt, indeed, has brought overdue attention to the trauma that ethnic Germans themselves experienced during the Third Reich and to the influence of that trauma on the self-conception of contemporary Germans. In 1997 and 1998, I was asked to work with a small group of ethnic German and Jewish–German analysts and therapists when they formed an organization to end "the silence" about the Holocaust-related issues that come up during clinical practice. I realized that such a "silence" was real and that it was difficult to deal with. (For details see: Volkan, Ast, & Greer, 2002, Chapter 9).

Beginning in the early 1950s, well-known psychoanalysts, both in the USA and Europe (A. Freud, 1954; Jacobson, 1954; Stone, 1954; Weigert, 1954) began to explore and write papers on a topic that became known as "the widening scope of psychoanalysis". Frosch (1954) summarized Anna Freud's concerns on this subject:

In the discussion [Arden House Conference, Harrison, May, 1954] Anna Freud referred to analytic situations which evoked variations in technique. She regretted, however, what she felt was the enormous expenditure of time and energy involved in the treatment of borderline and psychotic cases in view of the small ultimate results. In her opinion it would be more rewarding to devote such efforts to less severe cases with greater therapeutic promise. [p. 565]

We all know that, a couple of decades later, borderline patients and individuals with other personality disorders filled psychoanalysts' offices and psychoanalysts began writing about various new theories explaining borderline and other personality disorders and the technique for their treatment (Kernberg, 1975; Kohut, 1971; Volkan, 1976). Outside of new considerations about countertransference and other technical concepts, the widening scope of psychoanalysis was followed by studies on two movements in psychoanalytic practice:

1. There were efforts to come up with new psychoanalytic theories to understand the internal worlds of individuals whose superegos were not fully formed and integrated. Thus, there appeared a need to go beyond the application of the structural theory in order to explore the internal worlds of certain patients who were not simply "neurotics", and who were now referred to as "borderline" or "narcissistic" individuals. This led to the evolution of the type of object relations theory that primarily was systematized by Otto Kernberg (Kernberg, 1975), and I (Volkan, 1981) wrote about continuing to rely on the structural theory when analysing individuals with an integrated self-representation and utilizing the object-relations theory when treating persons with unintegrated self-representation.

2. It was noticed more and more how patients' internal and external worlds in general are intertwined. This, of course, was already known. Since "borderline" or "narcissistic" patients strongly and more openly react to their environments and often try to change them, or at least perceive them according to their internal demands, the intertwining of external and internal worlds in general began to receive more attention.

A primary reason to focus on these psychoanalytic movements, following discussions on the widening scope of psychoanalysis, seemed to be the fact that individuals with personality disorders, such as those with borderline or narcissistic personality organization, had began to attract psychoanalysts' attention. I think that there was also another reason. In the USA, in Europe, and in Israel analysts' resistances against recalling and re-experiencing the fearful external world of the Nazi period to a great extent had begun fading away by the 1970s, and more and more studies of the influence of the Third Reich on the psyche of the survivors (victims and perpetrators) had begun to surface. (For a review of the literature see: Kestenberg & Brenner, 1996; Volkan, Ast, & Greer, 2002.)

Psychoanalysts with a "classical" orientation began to realize that the specific nature of any given historical event is important when it symbolically becomes a mirror of our pre-Oedipal or Oedipal conflicts and our defences against them. In 1986, Abend wrote that "the impact of daily events, inner as well as *outer* plays upon our psychic integration and produces those fluctuations of mood, thought, and behavior which are part of our so-called normal personalities" (p. 565, my italics). He added that the analyst is constantly affected by shifting internal and external events. He suggested that the analyst cannot simply remain as a pure and non-changing "analyzing instrument".

In 1991, Arlow, another well-known American psychoanalyst, who was a key figure among the architects of the ego psychology that dominated the American psychoanalytic scene in the 1960s and 1970s, wrote,

> I think it is a fair statement that psychoanalysts today consider many more factors that contribute to the shaping of the individual— dynamic, biological, adaptive, developmental, experiential, and cultural factors. Where they differ is in the relative emphasis they give to one or another of these elements. [p. 60]

It is beyond the scope of this chapter to review the many studies on the reciprocal relationship between external reality and internal wishes, conflicts, defences, and unconscious fantasies, some of which, in spite of psychoanalysts' resistance to noticing them or focusing on them, indeed go back to Freud's own writings (e.g., see Freud, 1917d). What I am referring to here is the degree of "relative emphasis" that was given during psychoanalytic treatment to the intertwining of our analysands' experiences in wars, war-like conditions, and drastic political changes—and, we shall soon see, even of mental representations of our analysands' ancestors' historical events—that occurred in their internal worlds. World events following the collapse of the Soviet Empire, such as what happened in the former Yugoslavia, in Africa, and elsewhere in the 1990s, and now in the post-September 11 2001 world, have brought about an abundance of trauma studies and psychological studies of wars or war-like conditions. Such studies have also influenced psychoanalysts to a great extent. For example,

the theme of the 44th Annual Meeting of the International Psychoanalytic Association in Rio de Janeiro in the summer of 2005 was
"trauma", including trauma due to historical events. Psychoanalysts
have begun paying more and more attention to events in the external
world. There are, of course, many types of massive traumas in the
external world, some of them due to natural causes such as tsunami.
Keeping in mind the topic of this paper, I am focusing on traumas
related to wars, war-like conditions, drastic political changes, and
terrorism.

Meanwhile, beginning in the 1980s and spreading into the 1990s
and 2000s, a new phenomenon occurred in psychoanalysis that
became known as the new "pluralistic landscape of psychoanalysis"
(see, for example, Samberg, 2004, p. 243). In other words, many new
"schools" were put under the umbrella of "democracy in the field"
and each one of them claimed to be psychoanalytic. Under this
"democratic" approach, even some crucial classical concepts of psychoanalysis and psychoanalytic technique, including the concept of a
dynamic unconscious, were questioned by some "schools". In certain
circles, as far as I can see, the new "psychoanalytic technique" seemed
to have a sole focus on the patient's relationship with the external
world in general—not necessarily the external world related to wars,
war-like conditions, or political change—and the psychoanalyst's
"managing" the patient's life instead of trying to achieve an internal
structural change in the patient. Some "psychoanalysts", in my view,
have now begun exhibiting resistance against examining the analysand's unconscious dynamics at the expense of focusing on the
patient's relationships to their external world, bypassing the examination of the intertwining of the two—internal and external worlds—
in a sophisticated fashion.

Even those clinicians who continue with the tradition that what
counts in a proper psychoanalytic practice is the analysis of the
analysand's dynamic unconscious sometimes still resist dealing with
the influences current wars or chronic war-like situations have on
patients' internal worlds and on the analytic practice in general. Of
course, there is also recognition of such problems. For example, in
2004, Elliott, Bishop, and Stokes from the Irish Institute of Psycho-
Social Studies referred, among other things, to the troubles in Northern Ireland and stated that, "In the world of psychoanalysis there has
been a tendency, in addressing societal questions, to abandon the

rigour of the consulting room, and to resort to a long-distance speculation" (p. 1). Interestingly, they assert that social diversity "seriously
affects what is considered 'normal' and what is deemed 'pathological'.
Failure to address it may, moreover, contribute by counter-transfer-
ence to the formation of psychoanalytic 'schools' antipathetic toward
each other" (p. 14).

After September 11, the International Psychoanalytic Association
established a Terror and Terrorism Working Group, and Sverre Varvin
of Norway and I edited a volume of collected papers for this group
(Varvin & Volkan, 2004). The writings in this volume by colleagues
with Jewish and Arab backgrounds, I think, reflect my Irish colleagues' concerns. They, in my mind, include references to countertransference issues as well as blind spots concerning the situation in
the Middle East and its effects on the internal worlds of people from
different groups.

The influence of an ongoing dangerous external situation related
to wars or war-like situations on the psychoanalytic practice has
recently been described by the Israeli psychoanalyst Ilany Kogan
(2004). With two detailed case reports, Kogan illustrates the role of the
psychoanalyst in the analytic cure during times of chronic crises in
Israel. In her first case, Kogan is able to stay with fears evoked in her
patient by the traumatic external war-like situation. But, in her second
case, for a long time she was like Melanie Klein treating Richard in
Second World War Britain. The psychoanalyst's blind focus on her
patient's internal reality was an attempt to counteract her own sense
of passivity and helplessness, as she, like her patient, was surrounded
by a chronic life-threatening external world. The psychoanalysis was
being conducted when a chemical or biological attack on Israel was
perceived to be imminent. Kogan made psychoanalytic interpretations
of internal events, ignoring her own and her patient's fears. A turning
point occurred when another important external event occurred. The
psychoanalyst had a granddaughter. When babies were discharged
from a hospital at that time in Israel, they were put into little plastic
tents. This, it was thought, would keep them safe in case of a chemical or biological attack as they left the hospital. Kogan envisioned
what could happen during such an attack: young parents, her son and
her daughter-in-law, wearing gas masks while frantically attempting
to put the screaming baby into a plastic bag and not being able to
touch and calm her. This image made Kogan aware that she was not

coping with the existing situation. This broke her denial of the external danger and, in turn, she could deal with her patient's fears.

Chosen trauma

From the late 1970s until the mid-1980s, along with other psychoanalysts, such as Rafael Moses and Rena Moses-Hrushovski of Israel and John Mack of Boston, I was involved with a team, sponsored by the American Psychiatric Association, that brought influential Israelis and Arabs together for a series of unofficial diplomatic meetings (Volkan, 1987, 1988). From the mid-1980s until early 2000s, I also attended a series of unofficial diplomacy meetings between influential representatives of opposing large groups, such as the USA and the Soviet Union, Russia and Estonia, Serbia and Croatia, Turkey and Greece, Georgia and South Ossetia. When representatives of one side in such meetings felt attacked by the representatives of the opposing group, they usually reactivated a shared mental representation of their ancestors' history. For example, if the Russian delegates felt attacked by the Estonians, Russians spontaneously would start speaking of the Tartar invasion of Russia centuries earlier. I called such reactivated shared mental representations of history during which the ancestors felt victimized "chosen traumas" (Volkan, 1991, 2004a).

"Chosen trauma" refers to the shared mental representation of an event that has caused a large group's ancestors to face drastic losses, to feel helpless, to experience shame and humiliation at the hand of enemies, and to suffer from difficulty or inability to mourn losses. Although some colleagues have taken exception to my term *chosen* trauma, because a large group, such as an ethnic group, does not willingly choose to be victimized or suffer humiliation, I believe that, like an individual, a large group can be said to make unconscious "choices". Thus, the term *chosen* trauma accurately reflects a large group's unconscious "choice" to add a past generation's mental representation of a shared event to its own large-group identity. Although large groups might have experienced any number of massive traumas in their history, only certain of these become special and their shared mental representations remain with them over decades or centuries. The chosen trauma causes thousands and millions of people who are designated as "chosen" to be linked together through their shared mental representation of that past trauma. By reactivating their chosen traumas, the members of a large group connect themselves with one another and try to patch up the injury they felt was inflicted upon their large-group identity during current times or as they face current "enemy" representatives.

The story of Slobodan Milošević allowing and supporting the reappearance of the Serbian chosen trauma—the mental representation of the 28 June 1389 Battle of Kosovo—is well documented (Volkan, 1997). According to the myth that developed among the Serbs some seventy years after the Battle of Kosovo, the event and the Serbian characters of this battle, especially the Serbian leader, Prince Lazar, who was killed during the battle, mingled with elements and characters of Christianity. As decades passed, Prince Lazar became associated with Jesus Christ. For example, icons showing Lazar's representation decorated many Serbian churches throughout the six centuries following the battle. Even during the communist period, when the government discouraged hero worship, each day the Serbs were able to drink (introject) a bottle of red wine called "Prince Lazar".

As the six-hundredth anniversary of the Battle of Kosovo approached in 1989, with the permission and encouragement of Milošević, Lazar's 600-year-old remains, which had been kept north of Belgrade, were placed in a coffin and taken over the course of the year to almost every Serb village and town, where they were received by huge crowds of mourners dressed in black. Again and again during this long journey, Lazar's remains were symbolically buried and reincarnated, until they were buried for good at the original battleground in Kosovo on 28 June 1989. On this day, the six-hundredth anniversary of the Battle of Kosovo, a helicopter brought Milošević to the burial ground where earlier a huge monument made of red stone symbolizing blood had been built. In the mythology, Prince Lazar had chosen the Kingdom of Heaven over the Kingdom of earth. By design, Milošević descended from a helicopter, representing Prince Lazar coming to earth to find a new Kingdom, a Greater Serbia.

Thus, Milošević and his associates, by activating the mental representations of Lazar and the Battle of Kosovo, along with the peak emotions they generated, were able to create a year-long "time collapse" (Volkan, 1997). The perceptions, feelings, and expectations concerning a past hero and event were collapsed into the perceptions, feelings, and expectations about at a current "enemy", magnifying its threat. Milošević and his associates first encouraged a shared sense of victimization, followed by a shared sense of entitlement for revenge. This led to genocidal acts in Europe at the end of the twentieth century. In early June 2005, new tapes showing violent murders in the name of large-group identity shook the Serbian citizens—as well as the rest of us.

What I observed in the international relations arena and what I thought about large-group psychology made a big impact on my clinical practice and my expanding understanding of individual psychology. When I was in my clinical office, I began "hearing" more clearly my analysands' descriptions of political, social, and military events in the external world and the influence of such events on their large-group identities, and in turn on their internal worlds. Furthermore, I began noticing the influence of history, including one's ancestors' history, on analysands' wishes, defences, conscious fantasies, separation–individuation, and Oedipal issues.

Examples from my own experiences

Now, like Kogan, who presented material from her own life, I will also present data from my life (from my personal analysis) with the idea that to do so may help contribute to our understanding of how external and internal wars intertwine. My personal psychoanalysis had taken place before my exposure to unofficial diplomatic dialogues and before I visited many locations such as refugee camps, places where the effect of wars or war-like conditions on the internal worlds of the victims cannot be easily denied. After a successful personal analysis is completed, the analysand represses most aspects of its memory, as he or she typically represses childhood events. Thus, when I speak about my own analysis, we need to keep this fact in mind. Nevertheless, I am aware that the influence of two external historical war-related events entered my analysis.

The first story from my own analysis refers to my childhood in Cyprus, a Mediterranean island forty sea-miles south of Turkey, which then was a British colony. During the Second World War, Germans occupied Crete, another Mediterranean island, which belonged to Greece, and it was supposed that they would occupy Cyprus next. Accordingly, my father moved his family—my mother, my two older sisters, and me (then an Oedipal age boy)—to a village about twenty miles from the capital city of Nicosia where we lived. The idea was that the German aircraft would bomb Nicosia, and that living in this village away from the capital city would keep us safe. My father, a headmaster of an elementary school, however, remained in Nicosia, as his job required him to do so. At the weekends, he would take a bus and visit us in the village, only to return to Nicosia again during the week.

I recall German planes flying very low over the village. I recall even seeing the faces of the pilots. Of course, I do not know if my recalling their faces is real or fantasized. In reality, they would bomb Nicosia. From a hilltop I, along with other children from the village, could watch them dropping their bombs and we could hear the noise. I would wait with anxiety until I saw my father the next weekend. Today, I believe that this historical event, the bombing of Nicosia by the Nazi German aeroplanes, was intertwined with my Oedipal issues. Such bombing could kill my Oedipal rival, my father in Nicosia, while I could be safe with my mother and sisters in the village. I could remain as their little "prince" and have an Oedipal triumph, as well as guilt, of course. I think that this historical event played a role in my not feeling comfortable when I was physically close to my father during my youth. I was more appreciative of my father as a kind and a brave man after my personal analysis ended.

I am sure that I spoke of the German bombing of Cyprus during my personal analysis, although I do not recall my analyst making any remarks about it. On the other hand, knowing my analyst through his writings, I am sure that he appreciated the internal Oedipal reflections of my watching German planes dropping bombs on "my father". Most probably, he used this understanding, along with understanding other data, in interpreting my Oedipal issues, and helping me to work through them.

The second external war-related event actually took place while I was in analysis. Between 1963 and 1968 there was terrorism on the island and Cypriot Turks were terrorized. While I was safely in the USA, Cypriot Turks, who previously inhabited 37% of the island, were forced by Cypriot Greeks to live in 3% of the island in various en-claves surrounded by their enemies and in subhuman conditions. I knew that sixteen families had come to live in our house in Nicosia, literally on top of each other. I could not have direct communication with my parents, sisters, or friends. Sometimes, I would not hear from them for three months or so. I did not know if they were dead or alive. I knew that my long-time roommate from our days in medical school in Turkey had been shot to death by Greek-Cypriot terrorists. Obviously, I spoke about what was happening to my people in Cyprus while I was lying on my analyst's couch. I do not recall that my analyst and I openly discussed my concerns about the external events that were happening thousands of miles away and my survivor guilt.

My psychoanalyst was Jewish. Much later, after I finished my analysis, I wondered if his own history connected him directly with the Holocaust and if he had his own survivor guilt. I wondered if he felt that atrocities committed against the Cypriot Turks between 1963 and 1968 were, in a sense, insignificant compared to the enormity of the Holocaust. I also wondered if the opposite were true. Did my telling the story of Cypriot Turks living in ghettos for five years induce bad affects in my Jewish analyst, and that he wanted to deny them by not focusing on them during his work with me?

My psychoanalyst and I did not see one another after the late 1960s when I terminated my analysis, except occasionally when we ran into each other at some professional meetings and greeted one another. I always felt that I was lucky to have had him as my analyst. I read many of his papers as I developed professionally and always felt that he was a very gifted clinician and very good psychoanalyst for me. Some years after my analysis finished, I wrote a book on the ethnic conflict in Cyprus (Volkan, 1979). Was it, at least partly, my attempt at a kind of self-analysis of this ethnic conflict's influence on my internal world that was not examined on the couch?

Thirty plus years after I finished my psychoanalysis, my psychoanalyst died when I was out of the USA. After returning home, I attended an American Psychoanalytic Meeting. Unexpectedly I saw a notice on a board and learnt of his death. I soon found out how it is to mourn the loss of one's psychoanalyst. I felt very close to his mental representation, reviewed some of my experiences on the couch in analysis with him, and experienced sadness. I had an urge to visit his gravesite if he were buried and to say goodbye. In order to find out where he was buried, I wrote to one of his friends—another psychoanalyst—and enquired about my psychoanalyst's death. It turned out that this psychoanalyst had given the eulogy during the funeral. Without my asking him, he sent me a copy of what he had said at the ceremony. It was a moving eulogy. In it, he referred to his perception that there was an area in my psychoanalyst's mind that was very personal and that, in a sense, my analyst kept this part of himself "secret" from others. This increased my fantasy that this "private area", which I thought had something to do with his Jewish history, kept him from paying much attention to the dangerous external world my family lived in at the time of my analysis.

Ancestors' history

My references to external historical events in this paper until now have related to situations that directly affected the analysand as well as the psychoanalyst. I will go one step further: I will try to illustrate that historical events through which our ancestors lived, events that took place a century or so ago, can be factors that structure our psychic lives. I will turn my attention to a third historical event in my life that illustrates how large-group events in our ancestors' lives influence us. (I did not discuss this historical event with my psycho-analyst because I became preoccupied with it after I finished my analysis.)

My mother died in 1979, over ten years after my personal analysis ended. Soon after this, during a trip to Cyprus, my older sister, in passing, referred to an odd behaviour on my mother's part. She would never wash clothes! She would always find someone else to do this chore for her. I grew up with a mother who was above washing clothes. Obviously, as a child I perceived her "character trait" as a normal phenomenon. I do not recall ever wondering about her not washing clothes. As an adult, mostly living in the USA, I had forgotten it until my sister brought it up again.

This conversation with my sister was one of the reasons for my beginning to collect data about my ancestors on my mother's side. My mother was born when Cyprus was an Ottoman island. The Ottomans had conquered the island in 1570–1571 and taken it away from the Venetian Empire. My mother's paternal grandfather was a "kadı" (meaning something like a religious supreme court judge) and her maternal grandfather was the minister of vineyards (meaning something like the minister of agriculture). In 1878, a drastic historical event took place. The Ottomans "rented" the island to the British.

Great Britain took Cyprus "on trust" by treaty with the Ottoman Sultan, who was assured of protection against Russia in return. Cyprus would remain an Ottoman island, but the British would run it administratively. In 1914, at the start of the First World War, in which the Ottomans allied themselves with Imperial Germany, the British formally annexed Cyprus. There was no war on the island, no bloodshed. Overnight, the Ottomans lost it. Modern Turkey, the heir of the Ottoman Empire, recognized British rule in Cyprus under the Treaty of Lausanne in 1923, and Cyprus became a crown colony the following year.

Soon after the British took over the administration of the island in 1878, they transferred my mother's religious judge (kadı) grandfather from the capital city to a new, but rural, location. The kadı's wife, the daughter of the "minister of vineyards", refused to leave the capital city. He and his family were humiliated. Without going into detail, I should report that this historical event led to drastic family problems and to the collapse of the family fortunes.

After my mother's death, with the help of my niece and others, I began to further investigate my ancestors' history. Since they had high positions, there were historical Ottoman and British documents on record about them. Some of the older people in the family knew their history, but I do not recall my having any cohesive knowledge about family history when I was growing up. I came to the conclusion that my mother's "character trait" of not washing clothes was related to her attempt to keep a psychological link to the glorified times of the family. She could still pretend that she was the spoiled daughter of the Ottoman elite. My older sister, I learnt, had come to this conclusion a long time ago. What is interesting is my becoming aware that I had a similar character trait—a stubborn and narcissistic streak. Under certain circumstances, I would rather die than "lower" my standards and perform certain tasks.

My journey (briefly described above) into my ancestors' lives and my involvement in international relations made me clearly aware that it would be better, and even essential, that, during clinical analysis, the analyst pay attention to the role of the analysand's ancestors' history and transgenerational transmission. One result of this awareness has been my study with Gabriele Ast and William Greer of how "transgenerational transmissions" occur and how Holocaust-related historical mental representations were involved in transgenerational transmission in certain—Jewish, German, and one Gypsy—patients (Volkan, Ast, & Greer, 2002). Writing the Foreword to this book, Brenner (2002) refers to the still-existing controversy over including mental images of history in "classical" psychoanalysis.

Brenner reports how certain children "enter a psychological time tunnel" and "weave their parents' past into their own developmental experience" (p. xiii). When he was presenting a case to illustrate this to a group of analysts who met regularly, some talented "outsider" colleagues argued that

> since analysis deals with the realm of psychic reality only, we were introducing an unnecessary element that only "muddied the waters" and was unnecessary for successful treatment. As persuasive as many of these arguments were, we nevertheless felt that much would have remained unanalyzed without this extra step, which required an understanding of historical reality. [*ibid.*, p. xiii]

The "extra step" that Brenner speaks about is usually first taken by the analysand. All the analyst needs to do is to pay attention to it.

Ancestors' history during a psychoanalytic process

A man named Hamilton came to psychoanalysis in his late fifties (Volkan, 2004b). His primary symptom was an "addiction" to women. He kept a book that included the names of 100 women whom he could call. If he did not have a woman in his bed during the night-time, he would have "paranoid" symptoms. By the time little Hamilton was only four years old, his mother had delivered two daughters. After each delivery she suffered from post-partum depression, and Hamilton was taken care of by a black nanny. After his second younger sister was born, the nanny was fired. Thus, Hamilton had lost his idealized mother when she became pregnant with Hamilton's next sibling as well as his "second mother", the black nanny. The rest of his life he kept searching for a perfect woman. Furthermore, he was also physically abused by his mother and his father. When he was an Oedipal age and later, his father would beat him regularly with a razor strap in a bathroom that Hamilton nicknamed "a torture chamber" in order to make him develop a "good" character.

During Hamilton's developmental years, his paternal grand-mother, Dolly—who would regularly visit the family—was a promi-nent figure. Hamilton knew that Dolly was the mastermind behind the creation of the "torture chamber" and his receiving other physical punishments "for his own good". It was Dolly who would preach to her son and daughter-in-law, advocating a method of child-raising to develop "good character". Dolly was a follower of a "German doctor" who knew best how to raise children. During Hamilton's analysis, my analysand and I learned that the German doctor was Daniel Gottlieb Moritz Schreber. The memoirs of Schreber's son, Daniel Paul (Schre-ber, 1903), were examined by Freud (1911c). Freud's historical accu-racy and his understanding concerning Dr Schreber's child-rearing ideas have their critics (Israëls, 1989; Lothane, 1992), and I will not focus on this controversy here. What is important was Dolly's own interpretation of Schreber's harsh treatment of children for "character building".

From the beginning of Hamilton's analysis, I knew that his ances-tors in Virginia, who are, in fact, relatives of the British Royalty, were neighbours of Robert E. Lee. During the American Civil War, they fought for the Confederacy against the Yankees. When Robert E. Lee surrendered, they lost wealth, prestige, and influence. (You might hear an echo of my ancestors' fate.)

I worked with Hamilton four times a week for five years and he successfully finished his psychoanalytic work with me. In the fifth year, both of us began thinking of a successful termination of his analysis. But soon it became clear that following Saddam Hussein's invasion of Kuwait, America would go to war in the Gulf region. At this time, Hamilton took a spontaneous "extra step" and began to fill his psychoanalytic hours with curiosity about the American Civil War and its influence on his ancestors and, in turn, on himself. He had an opportunity for a "second look" (Novey, 1968) at his childhood.

Both Saddam Hussein and President Bush were perceived as the punishing fathers. He recalled how he used to think of me as a "terri-ble Turk" with a scimitar. He said that it amused him to realize that my scary image was very mild in comparison to his image of Presi-dent Bush with an IRM missile performing "surgical strikes" when the Gulf War began. As he watched the air assaults on television, he had an urgency to look at the important people in his past, even people he never met because he was born after they had died. Once more, he remembered how the image of the Civil War was present in his grand-mother Dolly's mind. He recalled a trunk in Dolly's house filled with American Civil War pictures. As a child, stories about these pictures were told and retold in the family. He related the following dream:

> Iraqi soldiers were shooting at me. Bullets were coming through a wooden board. I was shot and I died. I was put in a tomb. Although I was dead, I could see people around the tomb. They were all dressed up. My mother was there next to a woman who was wearing a beautiful fur coat. Then a strange thing happened. I had a rebirth. I got out of the tomb and began walking around. All the people began to become like mannequins, some of them black people. I wanted to put these mannequins into the tomb that I had just vacated.

The wooden board in the dream stood for the wooden board at the end of Hamilton's parents' bed. Earlier he had spent a great deal of time associating to this wooden board. As a little boy, whenever he had an ailment, his parents would put a crib next to the wooden foot-board of their bed and allow little Hamilton to sleep in their bedroom. Throughout the initial years of his analysis, Hamilton had many asso-ciations to this wooden board image: his isolation from his parents, their rejection of him, his wish to remove the board and join them, his Oedipal struggles and his rage. Iraqi soldiers' bullets going through the wooden board connected the war in Iraq with his childhood conflicts and emotions and then with the image of the American Civil War.

The woman next to his mother in the dream in fact was a wealthy Iranian woman whom Hamilton had met hours before at a dinner party. They spoke about Iran, Iraq, Israel, and the war. She insisted that Iranian children were well behaved because if they were not, they would be punished by their parents. This reminded Hamilton of his own childhood and childhood rage. He "misbehaved" at the dinner party and shouted at the Iranian woman, who represented his punish-ing parents and Dolly. This incident, in fact, was his dream's "day residue".

By associating to the mannequins in the dream, Hamilton spent *a month* on the couch examining them. He was also active outside my office and collected data about "them". The mannequins represented his ancestors and their black slaves. The most important aspect of this review was his finding out why Dolly became a disciple of Dr

Schreber and how this, in turn, played a most significant role in his having an abusive childhood and later developing his personality structure and symptoms. Here is Dolly's story.

She was the youngest of seven siblings. She was six years old when the South was defeated and the American Civil War ended. During the war, Dolly's father had gone to fight and the family, on a large farm, lived in fear of hunger, rape, and death. One aging slave on Dolly's family's farm, named King, had worked for Dolly's father and was considered trustworthy. When Dolly's father went to war, King was appointed her "protector". Hamilton recalled his grandmother saying on many occasions: "I loved King!"

When Dolly's traumatized father returned to his farm, King, without giving notice, escaped to the North. Realizing this, Hamilton understood that Dolly, like himself, was "loved and abandoned". A similar story would repeat itself when his beloved black nanny suddenly left little Hamilton. Now, Hamilton came to the conclusion that Dolly played a role in urging her son and daughter-in-law—Hamilton's parents—to "fire" their son's "second mother", the black nanny assigned to look after little Hamilton while Hamilton's mother was busy with her new babies and while she suffered post-partum depression. Dolly had never forgiven King, even though she continued to "love" him, as Hamilton continued to love his black nanny by having an inner obligation to seduce every attractive woman with dark complexion and dark hair. He even had to seduce women who wore black stockings!

After the Civil War, when all the siblings left the farm, the youngest child, Dolly, remained as an "old maid" to look after her war-traumatized parents. One male sibling went to Germany, studied medicine, and became a follower of Dr Schreber's ideas. In fact, Dr Schreber had died in 1861, the year the American Civil War began.

When Dolly's brother returned to the USA, he made his then-unmarried sister, Dolly, his "nigger" in an attempt to have an illusion of the old family tradition to have black slaves. He would literally say, "Nigger, bring me water!" "Nigger, bring me a chair!" Hamilton recalled Dolly saying that she "willingly" became her brother's slave. Hamilton and I thought that by "willingly" creating a "nigger–master" pair, Dolly was masochistically re-establishing her lost relationship with King, in a reverse fashion. This time she was the black slave taking care of her white brother.

Dolly married late in life and left her masochism behind, replacing it with sadism. She was sadistic towards Hamilton's father. Identifying with her doctor brother, she became her own version of Dr Schreber and later saw that little Hamilton was physically abused in order to develop his "character".

After examining the "mannequins" in his dream, Hamilton was ready to bury them for good in "the tomb" he had created. During this time, he and I took what Brenner called "the extra step", bringing the ancestors' drama and its influence on Hamilton to his analysis, and I believe that this allowed Hamilton to have a more comprehensive analysis. In turn, he became interested in his grandchildren even more and wanted to break any influence of their ancestors' problems, starting with the American Civil War.

Would Hamilton have successfully finished his analysis had he not examined his internal intertwining of his ancestors' reactions to historical events with his own personal traumas during his developmental years? Perhaps the answer is "yes". But his understanding of himself as a "reservoir" of the mental images of individuals who were humiliated and hurt by a war and left with masochistic and sadistic character traits, I believe, allowed Hamilton to obtain a better internal freedom in dealing with himself and his environment.

Last words

The controversy about bringing the danger resulting from wars, war-like conditions, and political change into the psychoanalytic process still continues. I am in favour of paying attention to wars, war-like conditions, and drastic political changes in the external world, and acute or chronic historical crises that might enter our physical environments. Furthermore, I tried to illustrate how the mental representation of our ancestors' historical events sometimes plays a crucial role in our psychological makeup. I am suggesting that the analyst should take into consideration the various types of transgenerational transmissions. I also wish to repeat that paying attention to history should only be done in a way that illustrates how past actual trauma, war, war-like conditions, and political changes—their mental representations—intertwine with our internal developmental issues, wishes, defences, conflicts, and fantasies. When, within the analytic setting, our analysands experience that some of their symptoms or character traits originally belonged to their ancestors, or were initiated by past historical events, they have a better chance of freeing themselves from the troubling influences of such symptoms or character traits. They will also have a better chance of working through the transference manifestations associated with ancestors and people who lived before their birth when they face wars, war-like conditions, or political change.

References

Abend, S. (1986). Countertransference, empathy, and the analytic ideal: the impact of life stresses on analytic capability. *Psychoanalytic Quarterly, 55*: 563–575.

Arlow, J. (1991). Derivative manifestations of perversions. In: G. Fogel & W. Myer (Eds.), *Perversions and Near-Perversions in Clinical Practice: New Psychoanalytic Perspectives* (pp. 59–74). New Haven, CT: Yale University Press.

Blum, H. P. (1985). Superego formation, adolescent transformation and the adult neurosis. *Journal of the American Psychoanalytic Association, 4*: 887–909.

Brenner, I. (2002). Foreword. In: V. Volkan (Ed.), *The Third Reich in the Unconscious* (pp. xi–xvii). New York: Brunner-Routledge.

Eckstaedt, A. (1989). *Nationalsozialismus in der "zweiten Generation": Psychoanalyse von Hörigkeitsverhältnissen* (National Socialism in the Second Generation: Psychoanalysis of Master–Slave Relationships). Frankfurt: Suhrkamp Verlag.

Elliott, M., Bishop, K., & Stokes, P. (2004). Societal PTSD? Historic shock in Northern Ireland. *Psychotherapy and Politics International, 2*: 1–16.

Freud, A. (1954). The widening scope of indications for psychoanalysis. *Journal of the American Psychoanalytic Association, 2*: 607–620.

Freud, S. (1911c). Psycho-analytic notes on an autobiographical account of a case of paranoia (dementia paranoides). *S.E., 12*: 3–82. London: Hogarth.

Freud, S. (1917d). Metapsychological supplement to the theory of dreams. *S.E., 14*: 219– London: Hogarth.

Frosch, J. (1954). Editor's note. *Journal of the American Psychoanalytic Association, 2*: 565–566.

Grubrich-Simitis, I. (1979). Extremtraumatisierung als kumulatives trauma: psychoanalytische studien über seelische nachwirkungen der konzentrationslagerhaft bei _berlebenden und ihren kindern (Extreme traumatization as a cumulative trauma: psychoanalytic studies on the mental effects of imprisonment in concentration camps on survivors and their children). *Psyche, 33*: 991–1023.

Israëls, H. (1989). *Schreber: Father and Son.* Amsterdam: Elandsstraat.

Jacobson, E. (1954). Transference problems in the psychoanalytic treatment of severely depressive patients. *Journal of the American Psychoanalytic Association, 2*: 595–606.

Jokl, A. M. (1997). *Zwei Fälle zum Thema "Bewältigung der Vergangenheit"* (Two Cases Referring to the Theme of "Mastering the Past"). Frankfurt: Jüdischer Verlag.

Kernberg, O. F. (1975). *Borderline Conditions and Pathological Narcissism.* New York: Jason Aronson.

Kestenberg, J. S., & Brenner, I. (1996). *The Last Witness.* Washington, DC: American Psychiatric Press.

Klein, M. (1961). *Narrative of a Child Analysis.* New York: Basic Books.

Kogan, I. (2004). The role of the analyst in the analytic cure during times of chronic crises. *Journal of the American Psychoanalytic Association, 52*: 735–757.

Kohut, H. (1971). *The Analysis of the Self.* New York: International Universities Press.

Lothane, Z. (1992). *In Defense of Schreber: Soul Murder and Psychiatry.* Hillsdale, NJ: Analytic Press.

Novey, S. (1968). *The Second Look: The Reconstruction of Personal History in Psychiatry and Psychoanalysis.* Baltimore, MD: Johns Hopkins University Press.

Samberg, E. (2004). Resistance: how do we think of it in the twenty-first century? *Journal of the American Psychoanalytic Association, 52*: 243–253.

Schreber, D. P. (1903). *Memoirs of My Nervous Illness.* Leipzig: Oswald Mutze.

Stone, L. (1954). The widening scope of indications for psychoanalysis. *Journal of the American Psychoanalytic Association, 2*: 567–594.

Streeck-Fischer, A. (1999). Naziskins in Germany: how traumatization deals with the past. *Mind and Human Interaction, 10*: 84–97.

Varvin, S., & Volkan, V. (Eds.) (2003). *Violence or Dialogue: Psychoanalytic Insights on Terror and Terrorism.* London: International Psychoanalytical Association.

Volkan, V. (1976). *Primitive Internalized Object Relations: A Clinical Study of Schizophrenic, Borderline, and Narcissistic Patients.* New York: International Universities Press.

Volkan, V. (1979). *Cyprus: War and Adaptation: A Psychoanalytic History of Two Ethnic Groups in Conflict*. Charlottesville, VA: University of Virginia Press.

Volkan, V. (1981). Transference and countertransference: an examination from the point of view of internalized object relations. In: S. Tuttman, C. Kaye, & M. Zimmerman (Eds.), *Object and Self: A Developmental Approach (Essays in Honor of Edith Jacobson)* (pp. 429–451). New York: International Universities Press.

Volkan, V. (1987). Psychological concepts useful in the building of political foundations between nations: Track II Diplomacy. *Journal of the American Psychoanalytic Association, 35*: 903–935.

Volkan, V. (1988). *The Need to Have Enemies and Allies: From Clinical Practice to International Relationships*. Northvale, NJ: Jason Aronson.

Volkan, V. (1991). On chosen trauma. *Mind and Human Interaction, 4*: 3–19.

Volkan, V. (1997). *Bloodlines: From Ethnic Pride to Ethnic Terrorism*. New York: Farrar, Straus and Giroux.

Volkan, V. (2004a). *Blind Trust: Large Groups and Their Leaders in Times of Crisis and Terror*. Charlottesville, VA: Pitchstone Publishing.

Volkan, V. (2004b). *Kusursuz Kadının Peşinde* (Searching for a Perfect Woman). Istanbul: Bağlam Yayınevi.

Volkan, V., Ast, G., & Greer, W. (2002). *The Third Reich in the Unconscious: Transgenerational Transmission and its Consequences*. New York: Brunner-Routledge.

Weigert, E. (1954). The importance of flexibility in psychoanalytic technique. *Journal of the American Psychoanalytic Association, 2*: 702–710.

CHAPTER SIX

Treatment resistance and the transmission of trauma

M. Gerard Fromm

Patient authority and treatment resistance

As 2010 is the one hundredth anniversary of the founding of the International Psychoanalytic Association, I would like to bracket this discussion with two of Freud's statements. The first famously outlines the clinical trajectory of psychoanalysis: "Where Id was, there Ego shall be" (1933a, p. 80). In a sense, this description of psychoanalysis launched the field of ego psychology, leading to a rich set of theoretical concepts and a point of view about clinical technique. The conceptual contributions included the potential neutralization of the drives, and the technical approach emphasized supporting the ego in its all-important efforts at synthesis and mastery.

As part of his radical "return to Freud", Lacan drew on Freud's original German and retranslated the above foundational quote as "Where It was, there I must come to be" (1977, p. 129). He thereby shifted the field of discourse from one of forces and their control—Freud's proverbial horse and rider—to the dimension of subjectivity. He recognized that it had been Freud's genius to discover a model of psychological treatment that reversed the ordinary positions of doctor and patient. Within a traditional medical model, the patient was to make himself the object of the doctor's knowledge and ministrations. But Freud, though he sometimes struggled with his startlingly new paradigm, set up a clinical situation in which *he* was to become the object of the patient's unconscious strivings. As this transference from the past was gradually interpreted, Freud would return to the patient his or her own, formerly inchoate, knowledge about the sources of the illness.

Lacan drew attention to a different task for clinical psychoanalysis: pathology reflected a position of objectification, and treatment facilitated a subject's coming into being. For Lacan, the essence of being human is our immersion in meanings, first of all what we mean to the other person, and the essence of human activity is our effort to grasp meaning for ourselves. The psychoanalytic situation was set up for exactly this purpose: to discover, within a therapeutic relationship, the unconscious meanings the patient was carrying, much to their psychic discomfort. The technique of clinical psychoanalysis was organized around this profoundly different understanding of the locus of authority within the treatment. In an earlier paper (Fromm, 1989), I outlined the analyst's role in setting the frame for the treatment, which reflects his authority, and the patient's role in using the analyst as a medium for emotional communication, which reflects the patient's authority.

This bears directly on the problem of treatment resistance. By the latter term, I mean something more specific than resistance in the usual psychoanalytic sense. I do not mean resistance to experiencing anxiety, or to unacceptable thoughts or feelings, or resistance as a specific transference to the analyst. Nor do I necessarily mean a negative therapeutic reaction, though, if space permitted, it would be useful to review this concept as an important form of treatment resistance. Rather, by treatment resistance, I simply mean negative treatment results over time and across a number of treaters.

My point of view in this chapter is that treatment resistance can be considered the response of some patients to treatments that do not take into account the critical issue of subjectivity, that is, of the core meaning-making dimension of human experience. And, of course, many treatments do not, for reasons that make sense within their frames of reference. Psychopharmacology operates within a traditional medical model and aims toward an objective assessment of symptoms, to be followed by a therapeutic action upon them. Cognitive–behavioural treatment invites the patient to isolate self-defeating thoughts and apply a more constructive way of thinking in those situations of anxiety where habitual, maladaptive thoughts arise.

These ordinary, non-psychodynamic approaches rely on patients lending themselves as both partners and objects to the treatment process. These approaches might work well for those people who can take themselves for granted as subjects and take the good intentions of the doctor for granted as well. But, assuming both good intentions and expertise on the doctor's part (and treatment resistance makes a different kind of sense when either of those cannot be assumed), it might be that many patients who eventually come to be regarded as treatment resistant can do neither. Instead, they cannot fully use treatments that do not address the role of meaning in their symptoms and of relationships in the origin of their disturbances and in their efforts to get well. They cannot surrender to the authority of the doctor if their own confused or disabled sense of authority is not recognized.

Freud's ideal clinical course, as reframed by Lacan, is about patient authority—the "I" that must become able to stand in the place where "It" was: "It", I would suggest, meaning unintegratable affective experience, regardless of its source in impulse life or external impingement. To the degree that such affective experience overwhelms the ego's capacities, we enter the realm of trauma, the variations of which open up a vast area for exploration. For the purpose of this discussion, suffice it to say that experience that might not be traumatic for a person who has developed a cohesive sense of self might be quite traumatic for a person who has not. For the latter patient, fantasies related to the trauma are concretized and lived out in and as reality. Their ability to use words to symbolize experience is compromised, and they need an interpersonal space to play out and, thereby, learn about their internal experience through the responses of others and the interpretative work of their therapy. This is the kind of space a psychodynamic hospital, such as the Austen Riggs Center, can provide.

Trauma and its transmission

It was, in fact, the issue of trauma that led Freud to a reconsideration of the ego and its operations "beyond the pleasure principle", this reconsideration resulting from his encounter with the psychological casualties of the First World War. Trauma studies have burgeoned in the past several years and moved clinical understanding beyond a narrow focus on post traumatic stress disorder to a broader apprecia-tion of states of extreme arousal, both sudden and sustained, in which the adaptive coping mechanisms of a person shut down in favour of massive organismic dissociation. This is a vast literature, which I cannot review here. Suffice it to say that, in the Austen Riggs Center's Follow-Along Study of 226 patients followed over a considerable length of time, an early finding documents the prevalence of trauma in the life histories of treatment resistant patients and the effect of specific kinds of trauma on later relationship patterns (Drapeau & Perry, 2004).

In this paper, I will focus on one aspect of the issue of trauma: its transmission from one generation to the next. The seminal paper on this subject, "Ghosts in the nursery", by Fraiberg and her colleagues (1975), describes vividly and painfully a mother who could not hear her baby's cries because, it turned out, she could not hear her own cries within her original family just as her parents could not hear her as a child either. At the time this paper was published, the problems of the children of Holocaust survivors were coming to light and being systematically studied for the first time. Although we have subse-quently learnt all too well the crude fact that abuse to one generation often begets abuse upon the next, Fraiberg's paper and the study of second-generation Holocaust survivors opened a new field of investi-gation, one that, I will argue, adds to our understanding of treatment resistance.

More than thirty years before Fraiberg's ground-breaking paper, Anna Freud and Dorothy Burlingham wrote their influential book, *Children in War* (1943). In it, they showed that during the London Blitz, children whose mothers were traumatized by the experience devel-oped trauma symptoms themselves, whereas this was not the case for children whose mothers were able to serve as "protective shields" despite the dire nature of the threat. Freud and Burlingham thus demonstrated that the potential effects of trauma were mediated by human relationships.

Since September 11 2001, a number of clinician-researchers have taken up similar studies of the traumatic consequences of the attacks on the World Trade Center. Coates, Rosenthal, and Schecter (2003) argue persuasively that trauma and human bonds are inversely related, that trauma is often a phenomenon of aloneness, and, on the other hand, going through a terrible situation with other people some-times mitigates its traumatic effects. In this same volume, Schecter (2003) tells the story of a little girl who seems to be holding not only her own terrifying experience, but her father's, too. She drew in red, yellow, and black the burning buildings she had seen on television and in which she, and her family too, had thought her father had died. But he had not been at the World Trade Center that day; he was doing errands, having exchanged his shift at its top-floor restaurant with a friend who did indeed die in the catastrophe. He was shocked to real-ize that his daughter believed he was nearly killed by the fire. Suffering agonizing survivor guilt about his friend and recurrent nightmares envisioning how he had died, this father had lost touch with his little girl.

"So your daughter is drawing your dreams," Dr Schechter said. His intervention put father and daughter back in conscious emotional touch with each other. Dr Coates and her colleagues illustrate power-fully the unconscious attunement between children and parents, espe-cially in situations of potential trauma. Dr Schechter's clinical vignette shows how child and parent can be both in unconscious resonance with, and also dangerous isolation from, each other. As I wrote else-where (Fromm, 2004, p. 9):

> Parents *mind* children. That verb connotes the holding-in-mind of the total child, including the developing mind of the child. When parents lose their minds under circumstances of extreme distress . . . *children mind their parents*. The critical question is whether the parent can hear the child's interpretation, an interpretation delivered in a drawing, a nightmare or disruptive behavior.

Fonagy and Target (2003) have developed the concepts of reflective functioning and the interpersonal interpretive function, both describ-ing the minding function. Their research takes up the relationship between the state of these capacities in a child and that child's prone-ness toward, or resilience in the face of, traumatization.

In another recent study, Davoine and Gaudilliere (2004) present findings from their psychotherapeutic work over many years with traumatized and psychotic patients. They are convinced that the psychotic patient is madly conducting a research into the rupture between his family and the social fabric, a rupture brought about through trauma and betrayal. They suggest that the unthinkable traumatic experience of the preceding generation lodges itself in highly charged but chaotic fragments in the troubled mind of the patient. In a sense, these patients are attempting to give a mind to that which has been cut out of the social discourse that surrounds them.

Davoine and Gaudilliere's work powerfully links the clinical arena with the historical and the political. Like Freud, their encounter with the First World War, particularly in the work of the military psychiatrist, Thomas Salmon, has led them to realize a remarkable similarity between his principles of treatment of traumatized soldiers and theirs with psychotic patients. One of their major points is embedded in the subtitle of their book: "Whereof one cannot speak, thereof one cannot stay silent". The experience of trauma must be communicated, or at least be communicable, if the traumatized person is to carry on as a whole person. When it cannot be communicated in words that carry genuine emotion, it is transmitted through action, a kind of unspoken, unspeakable speech, and, like Dr Schechter's three-year-old little girl, someone is listening.

Volkan's recent work (2002, 2004) argues cogently that the transmission of trauma from one generation to the next takes many forms. For example, anxiety or other feeling states could be passed from parent to child. Or unconscious fantasies about the cause, nature, and effects of the trauma might be passed on. Or sometimes an unconscious task is deposited in the child, for example, to avenge a parent's humiliation or to make up for a terrible loss. Holocaust studies and our clinical experience at Austen Riggs show that the effects of trauma are carried forward, not only into the next generation, but also into the second generation and perhaps succeeding generations as well. Indeed, Volkan (2004) has powerfully illustrated the political mobilization of a society's ancient "chosen trauma" to fuel contemporary ethnic conflict.

Finally, Faimberg captures one theme of this chapter in the title of her 2005 book, *The Telescoping of Generations*. She underscores the unconscious transmission of the parent's preoccupations with themselves into their intimate relationship to their children. These charged bits of unconscious but endangered narcissism necessarily make their way into the transference. Faimberg emphasizes the centrality of listening as a critical aspect of the analytic process at such moments—listening to the patient's private language, listening to how the patient listens to the analyst, and listening to silence.

The big history and the little history

The theorists discussed in the preceding section examine the intersection between the big history of wars, atrocities, diaspora, and social upheaval and the little history of a person in a family in a particular time and place. It has proven to be such a clinically compelling perspective to me that, if I find myself without the time to read the full case abstract at Riggs' case conferences, I begin with the story of the grandparents and the earliest part of the patient's life history. The following clinical vignette illustrates the intersection of the big history and the little history as well as a patient's being unconsciously assigned the task of making up for a parent's experience of loss.

A young woman brought up in London reported a dream after her therapist's vacation. "There were some ruined buildings. They were destroyed by fire. One was a pet shop. There were some guinea pigs in a cage, doing something sexual with each other." The next day, she remembered that the buildings were not destroyed by fire, but by rain. Spontaneously, as though it were more her thought than his, her therapist said, "There is a kind of rain that brings fire." The patient said, "Bombing" and suddenly remembered, for the first time, an event from her childhood.

Night after night, her father would watch newsreels of the bombing of London. He seemed to be looking for something. His eight-year-old daughter sat anxiously beside him and repeatedly asked him why he was looking at these films again and again. He made no reply. This took place just after the father's mother had died, with whom he had been quite close. In fact, mother and son had long since been left by the grandfather, so that when her son moved away to be with his own family, the patient's grandmother became desperately lonely and seemed to will herself into debilitation and death. The patient was named for this grandmother. She was later to learn that her father had lost his childhood home in the bombing of London when he was eight years old.

After his mother's death and the phase of searching newsreels for his destroyed home, the patient's father entered a long, subtle depression that his adoring daughter's liveliness and flirtatiousness were designed, though not destined, to cure. As she grew into adolescence, this former "pet" of her father felt that she had lost her father's presence and love completely. She became vulnerable to rejection in love relationships, deeply conflicted about sexuality, determinedly involved with wounded, remote men and increasingly convinced that no one could stand the anger, born of hurt and humiliation, she felt inside her. Eventually, she became recurrently and seriously preoccupied with death. Multiple near-fatal suicide attempts were interspersed with both outpatient treatments and short-term inpatient treatments, none of which led to sustained improvement. From one angle, she seemed to be following in her namesake's suicidal footsteps, as though to replace her grandmother as the object of her father's mourning. Perhaps, if she could not have access to his liveliness, she could at least access his depression.

There is a great deal that could be said about this case. Life stories are always complex and psychopathology is always multi-determined. In this chapter, I suggest that this vignette illustrates the way that trauma to one generation falls out upon or is, in a sense, given to the next. There is a paradox within this transmission. On the one hand, silence is a recurrent feature in the transmission of trauma, silence about something both terribly confusing and absolutely urgent. This eight-year-old experienced an urgent speechlessness from her father at the core of his trauma. Had it been possible for her father to speak, his choosing to be silent might have been designed to protect her. But, in her experience, it deprived her, and the subsequent, ongoing deprivation she felt from her father led to a retaliatory, deeply depriving motive within her suicidal actions.

From another angle, the unspeakability of her father's trauma spoke in different and very powerful ways to his daughter. It spoke with images, which, like their content, bombarded the little girl with affect-laden stimulation. She was saturated with her father's unspeakable grief, and, of all her siblings, she was the one to stay with him through it. This special place—the woman in the next generation with the same name as the lost woman from the preceding generation—might have meant that the patient had already been spoken to through her name, as though this naming was her father's unconscious act of encoding the past for the purpose of future recovery.

There is an Oedipal dimension to this special place. The patient was stimulated by her father's experience without the containment that would have been provided by his explaining to her that he was looking for his lost home in those films. An essential perspective was missing, which would have functioned as a Third (Muller, 1996), structuring, containing, and providing meaning to the patient's childhood affectivity and interpretations. Instead, like the patient's father, who had been left alone by his father to deal with, and perhaps cure, his mother, the patient was left alone with the arousing, terrifying, and ultimately futile task of curing her father.

To put the situation in slightly different terms, the loss of his mother, and all that she had meant to him in the traumatic history of his original family, led the patient's father to lose his mind in grief. But he had a daughter who—in her name, in her eight-year-old-ness, and in the dissociated experience he shared with her—*re-minded* him, for better or worse, of these losses. And indeed, it might have been for worse. One finding from the 9/11 studies (Coates, 2003) is that traumatized parents cannot bear the reminders of loss that their children bring to them in the most innocent and ordinary ways. To the degree that the patient's father could not bear what his daughter represented for him, she might have become the unconscious repository for a crucial bit of dissociated history, and, as children do, she took it personally. To her great peril, she misinterpreted the subsequent rupture with her father as the consequence of her Oedipal claims on him and her adolescent badness. More basically, she identified with the dissociated history she had shared with him. It was not that experience of his past or of his mother that he could not bear to see; it was *her*! Her suicide would not only have been a depriving retaliation, but the burial, once and for all, of her father's trauma.

Sometimes, a child's fulfilling this kind of role for a traumatized parent represents a form of mission, and naming is one way such missions are unconsciously assigned. This patient felt a charge from her father in the dual sense of that word: that is, the energy in his relentless searching of those images of destruction and, through their silent togetherness, an unconscious assignment that implicated her in his trauma. This goes beyond a patient's having a designated unconscious role in her family, in which she receives the unwanted projections of its members, though that, too, was part of this patient's experience. Rather, I mean to emphasize an unconscious sense of duty and authorization in the patient through which she is to represent and live out a dynamic at the intersection of her family's and the society's history. Especially if the family's issues are interwoven with societal trauma, the child's mission is not so much the restoration of the family's well-being, but the representation of its painful and dissociated history in language.

Treatment resistance in patients like this has to do with the unconscious task they are living out on behalf of their family. This patient was not only bringing her suicidal depression to treatment, but her father's and her grandmother's as well. Unconsciously, she was not seeking relief from her symptoms. In fact, she would experience efforts to provide her with relief as a current attempt at further dissociating a crucial bit of history, and she would experience actually feeling relief as a deep disloyalty. Instead, she seemed to be seeking in treatment a relational venue for bringing into discourse what I have come to think of as her "unconscious citizenship" (Fromm, 2000) in her family.

In a sense, the patient played out the transmission of trauma in the transference relationship to her therapist by allowing herself to react to his vacation with the feelings and images of abandonment in her dream. These nodal points of condensed meaning Lacan calls "signifiers". The dream image of buildings ruined by a fire-rain—and perhaps the history of images she had "bombarded" her therapist with over the course of her treatment—opened up a crucial bit of the patient's and her father's history and gave a completely new context of meaning to the sexuality about which she had been in such conflict. Sex now seemed like an effort to bring life into a context of death. Indeed, the work in her therapy following her dream and the de-repression of the memory of watching newsreels with her father led to major changes in her treatment resistant symptoms. She became far less given to the blindly passionate pursuit of damaged, inaccessible men, and, thus far, less prone to the self-destructiveness that regularly followed.

The act of dreaming this dream represented the patient's effort to formulate and take authority for what these images had meant in her family's life. Originally, she was to some degree an object in the presence of her father's trauma, but in treatment she attempted to become a subject in relation to it. Her actual access to her father as someone who could, in a sense, bear witness to her witnessing, helped her to build the emotional narrative of her family's life. This process of inscribing a dissociated history is not without peril for a patient, who might feel an inarticulable fear of destructiveness in speaking the formerly unspeakable. Speaking separates the patient from a person she needs and who needed her. It discharges the mission she has been carrying for someone she loves. Something life defining and deeply intimate is over. In addition, she is speaking something that her father could not or would not speak. In this way too, she leaves him. This real and painful separation might get to what Lacan means by his statement that the symbol is "the murder of the thing" (1977, p. 104) and is another source of treatment resistance for patients carrying the trauma of preceding generations.

"Something opened up"

"A year ago, something closed and something else opened up, and I can't close it again, and the person who could isn't here to." This person was a patient's father, who had died the year before her treatment at the Center. His death precipitated an intractable and volatile, treatment-resistant depression, including cutting and suicide attempts. The patient was a young, highly accomplished and driven lawyer whose father had also been a very successful lawyer as well as her mentor. She experienced his death as an unbearable abandonment. A story from her treatment is a more ordinary example of the unconscious transmission of trauma and its contribution to treatment resistance.

> Immediately after telling her therapist that she needed to speak with him about things she had done that she considered bad, she became extremely conflicted about speaking at all. She then came to her session having cut herself while in the woodworking area of the hospital's Activities Department. This was a major violation of a community norm against acting out in any way in this creative space. She felt she was showing her "badness" and perhaps trying to provoke her therapist into agreeing with this definition of herself and punishing her. This would have alleviated her guilt, but also protected her from having to say the things she felt she needed to say. Eventually her therapist said to her that she might be communicating something else to him in this act: "Cutting yourself in the Activities Department desecrates what people here consider to be a sacred space. Cutting can be seen as desecrating your body. Maybe you are trying to tell me about desecrating your body in a way that I can feel."

After the patient and her therapist worked through her defensive reactions to this interpretation, she got to what she had been afraid to say. She spoke in detail and in a tone of great seriousness about a complicated and ultimately destructive romantic entanglement with an older man who had "opened up the world" to her. She felt extremely guilty for the consequences of this relationship and had kept it to herself for years.

At this point in the therapy, the ongoing, agitated lament about her father changed completely into a quieter, deeper, and more alive anger at her mother, who had drifted into low-key but chronic medication abuse during the patient's early childhood. As she developed this material, the patient found, to her surprise, that she no longer wanted to cut herself and that she could look at pictures of her father again. She was no longer angry with him; instead she missed him, but felt she had him with her in a new way. The transference shifted from a paternal constellation to a maternal one, and, after further work in this area, the patient took the frightening step of asking her mother if they could speak frankly about their relationship. She also asked her therapist to take part in this meeting.

At the meeting, the patient spoke with her mother about how angry she had been at her for being emotionally absent during her childhood. She went into detail and spoke with feeling. Her mother replied, "You're right; I wasn't there; I'm so sorry." In the course of reflecting on the early years of her marriage, the patient's mother revealed to her daughter an early, complicated, and ultimately destructive romantic entanglement of her own. Its traumatic ending had been quite public and so terribly shameful and crushing to the mother that she had completely withdrawn from a promising and already accomplished artistic career. The patient's father came along at this time and rescued her from this catastrophe. She became pregnant with the patient soon after they married. But the shame and grief persisted, symptoms related to physical stress developed, and she found that she was medicating herself to deal with the strain of raising a lively child and responding to an ambitious husband. She did, however, devotedly encourage her daughter in the arts.

The patient's mother realized in this conversation the true extent of her grief at losing her artistic career. Performing had been for her "the most meaningful experience of my life, a glimpse of something beyond ordinary human experience. It needed concentration. I was in it. I wasn't really myself any more." It had also brought "a special joy" to her sad and withdrawn father. "He didn't talk about it, but we could meet there."

After this remarkable conversation, the patient felt she had rediscovered her mother as both a person and as a resource in her effort to get well.

This also seems to be a story about the transmission of trauma. In a family session, the patient's mother remembered, and disclosed to her daughter for the first time, a critical traumatic event in her early adulthood, an event remarkably similar to the traumatic relationship the patient eventually confesses in her therapy. Her mother's traumatic experience involved a love relationship that she felt to be enormously exciting but illicit. It had led to great shame and to a series of terrible losses, including of her artistic career. The latter represented the creative place where a wounded father and a loving, very talented daughter could "meet", and so, embedded in this young adult disaster was also the mother's despair at losing her own father.

In the next generation, the patient as a child felt this loss of her mother, but this painful experience was hidden behind the more overtly passionate relationship with, and eventual loss of, her father. Once the patient made emotional contact with this earlier loss in her therapy, she discontinued her cutting. She then began to recognize how she had attributed the early loss of her mother to her own badness. She had become convinced that her anger at her mother's absence would only lead to the further loss of this fragile person. It came to seem to her that it was in response to this conflict with her mother that she had directed her vitality toward her father, a move that felt both rescuing and illicit.

The patient's mother's willingness to open her own trauma to her daughter gave the patient a new context for her trouble. The parallels were remarkable even if totally unknown, at least consciously, by the patient. Like her mother, she had become entangled with a man in a way that led to shame, guilt, and painful losses. Both women shared a devotion to their fathers, and, like her mother, the loss of her father was cause for despair. Indeed, it seemed likely that the patient's mother had unconsciously sponsored the kind of relationship between father and daughter that she had had with her own father and then lost. She certainly sponsored her daughter's artistic interests and talents. All of this suggests the intricacies and the subtlety of a trauma's transmission.

The window into this transmission was opened by a major piece of acting out in the patient's treatment. She cut herself in the Activities Department. From one angle, this was the kind of assault on the treatment setting that provokes the designation "treatment resistant". But, from another, this action brought into the treatment two aspects of the trauma in her life and in her mother's. First, it enacted (as it simultaneously attempted to stay silent about) what she felt to be the illicit use of her body, just as her mother felt that her illicit use of her body had led to such humiliation and loss. Accompanying this in the transference was the wish for a punishing father, who would relieve the guilt of a sexually transgressing daughter and restore a damaged relationship.

Second, this action brought into the treatment the patient's assault on the creative life of other patients and staff in the Activities Department. This precisely replicated a childhood role she felt herself to have occupied. Her birth had indeed sealed her mother's decision to withdraw from creative life, and her anger at her mother's relative unresponsiveness compounded her sense that she was the destroyer of her mother's vitality. There was both painful irony and liberating understanding in this part of her analysis. The patient was certainly acting out an Oedipal issue. She secretly wanted her therapist to pair with her and forgive her attack on the creative space of other people, just as she wanted her father to take her side in the battle with her mother. But her action carried an echo from another generation. In fact, it replicated the trauma of her mother's early adulthood: it enacted shameful sexuality in displaced form and it had major consequences for the creative space she also loved. This is the kind of sobering realization that links the patient's symptoms with the family's history of trauma and frees a patient to use, rather than resist, treatment.

The unconscious as instrument

My second and closing quote from Freud is his remarkable, mysterious, and completely unelaborated declaration that "Everyone possesses in his own unconscious an instrument with which he can interpret the utterances of the unconscious in other people" (1913i, p. 320). Trauma seems to be transmitted from one generation to the next through this unconscious instrument, however much we still do not know about the specifics of its operation. Erikson noticed similar phenomena. He wrote about "the subtler methods by which children are induced to accept ... prototypes of good and evil" and the way that "minute displays of emotion ... transmit to the human child the outlines of what really counts" (1959, pp. 27–28).

My argument in this chapter is that treatment resistance for some patients reflects a complex authority issue. The experience of some children has been "authored", if you will, by the unspeakable traumas of their parents. Some have been especially, if unconsciously, "authorized" to carry their parent's trauma into the future. This "unthought known", in Bollas's apt phrase (1987), must come into being as emotional understanding if the patient is ultimately to take authority for his or her own life as distinct from that of the traumatized parent. Treatments that threaten to further dissociate this experience or threaten the unconscious mission to which the patient is deeply loyal will be resisted to the death, no matter how valuable they have objectively been for other patients.

In more practical terms, I am suggesting that the therapists of apparently treatment resistant patients consider the nature of the trauma those patients might be carrying from the preceding generation. This would mean that the therapist would be interested in the life stories of the patient's parents and grandparents, that the therapist would develop some sense of the social–historical context, especially its upheavals, in which these stories were taking place, that he would develop an "ear" for potential "signifiers" and perhaps be especially curious about the names people are given, that he would notice areas in the patient's life that are blanketed by silence, and that he would trust that his associations to the patient's material have potential meaning about the larger story the patient is trying to tell and come to know.

In the examples above, these larger meanings are told through a dream and an acting out. The therapists' responses are relatively spontaneous associations, but I would argue that they are, in fact, brought about by the patient's material. In other words, people to whom trauma is transmitted unconsciously must transmit it to the therapist and must use the same channel of unconscious communication that was used with them. Freud invited us to investigate this "instrument". Some treatment resistant patients invite us to use it to understand how it has been used with them.

References

Bollas, C. (1987). *The Shadow of the Object: Psychoanalysis of the Unthought Known*. London: Free Association Books.
Coates, S. (2003). Introduction: Trauma and human bonds. In: S. Coates, J. Rosenthal, & D. Schecter (Eds.), *September 11: Trauma and Human Bonds* (pp. 1–14). Hillsdale, NJ: Analytic Press.

Coates, S., Rosenthal, J., & Schecter, D. (Eds.) (2003). *September 11: Trauma and Human Bonds*. Hillsdale, NJ: Analytic Press.

Davoine, F., & Gaudilliere, J-M. (2004). *History Beyond Trauma*. New York: Other Press.

Drapeau, M., & Perry, J. (2004). Childhood trauma and adult interpersonal functioning: a study using the Core Conflictual Relationship Theme Method (CCRT). *Child Abuse and Neglect, 18*: 1049–1066.

Erikson, E. H. (1959). Identity and the life cycle. *Psychological Issues, Part 1* (pp. 1–171). New York: International Universities Press.

Faimberg, H. (2005). *The Telescoping of Generations*. New York: Routledge.

Fonagy, P., & Target, M. (2003). Evolution of the interpersonal interpretive function: clues for effective preventive intervention in early childhood. In: S. Coates, J. Rosenthal, & D. Schecter (Eds.), *September 11: Trauma and Human Bonds* (pp. 99–113). Hillsdale, NJ: Analytic Press.

Fraiberg, S., Adelson, E., & Shapiro, V. (1975). Ghosts in the nursery. *Journal of the American Academy of Child Psychiatry, 14*: 387–421.

Freud, A., & Burlingham, D. (1943). *Children in War*. New York: Medical War Books.

Freud, S. (1913i). The disposition to obsessional neurosis. *S.E., 12*: 313–226. London: Hogarth.

Freud, S. (1933a). The dissection of the psychical personality, Lecture XXXI. *New Introductory Lectures on Psycho-Analysis. S.E., 22*. London: Hogarth.

Fromm, M. G. (1989). Impasse and transitional relatedness. In: M. Fromm & B. Smith (Eds.), *The Facilitating Environment: Clinical Applications of Winnicotts's Theory* (pp. 179–204). Madison, CT: International Universities Press.

Fromm, M. G. (2000). The other in dreams. *Journal of Applied Psychoanalytic Studies, 2*: 287–298.

Fromm, M. G. (2004). Psychoanalysis and trauma: September 11 revisited. *Diogenes, 51*(3): 3–14.

Lacan, J. (1977). *Écrits: A Selection*. New York: W. W. Norton.

Muller, J. (1996). *Beyond the Psychoanalytic Dyad*. New York: Routledge.

Schecter, D. (2003). Intergenerational communication of maternal violent trauma: understanding the interplay of reflective functioning and posttraumatic psychotherapy. In: S. Coates, J. Rosenthal, & D. Schecter (Eds.), *September 11: Trauma and Human Bonds* (pp. 115–142). Hillsdale, NJ: Analytic Press.

Volkan, V. (2002). September 11 and societal regression. *Group Analysis, 35*(4): 456–483.

Volkan, V. (2004). *Blind Trust: Large Groups and Their Leaders in Times of Crisis and Terror*. Charlottesville, VA: Pitchstone Publishing.

CHAPTER SEVEN

Turns of a phrase: traumatic learning through the generations

Barri Belnap

Reading the language of the traumatized body, one sees evidence of a moment when rules and expectations are betrayed, leaving the victim in a sort of timeless zone in which no future is imaginable. The moment in which the traumatic mark is re-experienced is not normal time; time does not function as an expectable and reliable limit. Rather, time boundaries dissolve. "It is happening again." The body braces for a shattering return that repeats as if no time has passed, making present realities seem unreal. "It", the source of the destruction, is unclear. The sufferer searches and some-times finds present causes, but they only partially explain. Often, there are no words at all with which to understand what is happening. In other cases, though words are spoken, they do not find recognition in the listener, but instead evoke denial. A "no response" is registered and prevents the witnessing of what is at stake in such traumatic moments.

Repetitive jokes and teasing between family members often preserve in ritual form a bit of family trauma, an "It" that is sustained and simultaneously disavowed. The expectation that "It is happening again" gets generalized to contexts where it does not wholly belong. Because there is no spoken or observable link between the traumatic repetition and the present, it is as if not just time but the laws that govern social relations are suspended. "It", the source of the destruction, remains unclear and consequently potentially omnipresent. Considering the private pain suffered in such moments, the loyalty (conscious and unconscious) of sufferers to the preservation of their tie to "It" is both striking and puzzling.

Clinical work with trauma suggests that some experiences mark a turning upside down of what is "supposed to be", what one is "supposed to be able to rely on". The repetitions that keep these traumas alive do the same: for example, traumatic reactions unfold as if law does not hold, police do not protect, and neighbours become potential enemies. Some remembrances of trauma are passed down from ancestors in the form of *life lessons*. They are offered ostensibly to guide and protect, but are repeated curiously out of context, as if they need no explanation, and in a way that repeats some vestige of the trauma and the trauma's implications for social relations.

The trauma lessons I explore here are lessons enacted between parents and children. They can be distinguished from other learning by the *unspoken* demand in their rhetoric to survive "It", the trauma. This demand subtly replaces the more normative parental wish for the child to have his "own life", free to define himself in the present and future. The family's hope and attitude towards the future becomes based on the transmission to the child of the need to act in the future in a way that remembers and tries to be prepared for the trauma, which, like a father's name, has become a marker of the family line. "It" has become a part of who they are, a distinguishing mark of the family group, signifying a sense of belonging. Children are loyal to this tie despite its twisted nature (twisted in that the tie says your feeling must be the same as mine and refuses to recognize the child as other than the parent.). Through it we see how trauma can turn things upside down; for example, the future becomes the repetition of the past, leaving the child to be misrecognized as fatefully defined by it. In this way, the experience of the child as subject is foreclosed.

This double transmission—to remember the danger without understanding it and to survive it—happens via contradictions created between spoken words and the emotional situation in which they are delivered. In these frequently repeated rituals, what "It" is necessarily remains enigmatic to the child, yet the communication of "It" somehow defines the child in his parents' eyes. Both the child and the parents register that "It" is what they are looking for in him. Consequently, the child's sense of self includes the "It" mirrored back from his parents. "It" is deeply clung to because, through these lessons, something is turned upside down between the generations: the command to "survive" is grandiosely offered to a child *in place of* a natural faith in the family's capacity to belong to its community, the child's natural developmental capacities and his/her right to a life in the present world. In this way, trauma comes to be positioned as a primary symbolic link between the generations, a blood tie that the young person relies on to make his first pass into his unknown future.

It doesn't hurt

Mr A remembers a childhood game that became the signature of his relationship with his mother and a determinant of his future. In the game, his mother would take a hot cooking spoon and burn him from behind. He would cry out in pain, "That hurts." His mother would laugh, saying, "It doesn't hurt," and then repeat the game, despite her son's pleas for her to stop. Perhaps in a protective effort, he responded by becoming confused. It did not make sense. Why would his mother do this? He opted to trust in an explanation that preserved him as the son of a mother who loved him. He imagined that this hurtful game had reasons behind it that reflected the ethical laws he identified within the family, but laws that he now could not understand. The confusing effect of the game on him became the core of his identity; "It was confusing" became "he was confused". Symptomatically, this was expressed in a conviction that he contained an inexpressible badness and that, in some strange way, he did not exist in the same way that others did. This was reflected in the outsider status he occupied socially, his attitudes toward authority, and his inability to use his aggression effectively to meet that of others.

Clues to the significance of the childhood game came in a series of dreams. In the first, he wandered through a frozen underground world. He struggled to get out, but became paralysed with confusion when discovering himself, near the exit to the cave, frozen in a pillar of ice. In a later dream, he was crawling through a tube in which sharp protrusions cut into him as he moved toward the exit. In the next image, he was pounding his head on a stone wall so as *not* to feel pain.

In the last dream, a baby was taken by his mother and dropped off a cliff. His therapist reacted emotionally, claiming that a murder had been committed. He said, "No; it was an act of mercy," meant to protect the child from a life that was too cruel and painful. "It was what the mother could *do*." This dream led him to retell the story of his mother's childhood trauma, in which she witnessed extreme parental violence in the kitchen at mealtimes.

The location of his mother's traumatic experience became the location for his own life lesson. The mother's survival lesson instructed her son not to feel, but instead to laugh at and deaden a horrifically painful life she saw as his inevitable future. This determination was the result of perceiving her son's future as limited to an unstoppable repetition of the painful realities of her own childhood. The laughter at pain so central to the childhood game between them felt to the son like his mother's scornful repudiation of his right to his own life. Pain was to mark his life. Scornful laughter split the patient off from "normal" life, creating a state of exception assigned to him by his mother's actions: a place where really "it doesn't (or perhaps shouldn't) hurt".

In a parallel manner, the patient acted on the maternal injunction to "deaden the pain" by going into dissociated mental states in which he identified with the "mother of mercy" in his dream (who threw her child off a cliff) by perpetrating on himself near fatal suicide attempts. These were interrupted only by the accidental discovery of his dying body by passers-by, social accidents that undercut the grandiose maternal claim on her son as not a part of the "normal" world. Through these fortuitous rescues, the social world established its own claim on him, contradicting and potentially replacing the deadly maternal injunction by inviting him to live and take his place in the world beyond the maternal cave.

At the same time, it opened up the patient to a terrifying void; he could not look in his mother's eyes and see "love" for him. He could only see hatred and her effort to deaden the pain he now aroused in her. If he rejected the place he had occupied for her, where would he find a connection to the "people" to whom he belonged, a people who claimed him as their own? The mother's hatred and envy of "normal" unscathed life gave her son no opportunity for connection with her except by identifying with her vision. He felt he had no real alternatives.

In the repetition of the game between patient and therapist, the hot spoon became the threat of suicide. It was applied to the skin of the therapeutic work as the therapist felt the patient's attack on her analytic ideals. Interpreting from the countertransference, the therapist winced and said, "It (these self-destructive actions) hurt" their shared therapeutic work. In an identification with the mother of mercy, the injunction from the patient to the therapist was that she, the therapist, should feel nothing and that the "truth" of their connection depended on that. The patient's felt experience was that the meaningfulness of the connection with his therapist, the life of the therapy, depended on "not feeling it". The patient claimed that, as a professional, it was the therapist's duty to "sweep up dead bodies", as if this duty were an act of mercy. If the therapist could not deaden the patient's pain, then she should allow the mercy killing. In the therapeutic work, it appeared that the therapist's experience and expression of pain became the boundary around which a battle was fought. In this battle, the life or death of the therapy—and of the patient—hung in the balance. This was a battle that tested the "ethics" of the therapy and the social field in which the therapy was embedded: the demand that the patient's pain be embedded in the deadly maternal injunction for a mercy killing was pitted against an ethics that rejected this use of his suffering to sustain the masochistic union between mother and child.

The therapist, in keeping with social norms, recognized his pain as a signifier of his right to a life and as the expression of life-sustaining drives. The patient, at this moment, was acting from the position of his mother who was situating the therapist in the child–patient's place. At this critical juncture, the transference demanded that the therapist locate the pain in herself and at the centre of their work, even in the face of the patient's demand that it be denied. Doing so, the therapist laid claim to the patient's pain as a point of identification and commonality, so as to bring the patient out of the "state of exception" that he occupied with his mother and link him instead to a social effort to understand and compassionately respond to the painful position he was in with her.

Despite the patient's expectation of a malevolent maternal injunction, which had become his relation to the future, something different evolved in the therapy. The patient was no longer "numb"; he began to "feel." In "feeling" he showed to himself *with the analyst as witness* that he was no longer *deadened* to joys, emotions, or the painful anticipation of their loss. This new reality created between therapist and patient contradicted the "unreality" of his pain established by the "spoon game". This development frightened him because it threatened the deadly maternal bond, and he attacked this potential by becoming suicidal. In the countertransference, the therapist was aware of her own pain at what was unfolding, and identified her pain as grief: grief over the threatened loss of a new aliveness that unquestionably had become present in the therapy, of which they were both a part. This was a vital clue. The therapist, through her role as witness, was positioned between his past frozenness, his present aliveness, and a future "end to the tunnel", which the therapy claimed on his behalf.

At this juncture, the therapist felt her grief to represent a boundary around which the core issues of the therapy were unfolding. *Dead* as a signifier shifted, when he threatened suicide, from a merciful absence of pain, evoked by the dream image of hitting his head against a wall until he "felt nothing", to *dead* as the signifier of the loss of a particular life, the "new" life he had begun to have in the therapy, a life that had become dear to both the patient and his therapist. *Dead* might also have signified the deadening attachment to his mother's trauma that was also a dear one, but which he began to relinquish. The therapist's expression of grief at this potential loss put her in the position the patient could not occupy with his mother or himself. If grief functioned as a boundary to suicidal action, and to the connection to the grief-denying mother it represented, then the world as he knew it would be turned upside down. The patient would again be subject to something greater than the maternal demand on him to deaden unbearable pain through the sacrifice of his own life.

Indeed, the patient's dreams attested to a transformation that took him from a frozen place deep within to an underground tunnel that tore at his skin when he moved towards the hope to "get out". Not seeing the end of the tunnel, he had to take it on faith that the pain endured would be worth it as the price for freedom. The development promoted by the therapy meant inevitable pain. Agreeing to the process required an act of faith—faith in himself and in the society of which his therapy was a part. This faith was introduced into the therapy by the therapist's accepting the potential grief at losing him and her willingness to bear this pain in the conviction that growth and repair were possible. She, thus, challenged the omnipotence of the maternal claim on *her* patient, offering instead the possibility of identification with the *process* of grief as both a survivable and a healing experience. Grief as a process grounded in tradition placed both therapist and patient in a position to acknowledge death as a shared limit to which no one can claim exception. In that way, grieving represented a functional third to the dyad and a limit on the grandiosity that denied death.

This acknowledgement of grief created a new conflict between past and future. Witnessing his therapist's grief, the patient felt changed, and this initiated an impasse—a terrible "caught in between" state where he felt he had no place to stand. The image of "no place to stand" became a new battleground. The patient felt he had lost something because he could no longer conceive of killing himself without "feeling". Without that possibility, he was left with a terrible agony, which he felt powerless to address. He held his therapist responsible for this and was enraged at his new capacity to see and feel his therapist's grief as a reflection of his own. The development of this identification between patient and therapist prevented him from feeling isolated in a "state of exception". He no longer had the freedom to see his death as merciful. Accustomed to seeing hatred reflected in his mother's eyes, now he was seeing something different reflected back to him. He wished for the state before the encounter with his therapist. He attacked the morality of the psychotherapeutic work on this basis, claiming that it created suffering without an end. He felt he was now nowhere.

Again, the turning point away from this nowhere place was marked, after the fact, in a dream. He had been plagued by terrible headaches that made life a living hell. In the dream, he was in a room with a great aunt on the maternal side whom he had forgotten about. This ancestor had prepared a meal for the patient and sat in a rocking chair while he ate, and then. to his surprise in the dream. he was able to sleep under her watchful eye.

This ancestor represented a new link. It was a link to the idea of someone watching over him, of a kind of maternal role unencumbered by trauma. This maternal aunt was of the generation that *could* have cared for his mother. In the transference repetition, the therapist was ultimately distinguished from the mother and from the patient, creating the possibility of a new social link. It is on the basis of this new relationship that the maternal great aunt is remembered. In other words, the dream gives representation to an independent care-taking other outside the mother–child-oneness and outside the trauma-based relationship that the mother and son were enacting. Following the dream, his life began to follow the new course staked out by the dream, with caring relationships and social circumstances that did not bear the traumatic markers that had linked him to his mother.

At these critical junctures in the transference of trauma, there is the need for the formation of a new social link, an essential creative act that restores the subject to *his* place in relation to the ancestors, to living a life endorsed by them, and to a future in normal, non-traumatic time. This non-traumatic time recognizes death as a boundary. Suffering grief then can serve as the entry point to a *process* by which the finality of death is recognized as a limit, a limit on another's claim on the subject's life and a limit that underlines the subject's authority and responsibility to make something of his own life.

The darkness around them

Ms B, too, asked me as her therapist to help her die. In the past, she had made a suicide pact with a boyfriend. They planned to get drunk, overdose on drugs, and die together. She expected her death to free her from the pain of being alive. She meant to go through with it, but at the last minute, he failed her. His was the position the therapist was asked to step into.

Ms B spoke of being depressed because of things her mother would not or could not see. Several years earlier, when the depression began, the patient had asked her mother to visit her in the hospital after a suicide attempt. Ms B purposely kept her room dark for the visit. She wished that her mother would ask her about it. She hoped that the dark room might bring her mother into an experience of the darkness that had fallen around both of them. The patient had hoped to make her mother feel what she would not acknowledge in words. But Ms B's mother's response was to demand that she let the light in. To this the patient responded, "Look what you are doing to me." To the patient, this statement marked a lost opportunity for emotional contact about a shared trouble. Not losing hope, she became more ill.

When this moment repeated itself in the therapy, words seemed to fail, and silence became the darkness between patient and therapist. Ms B stared blankly and said she could not speak. The therapist expressed a wish to know this darkness and wondered out loud if it would be possible to bring "It" into the office in some other form, so that they might see "It" together. The patient considered painting "It", but the thought was terrifying. The proposition stimulated a strong wish to die in the patient. She became paranoid and spoke of how governments betrayed people for private and unacknowledged reasons. We wondered about her death wish, and the therapist asked if perhaps what needed to die was linked to this darkness that could not be spoken about.

Soon after she began therapy, the patient discovered an amazing ability to paint. She was gifted not only with a talent that made her a promising artist, but also with the capacity to show what she could not say. One of her early paintings was of light coming from under a door, and a chair around which the space vibrated with colours that seemed to record the mood of the people who had once occupied it. Most of her paintings depicted rooms in a house, rooms that seemed the backdrop for ordinary events, except that they gave the impression of something deeply unsettling. Shadows of different colours carried the resonance of hidden events. They seemed to trace something solid though unseen. Like music in a film that promises relief or disaster before the characters themselves deliver the action, shadows in her paintings were showing something that both had been and was yet to come.

Discussing the shadows in her paintings connected us to a memory, her first hallucination, of footsteps coming upstairs in her childhood home. The footsteps were the harbinger of the illness that brought her into treatment. She remembered the moment when she first heard them. She was "alone" in the house with a friend. The friend, a girl her own age, was her comrade through very difficult times, but the patient also felt betrayed by her. Indeed, in her life story, no human connection seemed untainted by betrayal. Among these betrayals was the memory of an aunt. While alive, her aunt "understood" her. The patient felt seen and introduced into a world she wanted to belong to, but the memory of this aunt was stained by the patient's feeling of being betrayed and left alone by her upon her death, so that even this memory could provide neither solace nor the promise of finding a similar relationship in the future.

At the moment of crisis, Ms B was speaking in therapy of these betrayals: the mother who told her she loved her but asked her to sacrifice herself to the mother's needs, the aunt who cared about her but died, and her best friend who promised to always be there but left anyway. At that point in her treatment, Ms B became psychotic and began to again hallucinate steps in the attic. She invited the therapist to interpret her hallucinations as evidence of her "craziness" and ripeness for death. She made an effort to get the therapist to discount them as madness, with the implication that, being "mad", she should be allowed to die. As her therapist, I decided to believe in the ghost in the attic. I asked her to imagine *who* was walking there. My belief in the psychic reality of the footsteps contradicted her claim that they were evidence of madness and therefore "nothing" to take seriously. My belief in the face of her refusal to believe became a new battle-ground.

She struggled to stay with me. She felt unable to resist the call to death. She raged at the medication that she held responsible for her inability to have a life. She wanted to join the invisible maker of the footsteps. Taking this statement as pointing to the trouble, I insisted on hearing the voice of the ghost that walked on the floors above her. These discussions led to our musing about "skeletons in the closet". Abruptly, stories of violence and neglect came to the surface. We would learn shortly about the parental refusal to acknowledge the violence, and instead how her mother's demand that the patient "understand" had eroded her developing self, stripping her down to a skeleton stuffed with parental assertions of "love" and "under-standing", which actually served as instructions for her to feel noth-ing but gratitude and to deny the actual pain and danger she felt.

She put "It" on paper: part painting, part sculpture. "It" had no shadows, only a deep, dark background that gave the impression of three dimensions through the effect of many layers of paint. It contained the first human form that she had represented in her art. A skeleton without head or legs was sewn to the canvas. It was stuffed with crumpled letters written by her mother to her. Against a black background was pasted a letter on which the mother's handwriting was clear: "I love you", it said. The letter was torn and smeared with black and red. The patient told me that she had mixed her own blood with the paint. Next to the skeleton, there was a torn paper valentine heart and a doll's hand broken away from the body.

As she and I looked at the painting, she felt rage at her mother for the "lies" she found written there. "Love" was what her mother wrote.

The patient's collage revealed her translation of "I love you" to be the mother's injunction for the patient to love her, defined idiosyncratically by her mother as an instruction not to feel hurt at those critical moments when, instead of acknowledgement, her mother said nothing: nothing when Ms B's brother beat her; nothing when her mother "killed" the patient's hopes to pursue interests that were alive in her. Her mother justified these actions by claiming she was "loving" her. The patient's art and her associations to it showed how she had felt stripped to a skeleton stuffed with crumpled letters of "love". There was no skin. The bare bones seemed to mean that she was full of her mother's demands to "understand", which meant, "You must not scream, cry out, be angry or demand more."

Love, translated into an injunction not to feel pain, became for her the "reason" she had no right to "complain". No complaint meant no reason to hope for change. Her conclusion: her pain was the product of her own failure. "I love you" equalled "You must understand", which meant, "You have no reason to feel hurt or injured". Consequently, Ms B's bad feelings had no human place in which to make sense. Death was the option left available. In her paintings, these injuries were reduced to shadows that lingered in rooms after the human beings had left. In light of this, the therapist wondered if the hallucination of footsteps represented this skeletal self that had refused to die, but had instead become a shadow that walked the floors of the house at a safe distance, perhaps like her now dead aunt.

In the shift of metaphor from skeleton as the marker of death to a live representation of deathblows dealt to aspects of her self, but also survived by her, she began to feel a place in a human world. The patient's illness, like the canvas, recorded these deathblows, keeping them present in the hope of transforming the "sick things" into a shared intimacy through maternal understanding. She began to tell me stories about the bits that were represented in the dark blood-black areas of the canvas. The stories she revealed were horrible, the kinds of things families cannot speak, things that makes the phrase "skeletons in the closet" come to mind with horrifying and paralysing connotations.

Important among these was the story her mother told about how her own father had punished her by pouring acid on her hand. Without elaboration about why he had done this or what her reaction was, this horrifying "fact" stood between mother and daughter. Based on what the grandfather did to her mother, the patient was asked to "understand" irrational behaviour in the family, including the mother's. In translation, this understanding carried another injunction: "You must understand that what I do to you is because of what my father did to me. It is not what I want to do to you. I care about you. I do not mean to hurt you. I have put you in the position to live what I was denied, not just what I experienced. You will have the opportunity (actually the duty) to live what I could not."

The patient took this to be a promise. If she could repair her mother's life by offering her the possibility of living vicariously through her, then her mother would love her in the way that she longed for. Perhaps this explains how the aunt's death was felt as a betrayal. Her aunt, her father's sister, represented the possible "good mother" that the patient brought to life in a relationship of real understanding, but, despite this, she died anyway. The detached hand on the canvas was a signifier, hiding in plain sight, representing the story of her mother's hand, detached from meaning and affect. Even further, the daughter was to be her mother's hand, the unscathed hand, almost a hand puppet living out what the mother had wanted in her life but was too damaged to achieve.

The ties that bind

Both of these patients were attempting to bring speech to an area of unknown trauma, transmitted in the turn of a phrase, the double messages of games between parents and children. These trauma lessons also occur and recur in moments of discipline or punishment. For example when a parent says to a child, "Shut your big mouth." Or in moments of anxiety, when a parent teases her child, "If you aren't good, we'll leave you. We'll give you away." These are moments that seem to be an exception to the usual rules of family life. They are the repeated "sayings" between parents and their children that stop normal time, moments marked by a chuckle, a sigh, or a burst of exasperation that invites them to pass as if they never happened. Children and parents seem to reduce the communication to the status of something that does not matter, something "she always says but doesn't mean", "just a joke", "just a silly game", while potential witnesses stay silent.

These messages do not seem to fit with the rest of the relationship. Nor do they fit with the speaker's image of herself or the family's image of itself. This is a kind of speaking that happens in a place of *exception*, where words can be said and people can claim, "It doesn't mean anything." Unable to be registered fully as to *how* they are meaningful, these words hang in the air and become part of what ties the family together, at least at the level of shared, only half-conscious experience, but also at the level of an identity to which family members can become unconsciously quite loyal. In this latter sense, they are examples of moments in which family members tell each other who they are in ways that carry the markers of unspoken and unspeakable trauma.

In the formation of an individual's subjectivity, there is a stage in which the subject asks, "Who am I?" This question is answered on many levels. Who am I as an individual? Who am I in terms of my community? Who am I to others? Who am I to my family? With regard to the latter, the ties between the subject and ancestors have an essential link to ethics, where ethics means that which gives legitimacy and constancy to the answers to these subject-defining questions. The subject, as part of coming to know who he or she is, must ask questions like the following: "What ties me to my family? Of these ties, how do I discriminate between those that can I reject and those that I cannot? What defines me as one of them?" This last area is critical: the ties that define the subject as "one of them", that claim him and link him to his ancestors in a way that, like the blood that runs in his or her veins, marks the lived connection to his or her "bloodline".

This, I would suggest, is an extension of Freud's notion of *Bejahung* (Freud, 1925h). In his paper on Negation, *Bejahung* is the affirmation, *Verneinung* the negation of some connection. What we see in these families is the way parents sustain a claim on the child through connecting him or her to parental trauma. Such a claim might be understood as both an inversion and an extension of Freud's notion of *Bejahung*.

For Freud, *Bejahung* is the inchoate subject's affirmation of an experience, the "yes" that joins together elements of experience. Lacan (1953–1954) adds to Freud's conception the idea that the child's affirmation takes place in the Other (the Other representing the symbolic order, culture, the Third) in so far as the Other is the locus of the shared code that makes it possible to use language to communicate about these experiences. Affirmation that comes from the other-of-trauma is a disaffirmation (not a negation because negation implies a prior affirmation). It is a perverted claim that says you are one of us in a way that disaffirms the child's experience. The child is placed in crisis: if he claims his own experience, he has to give up the link insisted upon by the family. This is a perverted act-of-claiming because in place of the larger societal code, the family has substituted its own upside down language, upside down because words are used in idiosyncratic ways to carry private, unconscious meanings: meanings that actually are meant to deny or correct a trauma from a different time and place, while in the present, they function to deny current subjective experience.

In these families, we can observe an extension of *Bejahung* that goes beyond the primordial affirmation of the subject necessary for symbolization and includes the other's response, the stance taken *by the other* to the subject's affirmation of trauma. There is a cycle of trauma here, which begins with transmission from parent to child, but also comes back from the child to the parent for its disaffirmation. The traumatic mark is not complete until the other fails to confirm the subject's *Bejahung*. In this disaffirmation, the other claims the child through a traumatic capture of his experience, substituting the logic of trauma for the child's experience. There are many clear examples of upside down language in the cases above: actual pain is no pain; the child's statement, "It hurts," comes back to him as "It doesn't hurt"; the parent's claim, "I understand you," means "Please understand me". The parent's plea for "understanding" becomes, in the family code, a claim that understanding precludes feeling hurt or criticized, so the child cannot both feel hurt and satisfy the parent's demand to be understood.

Bejahung, in this extended sense, is the mark a child receives from his family that says, "You are one of us", that affirms membership through the disaffirmation of experience. It links the child to the fragments of a parent's traumatic past, which the child feels the effects of and becomes defined by, but without being able to know the referent. Worse than not knowing the specific referent of the parent's trauma is the aberrant nature of the new code—the different ethics and set of relations—that suddenly seems operative. The child experiences the shift from one code to another as disorientating. Confusion is created by the absence of an explanation for "ethical failure": the failure of law and the agreements that otherwise family members live by. The damage this does to the ordinary living out of ethical relationships within the family becomes the greater problem: the shift from rules that liberate to rules that constrict in the name of something unknowable and beyond understanding. One's place in the family is no longer assured simply by virtue of birth, but rather is deeply implicated in the trauma that he or she is given to both carry and deny.

These markers are not only important or powerful because of the horror of the actual trauma of which they are the remnant. The power of these markers derives, in addition, from the process by which the family defines itself. Trauma marks people in terms of *who* they are, what is expected of them, and what expectations they can have in relation to the world around them. When families define children in relation to traumatic markers, they set up omens, signs of the "actual nature of things", a way of communicating something urgent about the world without really understanding it. This gives the traumatic lesson its power and inevitably leads to the repetition of the ethical failures that accompanied it originally, ethical failures that are destructive because they, of necessity, are outside the law. Not being spoken, they cannot be predictably and safely confronted or, in a sense, adjudicated in terms of the needs of these family members in the reality of their current lives.

Ideological positions or values that a family uses to define "who we are" or to define their links to a larger group—for example, a political or religious organization—can become the vehicle for the trauma lesson. These positions identify not only who "we" can trust, but locate an enemy as the source of danger. People sometimes come together in marriage around their identification with the trauma each has endured. Feeling damaged and potentially damaging to their children, the marriage and the children it produces can be meant to draw a line between the traumatic past and a healthier present. But trauma can then function as a hole in the fabric of family life, identifiable by the extreme efforts to stop it up, to correct it, to do good where bad had been done.

Children born into such a family might come to see themselves as born to end their parents' suffering at the hands of previous generations. Without knowing it, they identify themselves with repairing trauma, which, ironically, compels them to try to discover the pain the parents are trying to put behind them. In an effort to connect, they reinflict something on the parents, who unconsciously push the child aside along with the reopened traumatic experience, thus leaving the child to face something alone. This constitutes another part of the repetition.

Trauma lessons of the sort described in this chapter create holes in the centre of identity and disrupt the meaning-making effort that is part of the epistemological drive to know who we are and what we mean to others. They also put trauma at the centre of family and social relationships, through the replacement of the authorization to live with an injunction to survive and even to represent "It", the trauma that the family unconsciously situates as central to its place in the social world.

References

Freud, S. (1925h). Negation. *S.E.*, *19*: 235–239. London: Hogarth.
Lacan, J. (1953–1954). *The Seminars of Jacques Lacan: Book I—Freud's Papers on Technique*, J.-A. Miller (Ed.). Cambridge: Cambridge University Press, 1988.

CHAPTER EIGHT

Intergenerational violence and the family myth

E. Virginia Demos

This is an exploration of how the trauma of loss and abuse, in a context of uprootedness, seems to have been transmitted across generations. It describes one young woman's painful struggle to learn to trust her own experience, to come to terms with her parents' commitment to a family myth that obliterated her reality, and to recognize how she was in danger of repeating their defensive patterns, thereby perpetuating the trauma. Her story unfolded gradually.

The patient

Ms L was an attractive, articulate, engaging twenty-year-old college junior, who had taken a medical leave of absence because of her daily drinking, her inability to concentrate and function in the college setting, and her suicidal wish to jump in front of a train. Consciously, she identified with the tragic death of Anna Karenina; over time, her story suggested deeper roots, not only in a fated romance, but in a more profound, unconscious identification with her mother, who, in her teenage years, had been struck by a vehicle.

When we began our psychotherapeutic work, she described her troubles as follows: "Things have fallen apart and I don't understand why." Her defensive style was one of repression in the context of a false-self organization. It was difficult for her to explore her problems without quickly feeling she was a total failure who would become non-functional, as she perceived her mother to be. She had always pushed herself hard to achieve, with little realistic sense of her physical and intellectual limits. Her world was rigidly polarized. The only alternative to being the "best" was to feel she was lazy, worthless, and bad. This deep sense of badness was the most enduring and certain thing she knew about herself. When her grandiose sense of her powers began to fall apart in mid-college, she was left only with badness, and became more and more focused on suicide.

Her particular suicidal image might also have represented an unconscious wish to stop the runaway train of performance she had boarded for emotional reasons unknown to her. It was an enormously expensive journey—in terms of the psychic energy and self-reproach she put into it—but for no destination she could yet call her own. She stated on several occasions that she really did not know who she was or what she wanted. Her only options seemed either to identify with her angry, frightening, yet idealized and successful father, or with her depressed, dysfunctional mother. The latter alternative was unacceptable, and the former no longer worked.

The family

Both of Ms L's parents were children of immigrants to this country from Southern Europe. On her father's side, his mother and uncle were the only survivors of many children. The uncle never married; the paternal grandmother did marry, but to an alcoholic, who abandoned her when Ms L's father was a toddler. The grandmother worked hard to educate herself and pursue a career, leaving her young son in the care of her mother and uncle, who beat his young nephew throughout his childhood.

Ms L's father never felt close to his uncle or to his grandmother, but he did feel close to and proud of his mother. Yet, according to Ms L, he treated her badly, yelling at her and arguing. After his early childhood, he saw his father only once; as a teenager, he met with his father and came away enraged and frustrated, his father being so drunk his son could not tell him how angry he was at him. A few years later, his father died. Like his mother upon her own abandonment by this man, Ms L's father focused on achievement; he graduated from college, earned an advanced degree and became a successful businessman. Thus, on the father's side, the family trauma of being uprooted and of loss seemed dealt with through hard work and achievement, denial of dependency, and enacting the rage at loss by physically abusing a helpless other.

Ms L's mother's life history was less clear. She had trained in fashion, but did not want to work for others, fearing they would take credit for her designs. She met her husband through an ethnic youth group, and they soon married. When she was pregnant with Ms L, (her first child), her mother died, and she named Ms L after her mother. The young family then moved near to her father. Over the next few years, two more children were born. When the maternal grandfather died, Ms L's mother and older brother had a falling out over the settlement of the father's estate, after which they never spoke again. As mentioned, Ms L's mother, as a teenager, had been struck by a car and injured in a way that immobilized her for a period of time. The settlement from that accident enabled the family to buy their own house. Thus, on the maternal side, issues of loss were also prominent, specifically the death of the maternal grandmother at a time when her daughter was expecting her first child. Naming Ms L after the grandmother while in the midst of complicated grief might indicate some kind of transmission. In addition, sibling rivalry seemed intense in the mother's story, and disability had led to gain while it also interrupted adolescent development.

According to Ms L, once the prized son was born, her mother seemed to ignore her daughters, assigning to Ms L, at an early age, the job of caring for her little sister. Otherwise, the family seemed to function relatively well in the early years. Mother made school lunches, took the children to and from school, and birthdays were celebrated with parties in the back yard. But one day, when Ms L was in the fourth grade, her mother did not arrive to pick the children up from school; her father eventually came. When they returned home, the house was dark and mother was in bed. So began the mother's inexplicable sudden and dramatic decline in functioning. From that day on, according to Ms L, her mother rarely left the house, no longer saw friends, and ceased to function adequately as a parent or as a house-keeper. No one in the family ever named this problem. The mother denied she was depressed or that there was anything wrong with her, and the father denied that anything had changed. The timing of this event seemed to coincide with the youngest child's (her only son's) entry into school, which might have been experienced by the mother as an emotional abandonment or a profound loss of role, leaving her alone and unable to function all day at home.

Several powerful indicators of the potential for the intergenera-tional transmission of trauma had emerged in the family history. First, the parents' life stories suggested an inability to process intensely painful emotions, particularly around loss and separation, a deficit not uncommonly associated with the profound uprootedness of immigra-tion. As is so often the case in immigrant families, over-achievement seemed to defensively compensate for loss as it also ensured survival in the new country. But, in this family, intense anger related to depri-vation and humiliation seemed constantly to break through. Second, the parents were joined in their denial that a very obvious, sudden change had occurred in the mother. And third, there was an unac-knowledged inversion of parental roles, as Ms L, from mid-childhood on, had to take over the care of both of her younger siblings. As the therapeutic work deepened and Ms L was able to speak openly about the abuse and neglect in the family, these three dynamics became very prominent. I will focus my discussion on how they affected Ms L's psychological development, her attempted solutions, and her painful struggle to free herself from her parent's attempts to lean on her psyche, in order to protect themselves from their own unresolved losses, hurts, and fears, and from her own wish to hang onto her special role in the family.

A family meeting

The early part of our work focused on Ms L's deep ambivalence about dependency. It was manifested both toward her mother, alternating between contempt for her neediness and a loving desire to help her, and toward herself, alternating between her fear that needing anybody represented being a loser, in danger of being exploited, and her painful longings to be taken care of. She began to recognize her long-standing pattern of suppressing her needs and feelings in order to please and take care of others, and how this pattern dominated her relationships with friends and with men. She hated herself for lacking the courage to stand up for herself in relation to others. In this context, her school achievement looked like a desperate attempt to fend off feelings of being a loser, like her mother, and to please and be like her successful father.

Early in treatment, we had a series of family meetings. I arranged to meet with the three siblings before meeting with the whole family in order to hear their versions of family life and to begin to help rebuild an alliance that had become badly frayed within this generation. Both siblings had had trouble with schoolwork and with their anger as well. In our meeting, Ms L's younger sister and brother verified the story of their mother's collapse and their father's rages, but were freer than Ms L to express their anger and rebellion toward both parents; they simply wanted to get away from home as soon as possible and could not understand their sister's wish to die. Ms L was more enmeshed with her parents than were her siblings. From the point of view of transmission, this sibling picture raises interesting questions: did Ms L, as the first-born, receive the transmission more fully, thus to some extent freeing her siblings? Or is their wish to make a hard separation from their parents a denial of their dependency and thus more likely to lead to unconscious enactments in the future?

In the full family meeting, Ms L's sister was most able to confront her parents. Near the end of the first session, the patient's mother said she felt that Ms L did not respect her and saw her as a failure. Ms L could not acknowledge the truth in this and tried to take care of her mother. We attempted to address the two versions of reality in the family: the children's experience of their mother's dysfunction and of parental fighting, as well as the effects these had had on them, and the parents' perspective, which focused on how spoiled these children were and how they took advantage of their mother. When we tried to sort out parental responsibility for managing marital problems and for child-care, the parents, after a brief acknowledgement, again blamed their children and insisted that it was their job to take care of the parents. They seemed pathologically certain, righteous and long-suffering about this, as though presenting a grotesque exaggeration of the Southern European culture from which their families had come. They seemed to hoard all the goodness for themselves and project all

blame onto their "ungrateful and uncaring children". They also manifested the same deep ambivalence about dependency needs that Ms L
had articulated earlier: that to need others is to be a spoiled nuisance,
which they located in their children. Yet, they longed for and expected
their children to take care of them, and felt exploited by their children's needs. The children did their best to defend themselves against
these charges: Ms L. tried to placate her parents; her siblings simply
retorted angrily.

The discussion was volatile. The children found it painful but help-
ful, in that they had never before discussed with each other or in the
family the troubles they had been experiencing. Ms L reported that
during lunch, when the parents had challenged this idea of two realities in the family narrative, the children had stuck together and re-
iterated their version of family events. Also, at one point, when the
parents fought and walked off in different directions, none of the children went after either parent to take care of them. Ms L said this was
a first for all of them. Thus, this initial attempt to re-establish generational boundaries seemed to have met with some success, at least with
the children, but had opened up an intense struggle within Ms L.

The psychotherapy

Although during the family meeting Ms L had continued to try to
please her parents, later, she expressed her shock and disillusionment
at her father's defensiveness and closed-mindedness. She had also
been surprised by her mother's ability to say as much as she did and
her own inability to speak up. As a result of her strengthened alliance
with her siblings and her father's behaviour in these meetings, she
experienced a massive and sudden de-idealization of her father, which
confused her. She no longer knew whom to look up to or to seek
advice from. But she did not feel entitled to her anger at her father and
reported that she could not sustain it outside of our sessions. At the
same time, she could no longer switch into a happy mood either, and
thus would go numb when she left my office.

This inability to hold on to her own reality in contrast to her
parent's reality represented one of the major effects on her psyche of
the parent's pathological certainty. Their united front in denying the
trouble in the family, their inability to process painful emotions, and

their leaning on her to take care of them combined to undermine their oldest child's confidence in her own perceptions and experience. Her struggle to claim her own reality, to feel entitled to her feelings and her needs, and to give up her assigned role in the family became the work of her treatment. Indeed, a central problem in the context of her father's frightening anger was Ms L's fear of losing control over her aggression, such that her own anger might become lethal. She also realized how these fears had crippled her capacity to defend herself or to speak up when needed, and how they had left her feeling enormously guilty and suicidal, especially for her rageful, even murderous wishes toward her collapsed mother.

During this same period, she had two nightmares, one about her father attacking her and being out of control, and the other about his dying as a result of her anger at him, which left her feeling frightened and guilty. A few days later she had more nightmares, one in which her father was yelling and hitting her, and another in which he was approaching her seductively. Ms L was terrified by the powerful feelings evoked in these dreams and by her inability to process these feelings when alone. She needed help, but this left her with her anxiety about dependency; she felt weak and in danger of my having power over her.

As she struggled with this intensification of her feelings, she became more suicidal and took a non-lethal dose of prescribed medication. She told no one for two days. Eventually, she acknowledged that the pills were the first step in a suicide plan that included tying herself to the railroad tracks, numbing herself with medication and not fighting to free herself. I pressed her hard about her commitment to staying alive and to the therapeutic work. She spoke about her deepest dilemma: that her rage was unacceptable to her because, if her parents knew about it, she feared they could never love her. Thus, she was up against an impossible choice: to be real and banished from parental love or to be false and banished from herself. Her awareness of always having to choose between being known or suppressing herself to get love was now becoming much more available to her. This new awareness allowed her to begin to notice how others managed anger and still cared about each other, and how when I was angry with her (e.g., around her pill-taking), I did not yell at her, but wanted to talk about what this action meant, which amazed her. She was embarrassed to say she was glad to be alive.

The sexual dream led us to explore a powerful Oedipal configuration in the family, in which her mother's weakness and collapse had strengthened Ms L's own sense of being a more desirable and better companion for her father. She spoke of her fantasies that she would dress up and go out with him as his date to various dinners, which her mother had no wish to attend. She felt she loved her father more than her mother did.

Then, several events occurred in quick succession. Her family did not acknowledge her twenty-first birthday, which hurt her deeply. She also went through a complicated grieving process about not being able to return to school. And she had again acted out, this time by drinking with under-age friends, in a way such that some real consequences might have occurred. Together, these events led to a painful sadness, which was new to her, representing a real break with her family's avoidance of sadness. She stated she had lost her way and would have to trust my saying that the sadness was healthy and important. She also reported a dream about people wearing elaborate disguises and then taking them off at night. She experienced herself as one of these people, but she could not take off the disguise, even when alone. She felt intense anger at her parents, then immediate guilt, and then a strong need to be hugged by them and reassured. She longed to be a small child again and sobbed.

This access to her grief, which seemed to validate longings that had been deeply suppressed for years, ushered in a flood of memories of physical and psychological abuse that had occurred in the family, especially regular beatings by her father, which were terrifying. Often her mother initiated them by blaming the children for something, (e.g., they had taken her pen or spilled something) and then threatening, "Wait until your father comes home!" Anticipating his arrival was torture. The patient felt her mother was so unaware that Ms L could sometimes set up her sister to get beaten, so as to avoid it herself. At one point, when her younger brother went to school with a handprint on his face, social services were called and made a home visit. Ms L reported that her parents told their children, "You can tell the truth, but if you do, they will take you away and you will never see us again." The implication seemed clear: that her parents understood the consequences of what they were doing, but made no effort to change, thus leaving Ms L and her siblings with the impossible choice of continuing to be abused or losing their parents. They chose not to talk about what was happening at home.

A second family meeting

In a subsequent family meeting, Ms L's father minimized the effects of these beatings, stating that his having been beaten as a child had never affected him and that his children should realize that he loved them. He simply could not process the intensity of fear that Ms L had experienced as a child and continued to live with, just as he had been unable to access his own fear from his childhood beatings. This denial of fear might well have enabled him to project self-hatred for his own early weakness, neediness, and imagined badness on to his needy, helpless, and allegedly bad children, thereby giving him free rein for his righteous but also vengeful rage.

Ms L feared her sister would not validate her experience of these beatings, or would see her as disloyal for speaking about the abuse. Her sister, however, did indeed validate Ms L's memories of both the beatings and her mother's emotional unavailability. She did not, however, share Ms L's contempt for their mother or her idealization of their father. She seemed to feel no disloyalty; rather, her impulse was to get away from her parents. Ms L felt deeply jealous of her sister's ability to disentangle herself from the family. She also felt shock and shame at how much gratification she had obtained from feeling that she was better than her sister. She was enraged that her sister understood some things better than she did and recognized in herself a mean streak, remembering that, as a child, she had been glad when her sister took the beatings that should have come to her. She briefly became suicidal again as she came up against her sadism and her unwillingness to give up being the best and "the chosen one".

This internal struggle between clinging to her "special" position in the family *vs.* seeing her parents and herself more clearly, if also very painfully, manifested itself over the next several weeks in exhausting fluctuations of feeling. Each visit home would convince her that her father or mother needed her and that she should leave treatment and go back to school. She would then feel a strong need for me, and yet feel guilty about spending her father's money while revealing his abuse. She could not integrate the abusive father with the father she adored and had tried so hard to please. She re-examined details of his physical and emotional abuse and of her conflicted romantic fantasies about him in the context of her mother's collapse. Her parents had deferred to her in several major decisions, leading her to believe she could do anything in the family. This was a heady, all too believable possibility. The part of her that imagined she could actually marry her father felt angry and spurned by him, recognizing that he seemed more interested in protecting his dysfunctional wife than in her.

These sessions were intensely emotional. The transference was highly dependent; Ms L wished I would take her home and mother her. But bringing into the transference relationship the raw honesty of her feelings seemed to release her to be interested in her peers, including a young man. She decided she could not make a holiday trip home, because, given her intense conflicted feelings towards her parents, she no longer knew how to relate to them. Soon after she communicated her decision, her father announced that he was reducing the funds he had made available for treatment.

In a third family session, Ms L's father said he was sad and hurt by her decision, but not angry, though his behaviour and metaphors ("putting daggers in our hearts") suggested otherwise. While he denied that his limiting the funds for treatment had anything to do with Ms L's decision not to come home for the holiday, he did seem to experience this decision as a massive separation threat and betrayal. The vehemence with which he tried to deny Ms L's experience brought to the therapist's mind Shengold's work on "soul murder" (1989). His reality as the good parent, who was being hurt and abandoned, was the only one possible in this family. Therefore, he felt entitled to use his rage and his money to try to fight off any threat to the myth of a happy family, even if it meant the destruction of his child's sense of herself. Ms L, too, had been captured and seduced by this family myth, but she was now in the midst of an intense struggle for what might be thought of as a more true self. She was deeply shocked and upset by her father's actions, but was determined to find a way to continue her therapy.

The psychotherapy continues

The next several months were extremely difficult. Ms L alternated many times between feeling enraged, like a "spoiled brat" who wanted to be taken care of, *vs.* accepting responsibility for herself and doing what she needed to do. She kept coming back to her shock and sudden realization that her father could act so vengefully. She wanted to escape this pain and do only what she wanted to do, but she realized that this was the way her mother lived, numbing herself and abdicating her responsibilities. Her mother had given up the struggle to have her own point of view.

Ms L then, for the first time, missed several sessions, leaving me a note about her anger at my being unable either to protect her from her father's retaliation or to change his mind. I had become the representation of reality and limitations; in spite of her efforts to corrupt me, I had not taken her home with me. She also hated that I made sense. She then confessed that some of her anger at me was because she could not express her anger at her parents for fear of things getting worse. After this episode, she began to feel a small, fragile self beginning to form, a self she could bring to therapy and show sometimes to her boyfriend, but could not take home.

Ms L wanted to pay for her therapy, but getting a job was conflicted for her. It seemed to symbolize a major step in asserting her independence and giving up on the wish to be loved and taken care of by her parents. It meant accepting the reality of her abusive childhood, with all the pain involved in that, and giving up her special, favoured fantasy position. She felt paralysed, but she also felt bored doing nothing, which helped her to see that she was really not like her mother. She seemed to be struggling to sort out what kind of woman she wanted to be.

At the same time, her relationship with her boyfriend was deepening, and she realized how frightened she was of real closeness. Her dreams were about losing him to another woman, which seemed to connect to her deep hurt in relation to her father and his abandonment of her for his sick wife. She had trouble differentiating this new love from her feelings for her father, and found it hard to accept that one could and should have a love relationship that was not abusive. During this period she suddenly and unilaterally decided to discontinue her medications, resulting in intense physical withdrawal symptoms and an intensification of her emotions. She was determined to get through these crises without medication and noticed that she was not suicidal, a self-discovery that was perhaps necessary for her to begin to trust herself.

While I was on vacation, she and her boyfriend spent a day in New York, riding the subways, and she reported that she had finally mastered her fear of trains. She also made a trip home, during which she watched home movies of her childhood. They were awful, full of her mother's yelling and of Ms L's being mean to her sister after her mother had been mean to her. The movies left her feeling very sad. Watching them seemed to be another step in the destruction of her fantasy of a happy childhood, which she had somehow maintained in the face of physical and verbal abuse.

As she became ready to return to school, Ms L had to once again negotiate with her family about money issues. She reported that in a long telephone conversation with her parents, she had been direct with them. In response to an angry outburst by her father, she was able to say, "If you keep yelling at me, I'll hang up," and he stopped. At the end, they thanked her for what felt like a very different kind of exchange. They agreed that she had to get a job and contribute toward her educational expenses, but her father also agreed to contribute toward the cost of her therapy. He seemed to have softened a little, perhaps because Ms L was still talking to him and still needed his support, and perhaps because he was relieved that she was no longer suicidal and indeed was considerably better. She accepted her side of the bargain.

Re-entry into school was a mixed experience. Socially, she was very lonely and isolated; all her friends had moved on, and she had not yet developed a new public persona. But her approach to work had changed markedly. She was no longer driven to be the best. She worked efficiently, with little stress and got eight hours of sleep every night. She seemed both pleased and perplexed, saying, "It's just happening." She was also less idealizing of her adviser and more able to see some of his limitations.

Her unbounded fear could still be aroused by hearing coyotes on campus: she found herself scared they might attack her in her room. This fantasy evoked vivid images of her father's crazed, angry look, with veins sticking out of his red face. She even imagined his sharp teeth. These links helped her calm down. She also began to recognize that she was repeating her family's pattern of taking out her fears and frustrations on her boyfriend by blaming him for things. She did not want to keep doing this, but described how she disconnected from her hurt and distress and then became very judgemental and angry at him. Recognizing this in herself helped her see how her parents, too, had protected their hurt feelings behind a wall of defensive anger. She asked, "If I repeat things, is it my fault or theirs?" I said it was now her responsibility to deal with what had happened to her by staying connected to, and working through, the kinds of fears and hurts that had led her parents to become abusive.

As she struggled with whether or not she could have separate feelings from her boyfriend (e.g., could she feel happy if he was depressed), she began to get in touch again with her rage at her parents. Her mother was so depressed, and Ms L never understood why. She reported revenge dreams in which she told her mother all the ways she had hurt her. She recognized all the things she wanted to change in herself before she would have any children. She arranged an important telephone conversation with her mother, in which she told her how angry she was at her for setting up the beatings, that she did not want apologies, but only wanted them to speak honestly with each other. She told her mother how she still lived with the consequences of those beatings every day; for example, her fear of making mistakes and her apologizing for everything. Her mother was able to listen and to acknowledge that she had never let herself think about the potential consequences of what happened. Her response and validation of Ms L's experience enabled Ms L to feel that maybe now she could bring both realities together.

Quite suddenly, Ms L's father lost his job, and she was pulled back briefly into believing she had the power to help him, which she also wanted. But she also felt she was owed a debt that she temporarily found it hard to let go of. This manifested itself in her not wanting to continue working. She had done so much already; she had taken care of her parents and her siblings, and now her parents owed her. It was somehow unfair that she should have to support herself. In the end, however, she found a very good job in her field, and felt excited to be working.

Discussion

The thread of trauma can be more easily traced in Ms L's father's family. His maternal grandparents lost many of their children, and the survivors might have had little capacity for experiencing loss, for managing violent feelings, and for nurturing the next generation. His mother lost her husband and turned her energies to work. The patient's father thereby not only lost his father, but also his mother as his primary care-taker. He learned early that his needs, losses, and helplessness were quickly met with anger, blame, and abuse. To survive, he adopted the same defensive stance.

Tomkins (1990) has suggested that the need to debase others is dynamically linked to the need to idealize the self and to polarize the world into the perfect and the deeply flawed, which he has called a decontamination script. This polarizing dynamic is fuelled by a deep self-hatred and the affect of disgust, which reflects a seduction that has become spoiled or contaminated. A grandiose exaggeration of both poles develops, which involves a conviction that one's badness consists of an inherent rottenness that could never be endured or faced, and leads to a belief that one could purify or decontaminate this badness by seeking a perfect world in which one would never have to suffer or feel pain. Emigration can come to signify this split—the old, bad world of pain being left behind for a new perfected world, in which there will be a new generation dissociatively separated from the traumatic past.

It seems that Ms L's father, and perhaps his mother too, had put much of their capacity for generativity into the role of breadwinner, while giving up responsibility for emotionally nurturing the next generation (Erikson, 1968). This seems to have allowed him to idealize the idea of family and his role as a "caring" father, while denying his limitations and his fears about his capacity to emotionally connect to others. A family myth was constructed as a defence against this painful reality.

The source of trauma on the mother's side of the family was never explicitly identified, but the capacity to tolerate separation or differences seemed undeveloped. This deficit might have been embedded in the unprocessed losses of the immigration process and mobilized further through the untimely death of her mother. Thus, Ms L's mother names her firstborn after her own recently deceased mother and moves near the family home, perhaps submerging her loss by taking care of her father. Around the time that her youngest child entered school, she collapsed into a major depression and felt entitled to her children's taking care of her. Her dependency and emotional dysfunction were denied, and she became prone to the same polarizing dynamic of debasement and idealization her husband seemed to have adopted.

Ms L's parents managed to form a bond in which the father was loyal to his wife, allowing for no criticism of her. Like his reported relationship with his own mother, someone he idolized while violence occurred all around them, he helped create an idealized myth of a loving, happy family. Ms L's mother seemed more overtly dysfunctional, perhaps even paranoid, as a person so dependent on denial must be. But there might have been a deeper, more intergenerational aspect to her paranoia. Her bitter stance with her children of "why should I cook or clean for you!" suggests a deep competition about who is to take care of whom, and her fury that they would steal something from her echoes a much older anxiety that people at work would steal the credit for her fashion designs or that her brother would cheat her of her inheritance from her father. Thus, intense feelings of envy and jealousy in one generation can be transmitted to the next generation as though children are unconsciously really siblings. When this happens, relations between actual siblings are deeply affected, as they were for Ms L.

Ms L's two younger siblings seemed disgusted with their parents and just wanted to get away, believing, perhaps, that they had not been damaged by the neglect and abuse they had experienced. But Ms L had been seduced into an intense Oedipal struggle by her mother's collapse and by her parents' denial of trouble in the family, leading her to embrace her father's idealized view of the family and to take on their emotional burdens. She must have been a lively, appealing, and gifted child, an easy target for parental projections of their own goodness. But any sign of her needs for nurturance or autonomy or any complaints would elicit immediate negative projections of their disowned and hated weaknesses and mobilize defensive righteous entitlement and punitive anger in them.

This is a potent, confusing mix for a child to make sense of. The parents seemed to hoard all goodness and to project all badness on to their children. If the child is seduced into trying to join that goodness, as Ms L was, any recognition of anger in herself or longings to be taken care of only confirms the child's sense of badness, which must then be denied in order to protect the fantasy of joining the parental goodness. (See Demos, 1998, for a more detailed description of these dynamics.) Ms L was caught in this deep ambivalence toward herself, her own needs, and her parents' needs, and this conflict was greatly intensified by the heated Oedipal situation that emerged in relation to the mother's abdication of her role.

After the mother's mysterious collapse, both parents expected Ms L to protect their shared myth of the normal functioning family by her simply taking over the mother's job. There seemed to be an unconscious bargain on both sides. On the parental side, "You take care of us, never leave us, cover up our weaknesses so we never have to suffer, and pretend this is normal, and we will pay for your schooling and other material needs." On Ms L's side, "I will deny your weaknesses and anxieties, your misuse and abuse of me, the legitimacy of my needs and my rage at you, in exchange for your love and money, and maybe the chance to win the big prize, namely, marrying daddy." But when, as a young adult, Ms L began to fall apart and became suicidal, the family myth was sorely challenged.

The real attack on the myth did not occur, however, until Ms L decided not to go home for the holiday. This was experienced by her parents as a deep betrayal of the bargain, which led her father to retaliate financially. His action shattered Ms L's belief that he would always take care of her. Her subsequent deep sense of being owed a debt and her rage at having to work spoke of her sense of a betrayal of the unspoken bargain she felt both had agreed to and to her intense fear of being on her own. The struggle of her therapy was for her to slowly believe in and value her experience, to accept a less grandiose reality of her and others' strengths and limitations, to embrace the legitimacy and normality of the full range of her negative emotions and to accept her conflict of loyalties, so as not to repeat, in the next generation, the patterns of denial and abuse she had endured herself.

References

Demos, E. V. (1998). Differentiating the repetition compulsion from trauma through the lens of Tomkins' script theory: a response to Russell. In: J. Tiecholz & D. Kriegman (Eds.), *Trauma, Repetition, and Affect Regulation: The Work of Paul Russell* (pp. 67–104). New York: Other Press.

Erikson, E. H. (1968). *Identity: Youth and Crisis*. New York: Norton.

Shengold, L. (1989). *Soul Murder*. New Haven, CT: Yale University Press.
Tomkins, S. S. (1990). Revisions in script theory. In: E. V. Demos (Ed.), *Exploring Affect: The Selected Writings of Silvan S. Tomkins* (pp. 389–396). New York: Cambridge University Press, 1995.

CHAPTER NINE

A quixotic approach to trauma and psychosis

Françoise Davoine

"Quixotic" is one way to describe the intergenerational transmission of trauma—on the side of both the patient and the
analyst—insofar as it is linked with the clinical experience of
psychosis and the societal inscription of history.

Aborigine psychodynamics

We recently came back from an international symposium in Australia
on the psychotherapy of schizophrenia, sponsored by an organization
originally founded in the 1950s by Gaetano Benedetti. At that earlier
time, it gathered psychoanalysts from Europe and the USA, especially
from the Austen Riggs Center and Chestnut Lodge, who knew how to
work with such severe cases. But this conference appeared to us actually to have been hijacked by numbers; we spent most of the time
watching its members worship statistics and present cases as though
the patients were things.

Only a New Zealander, John Read, stated that psychosis among
children was linked to abuse half the time. He and Anne Silver from
the late Chestnut Lodge boldly fought for the psychodynamic tradition

against an enslavement to pseudo-scientific treatment approaches that seemed to rely on therapy, but were saturated with a rhetoric of objectification. Not a word about the patient's dreams, not to mention the therapist's dreams—the latter so characteristic of Benedetti's technique—especially in a land where knowledge proceeds from "The Dreaming" among aborigines.

In this context, we realized that *we* were the aborigines of a "psychodynamic" primitive culture, dealing with primitive primary processes with our old fashioned, errant, intensive, psychoanalytic psychotherapy. We represented an unpalatable tradition, especially with my French accent, compared to CBT, DBT, DSM, ECT, and so on. Anyway, our work takes too much time, attends to too many stupid details, and wastes energy on literature, not to mention on the embarrassing contact with sticky "subjective" creatures unable to follow follow-up studies.

As many analysts say in a hushed tone in supervision—at least to me—about their impossible patients: "I have to tell you something that I'm afraid is perhaps not psychoanalysis, but it worked. I would never dare to speak about this in a conference." Usually it is about blunders, which, it often turns out, open a breach in the compactness of unsymbolized matters and constitute, in the aftermath, a turning point in the therapy. Provided they are put into words on both sides of, and beyond, the psychoanalytic dyad (Muller, 1996), these ridiculous bits and pieces initiate a "new loyalty".

I owe this expression to the British neurologist, anthropologist, and pioneer psychoanalyst, W. H. Rivers (see Barker, 1992), who used the psychoanalytic approach in order to reach and heal traumatized soldiers during the First World War. As demonstrated by the follow-up poetry of his famous patient, Siegfried Sassoon (1937), their psychotherapeutic encounter, and resistance to chemical and electric therapies, initiated a new beginning out of a frozen temporality, which otherwise would have been bound to have been transmitted as such through generations. In traumatic and psychotic areas, time stops. In consequence, one cannot say, "I or you or we are mad because of such a trauma." Causality makes no sense for this kind of timeless transmission because cause and consequences imply a past and a future. In catastrophic areas, psychosis deals with the haunting present of a trauma, even if the traumatic events occurred long ago.

So, my title, "A quixotic approach to trauma and psychosis", is about that kind of timeless transference, which nowadays appears out of date. At a previous Fall Conference at Austen Riggs in 1998 on "Psychosis and the social context", a senior psychotherapist told me, "Those patients make us very often fall on our faces, and they also forgive us for that." In between these falls—where we lose face—and this forgiveness—where we take the time to establish a new loyalty with subjects betrayed by falsified histories—lies the space and time for trust, speech, and affects to emerge from the brutal knowledge of trauma. But this "dynamic" is indeed a stumbling place. We are pushed into shameful adventures that we quickly try to repress or even to suppress. I will now waste some time about one of those ridiculous situations.

A ridiculous situation

In July 1998, just before the Fall Conference at Austen Riggs, we travelled in a country far away from our home for a presentation on the topic of our current seminar in Paris: "Madness and the social link". My paper was about the specific, inaugural "Yes, it is possible, with psychoanalysis, to get out of craziness or trauma", and how this "Yes" has to be reinvented with each patient. The conference was just starting, and I was supposed to speak. Suddenly, the analyst who had organized this meeting and was sitting at the table next to me held out her cell phone; "It's for you," she said. Then I heard the voice of a patient in Paris: "I am going to commit suicide. Your therapy does not work. Why do you do this job? It's hopeless." My heart started to bang, bang, bang, fast and loud; everybody could hear it, I thought. I answered that I would call him back after the conference. "OK," he said with a terrible voice, and he cut off the communication. I managed then to give my paper.

Still, at the very moment of opening my mouth, I felt changed into a totalitarian Führer: Hitler, Stalin, Mao's wife, anybody of this kind: a tyrant like the one who had actually been in close relationship with the patient's country and family life. I felt as if I was about to give a propaganda talk for psychoanalysis, while people back home were being tortured and killed through my fault. As a matter of fact, when the seminar was over, I called the patient back, but not right away. I waited—a little sadistically—so that I woke him up in the middle of the night, saying, "Sorry, I forgot the time difference." Then I told him that I would see him a few days later, just after my landing in Paris.

You might wonder, as I did, how he had found me. The mystery was quickly cleared up. He had come to France some fifteen years ago. The conference was held in a country close to his homeland. Gossip had given him the information. His parents had been strong support-ers of one of the most totalitarian regimes on the planet. As a very young child, he had been involved in this favourite occupation of theirs and threatened with death, so he thought and so they said, if he were to have been caught by the wrong people. He had been morally used and abused, even in his friendships with the children of his parents' many fake friends. That was the way life was; he had been well trained in it and had kept some of that training. As a child, he felt absolutely no fear of any kind.

When he had progressively taken his distance from his parents' faith, big fights had occurred with his father, who had knocked him down on several occasions in front of his brainwashed mother. He had started to tell an analyst about these "secrets". He had studied in order to become a researcher. When violence overwhelmed his country, some of his best friends were killed, became crazy, or committed suicide; he came to France and, after a while, broke down.

Only then could he experience terror, almost unfelt until that collapse. The terror took the form of a constant feeling of imminent death with strong impulses to commit suicide. All boundaries had crashed. Now was then, here was there, inside was outside, there was no more hope, no more self, no more other either. According to the words of Barrois (1990) a French psychoanalyst of trauma, he was inescapably up against the haunting presence, "the souvenir of hell and the hell of the souvenir".

Looking for psychoanalysis, which meant survival to him, he had tried a dozen famous couches in different psychoanalytical schools in Paris, until he had no more money and no job and had to be supported by social security. When his last psychoanalyst put him on heavy medications, he felt betrayed, in spite of his own approval of this happy, though brainwashed, condition. When he showed up for his first appointment in my office, he was staggering in a medicated stupor and said that he had spent all day in his bed in his little apart-ment, which he described as a mess of papers and books. As I was reading over and over Cervantes' novel for our seminar that very year, I thought of Don Quixote's library.

*   *   *

Quixotic indeed was this patient, conscious of being the fool now in many social situations. Later on, he would blame the medications, but, for the time being, in his current state he seemed to have no clue, even about his age. He knew he was around forty, but thought of himself as a youngster. He had no clue about privacy and told his life to everybody. He felt at the same time robotized, insensitive, easygoing, happy, buffoon-like, and terrified.

Was he Don Quixote? After his phone call to me at the conference, I had felt summoned to be faithful to our work, instead of speaking for the sake of my own reputation. According to Don Quixote's uncompromising motto, one must first of all defend the honour of abused children, like the patient, then widows and young maids, "whose virginity is as intact as the mother who gave them birth", so he says in his idealistic and, at the same time, disillusioned tune.

Was I, then, Don Quixote? Especially today, when psychoanalysis is our Dulcinea, a century old and quite out of fashion—beyond menopause, Cervantes might suggest as he puts on stage in the second book (Cervantes, 1615) a squadron of bearded "Duegnas" dancing a real Broadway musical. This overture will be followed, ten chapters later, by a quasi-psychoanalytic session between Don Quixote and the rigid, fussy mother of an abused daughter (Cervantes, 1615). He saves her momentarily from her submission to perverse patrons: a duke and a duchess, prefiguring the sadistic characters of the divine Marquis (de Sade, 1797). It is as if Don Quixote's folly was a taskforce meant to fight a tyrannical discourse and social structure, where real people were unwittingly manipulated as superfluous puppets, in fictitious scenarios created by the masters of the social order.

So was I, in my turn, trying to defend our century old psychoanalysis as though it were a desperate cause, discredited, at first by Freud himself, when it comes to trauma. I, too, was fighting windmills during this seminar, especially in a country where young, quick therapies and up-to-date Parisian theories were rather enjoyed. Holding the cell phone, I had felt ridiculous, close to giving up this quixotic job, close also to discovering, thanks to this clash, why I was doing it. In consequence, I realized that Don Quixote was neither this patient nor I, but the name of our transference.

Don Quixote, as the saying goes, is the title of the second best seller after the Bible. I think of it as the first, best analysis of a psychotic transference, which is itself a dynamic process designed to heal catastrophic blows received by survivors or their descendants. The two books are the best antidepressants to heal trauma and the best handbooks to teach about them. Their first effect is to make us laugh, triggering the unconscious, not so much the repressed unconscious, articulated with the signifiers of dreams and Freudian slips, but the cut-out unconscious, coming back as the uncanny, not yet articulated. Sancho Pança urges his master about the necessity of a talking cure after each of their falls. Otherwise, we are left with corruption "coming from rotten words decaying in our stomachs", where they have been silenced.

This silencing explodes in episodes of acting out, the world-famous episodes from which the hero and his squire recover—in the middle of mud, shit, and vomit, with broken teeth and bruised limbs—by talking and talking together. So, this psychodynamic cure takes up the greater part of the book, in between the powerlessness of despair and the empowerment of speech and laughter. The hero might be misdiagnosed as melancholic or bipolar, given the two poles of his sad countenance and his exalted assaults, but the truth is that he gives away an amazing healing energy that is one hundred per cent efficient.

Don Quixote calls what he does his "work" and his "science": a science that fights with what Cervantes calls "honour", something "familiar to the poor but foreign to the perverse" (Cervantes, 1615). In the last pages, he describes his pen as his spear: a weapon and a tool to restore speech and words in an area of death. Cervantes also comes from this area of death. As a veteran of the wars against the Turks and afterward as a POW and prisoner for ransom, he insists on this quality of being a veteran, especially in the second book, written and published just before his death in 1616. In the preface, he presents himself as a lame, one-handed ("manco" in Spanish is heard in "De la Mancha"), and poor old soldier. In spite of his fame (the first book was known in Europe and even in South America), money never reached him. Thieves had stolen it. But he would not be stripped of the pride of his wounds, "received in the most glorious naval battle of the century", at Lepante, where the Ottoman Empire was defeated by the European League in 1571.

The inscription of unspoken wounds and unsung battles in between two traumas

My patient, too, was a kind of veteran. At our first encounter, I acknowledged that he was a warrior child, like those all over the world who are used and abused as child-soldiers, for instance, in Columbia, Sierra Leone, and Sri Lanka. In fact, his first ghostly appearance in my office was as an old, cranky child, a baby veteran who had fought the wars of his ancestors, at times against, but more recently allied with, omnipotent tyrants. Now, with me, he constantly showed what could not be said: the corruption and decay of a world ruled by double talk, which he knew all too well but which was unbelievable to others, even to myself.

After one year, he decided to stop his medications completely. He improved, but not for long. He became worse, then better, then worse, ultimately always bringing us back to square one. No progress seemed to have been made. The worst things happened when I was going away on vacation. The course of his therapy was following the same chaotic tempo as Don Quixote's adventures, which, while the reader enjoys its dynamism, forces little by little the opening of an area of foreclosed speech and thought. In this catastrophic area, the symbolic order has collapsed, silences are thick, and only materialism prevails. "The disastrous perversity" of his century, described by Cervantes, is true for every century, including ours, and Don Quixote is more necessary now than ever.

With the same rhythm as my patient's failing and defeating me, Don Quixote regularly falls almost dead and rises again amid delusional upheavals. This dynamic is exactly the catastrophic rhythm of the psychoanalysis of trauma and psychosis. It is the beat of our psychotherapies: "On the road" (Kerouac, 1991) sings Don Quixote, "on the road again", with syncopated notes, in just the way that our fragile, erratic constructions faint and recover with a new energy. What is the source of this energy? That is the question I address now.

In the novel, we can see very clearly the successive delusional attacks of the hero as a series of traumatic revivals, triggered by tiny details: dust, light, glimmers, sounds, and coincidences, such as that seminar held in a country close to my patient's homeland, a visit which had nothing to do with him, or, at least, that is what I thought. This apparent accident triggered his attack on my safe space and revealed to me how my speech could be changed into mere propaganda, or, at least, a kind of marketing that disguises the facts.

In this case, as it is for the reader of the novel, the traumatic revival forced me to admit and accept the actuality of warfare in the apparent comfort of peacetime. We generally prefer to think of ourselves as humane and nice, but actually, when trauma enters the sessions, war is not nice: mud, blood, violence, scarce sleep, no food, stench, shit, vomit, shame, and absolute loneliness are the rule. In the novel, as in therapy, these erratic cross-accidents—my presentation near his country—seem to lead nowhere, but, imperceptibly, they broaden the field of investigation for a genuine psychoanalysis of trauma.

Believe it or not, in the last quarter of the first book (Cervantes, 1605), Don Quixote himself becomes a genuine psychoanalyst for a real madman. He asks his patient to lie on the couch—actually on the grass—in order to talk freely and tell his story. The madman accepts all of this on the condition that he not be interrupted. Of course, Don Quixote, like any quixotic, talkative analyst—which I confess to be—has a hard time keeping this promise. So, he cannot help interfering with the madman's tale. Predictably, a fight follows, but, finally, our hero persists and gives us a lesson about the tenacity that is essential for us in this field. The psychoanalysis eventually succeeds, despite many pitfalls. Finally, Cardenio, the madman of the Sierra Morena, is healed. As we are rediscovering today, his traumatic madness starts with betrayal by his noble hierarchy. His best friend and suzerain stole his girlfriend from him! This is what happened to Achilles, who became berserk after his commander, Agamemnon, took Briséis, Achilles' captive during the Trojan War (Shay, 1995).

So, from several perspectives, Don Quixote gives us a paradigm of psychodynamic analysis, including its reputation of no results for quite a while. Starting with the attack on the giant windmills, Don Quixote's target is progressively enlarged to become a whole international world war; he names precisely all the chiefs and armies and platoons and so on—which turn out, of course, to be a flock of sheep.

Nevertheless, we seem to be attending the psychoanalysis of a battle, as it has actually been performed during the Second World War in the Pacific (Marshall, 1944).

Finally, the hero trespasses the limits of our world and finds himself in hell, which turns out, of course, to be the infernal hammering of a mill. But, when Don Quixote enters hell, he enters history by crossing the threshold of the unwritten story of Cervantes. At the same time, after Don Quixote has proved able to heal the madman, the inscription of the unsung battles of his father, Cervantes, as he calls himself in the preface of the first book, may begin.

Miguel Cervantes de Saavedra (1547–1616) volunteered at age twenty to join the Spanish army in Italy, where a European coalition was waging war against the Turks. He was wounded in the chest during the battle of Lepante and lost the use of his left hand. He was twenty-five and had the title of an elite soldier. Sailing back to Spain, his boat was hijacked by Algerian pirates. He became a slave in Algieria for five years, where torture and execution were everyday threats, especially since he tried to escape once a year, five times altogether, but each time was miraculously spared the death penalty. The reason for this was said to be the very high price of his ransom. His life was finally redeemed by a religious order, which his parents had to remunerate for many years. When he came back to Spain, he was a poor, unfit veteran. He was thirty-three years old, worked as a tax collector, and wrote pastoral poetry and theatre.

Then, twenty years later, the second trauma occurred, well described by Claude Barrois and Jonathan Shay. The specific event that triggered the traumatic revival was again betrayal by his own command, when the nobleman for whom he collected taxes kept the money and went bankrupt. Cervantes was sent to jail in Seville in Andalusia. He was fifty. There, among beggars, prostitutes, and crooks, called *picaros* at that time, he gave birth "to his old cranky child", Don Quixote. He wrote the novel after the death in 1600, during the war in Flanders, of his beloved brother, Rodrigo, who had been his companion during their trials at sea and in Algeria. The first book was published when he was fifty-eight; it was translated all over Europe and carried by Conquistadores into the new world.

Then, another betrayal occurred. Crooks got rich; Cervantes stayed poor. The book, this time, was hijacked by a forger, who wrote followup adventures in order to steal extra money from Cervantes' bestseller.

Cervantes then decided to make his own version of the follow-up adventures; he decided to have his hero die, so that no further rubbish might rape his writing again. The second Don Quixote was another masterpiece. Cervantes was sixty-eight. At the end, Don Quixote passes away in a beautiful legacy of last words, completely cured, so that we may use the resources of his folly. Cervantes died the year after his hero, in 1616, along with Shakespeare.

PTSDQ: post trauma son, Don Quixote

"Quixotic" here emphasizes a link between trauma and psychosis as the relation of two catastrophes: the first when life survival is at stake, and the second, a symbolic one, when survival is about trust. In between lies an area of death where people are treated like things. There, Cervantes explicitly gives two successive missions to his cranky son.

The first is to heal his father's—Cervantes'—and ancestors' stains. Cervantes calls Don Quixote "de la Mancha", which might be heard as a Lacanian pun. "Mancha" means "stain" in Spanish, and also, as with the French word, *manchot*, it sounds like the word for "one-handed". Some authors have pointed out that the stain could be related to a Jewish ancestor, at a time of general suspicion and perse-cution against the Jews in Spain by the Inquisition. But I will limit myself to what his French biographer, Canavaggio (1986) and Cer-vantes himself assert: that the stain, "mancha", is the stain of war trauma. By putting his stains and those of his family on the public stage, Cervantes transforms them into an epic. In the same way, my patient re-enacted his father's totalitarian world, with the same delay of twenty years between the first life-threatening trauma of his youth and the second symbolic collapse, brought about by the betrayal of his parents and, so he said, of his analysts.

The second mission for Don Quixote is to free his father from being a hostage of tyrannical manipulation. Throughout the two books, the old-fashioned symbolic order, founded on speech and on loyalty, is constantly called on to arise. In the second *Don Quixote*, traumatic revivals are healed, acting out is over, and the hero's work and science is devoted to the building of free speech and of thought, this despite the disasters of a century plagued by epidemics, religious wars, geno-cides, hijackings, and abuse, still in the headlines today.

Don Quixote is also the name of transference
in traumatic and psychotic cases

One could very well object that Don Quixote is a character of fiction;
how can I apply his case to my patient? But this patient was precisely
telling me about a "fictitious world" in which he wandered, totally
"superfluous", looking for a reliable other, as Arendt says in *The
Origins of Totalitarianism* (1948). How did I provide him with that
fragile quality of reliability? Not by merely saying, "I listen to you, you
can count on me." I had to give him some kind of token. Don Quixote,
too, challenges everybody he meets in order to test their quality of reliability. His disastrous adventures work as a process of the selection of
trustworthy others. What matters is not so much the cause of his folly,
but its target: the birth of a subject of speech and desire, out of its
violent negation: for instance, when he is disqualified as a fool.

The most fascinating feature of the hero is how he never lets
himself be pitied or victimized, even when he is in the worst shape. His
duty is to give existence to worlds and subjects eradicated from existence. How? Mostly by illuminating the meaning of little, ridiculous
details that psychoanalysts are keen on and that are so unwelcome in
symposiums. For instance, the famous shaving dish that becomes a
helmet on Don Quixote's head (Cervantes, 1605). The ridiculous
bonnet of a fool, but, on the hero's head, it is an emblem of the name of
the father. Cervantes was the son of a deaf and humiliated barber,
Rodrigo de Cervantes, who also had once been put in jail for debts, the
same jail in which his own father Juan, a well-known lawyer, had once
been imprisoned, as would be his grandson, Miguel, later on.

This quixotic quality of the transference, which stresses the positive side of belittling matters, brings us to the intergenerational transmission of trauma. My patient was also the grandson of a humiliated
Jewish grandfather who was forgotten in a remote province and said
to be dead. He had been ostracized by his own son because he had
dropped out of his son's political activities. When the disowned
grandfather one day reappeared out of the blue, to his grandchild's
eyes he seemed to be a ghost, at the same time both alive and dead.
Discarded as a *Schlemiehl*, a Jewish "has been" shopkeeper, he was not
the right stuff for the progress of humanity.

About this matter of the living dead, I will mention another detail
from my experience. One night, long after his phone call at the

seminar abroad, as the patient remained chronically suicidal, I dreamt that I was shouting at him: "Go ahead. Kill yourself, and let us drop the subject." Then I forgot all about it. The next session, as he was, as usual, close to killing himself, my dream came back. With carefully chosen words, I told him about this unconscious message, apologizing, "It's not me who says it; it's my dream."

To my surprise, he laughed heartily and thanked me for taking care of the "subject" that had "dropped" into my dream. His interpretation was that I had, on the one hand, killed the living death dear to his parents, who thought of themselves as immortal; on the other, I had dropped in my dream the "subject" discarded by their materialistic ideology. My dream had, so to speak, in an evocative sentence, made a claim on a "subject" who had otherwise been made an outcast by the laws of numbers and objectification. My dream had addressed him as a "you", so that in this interference between him and his analyst, a "drop" of subjectivity could grow as a "thou". My dream had echoed the murderous injunctions of his childhood to kill his individual subjectivity for the sake of the collective good. At the same time, it had expressed, from the place of the dreaming other, a witnessing of this historical soul murder, allowing on his part what Felman and Laub (1992) call "a witness from inside" to be authorized.

To my surprise, he added, "By the way, Lacan's conception of the subject is not at all accurate. I hate his disciples' submission, as well as the French expression 'masters of thought', '*maîtres à penser*'." It seemed to imply slaves to the thought. From that time, he got definitively better, slowly resuming his research. One day, as a test of his intelligence, he gave a paper on the use of the pronoun "thou" in his native tongue to a seminar he used to attend ten years earlier. Today, he works in his field and enjoys it.

In the meantime, he gave me a wonderful gift. Before my departure for summer vacation that year, he brought a clipping announcing the publication in French of the conference given in 1923 by the famous art historian, Aby Warburg (Warburg, 2003). This conference had been carried out, as had his seminar, on the threshold of life and death. Aby Warburg had been confined for three years, completely crazy, in Switzerland, in Kreuzlingen, the private hospital of Ludwig Binswanger, when he produced this piece of knowledge. Aby had become delusional (Chernow, 1993) during the First World War in Hamburg, where his brothers were powerful bankers. At some point in his hospitalization, he hollered every morning that the Jews were going to be exterminated and that Binswanger was the chief perpetrator, feeding his patients with human flesh. Screaming that he wanted to get out of this hell, the patient managed to get his famous psychoanalyst to take him at his word.

As a matter of fact, Aby calmed down every afternoon and had tea with Binswanger, who was very fond of his intelligence and of his work. So came Binswanger's bright and challenging idea. Would Aby give a conference for the other patients, a group that included Nijinski, the feminist Bertha Pappenheim (Freud's Anna O), and the writer Joseph Roth, in this smart hospital of Bellevue on the Bodensee? If he were able to resume his research and show his ability by giving a presentation to them, he would be released.

A masterpiece came out of this challenge. Aby Warburg gave a one-hour talk on the Hopi Indian's snake ritual and other ceremonies among Pueblo Indians, whom he had visited in New Mexico in 1896. His topic was audaciously transcultural and interdisciplinary, connecting the therapeutic use of ceremonies to the art of Antiquity and of the Renaissance as a healing process in cases of trauma. His conference was, at the same time, a piece of research on healing processes and a healing process for himself. True to his word, Binswanger discharged him after this, and Aby took up the task of caring for his famous library, which he called "Mnemosyne", now the Warbug Institute in London, where his books were smuggled in the 1930s, after his death, to escape their being burned in the Nazis' *auto-da-fe*. So, this patient gave me access to the story of a prophetic researcher, who, according to Caruth (1995), "addresses as a survivor the survivors of another culture, and creates a whole field of research from trauma itself, providing the very link between cultures".

Entering together an unsaid bit of history

But again, what dynamic allowed me that assault toward him in my dream, just before he was able to deliver a talk on his research after so many years of interruption? To understand this, we have to go back to the previous quixotic clash, occurring just before my own talk in the foreign country. This clash at the very brink of talking is probably the source of my scream in this dream. I understood it when, on my return from this conference in July 1998, I landed in Paris. "Quixotic" here qualifies as a description of the transmission of trauma, not only between generations, but also between patient and analyst.

The day after we landed, the Champs Elysées in Paris was crowded. People cheered for a victory with little national flags that nobody had seen in people's hands since 1945, when Paris was liberated. We had won the World Cup in football! Personally, I am not very excited by this game. Still, not knowing what I was doing, but pushed by some imperious necessity, I phoned this patient to cancel our appointment, in spite of the emergency. I told him that we would meet the day after. Then I rushed into the middle of the crowd, not so much interested by the dream team than, I realized only then, by those damned flags. When the patient and I met the day after, he told me that he loved football and was so happy to see that I, too, was a supporter. I had to disenchant him, exactly the way Sancho tries to disenchant Don Quixote by transforming Dulcinea into a peasant girl of easy virtue, sweating and smelling of garlic. So, thanks to his misinterpretation, I had to explain what I had done. This moment became a turning point in his analysis.

The answer I gave him led me to discover part of the answer to his question: why do you do this hopeless job? I was two years old in 1945, when the flags flourished at the windows of the houses in the valley of the Alps where I was born. But they had to be quickly removed. The country was moving towards peace, but not in the mountains. After the cease-fire, violent fights resumed on the passes towards Italy, between French Alpine troops who had not disarmed and the retreating German army, who had nothing more to lose. Danger for the civilian population was everywhere. After the cease-fire, there had been atrocities. But, strangely, this episode was afterwards erased from the official history. At the Liberation, everybody was very concerned to appear on the good side of the Resistance. That is why this page of history is usually ignored outside of this province called Savoy.

By telling him about that bit of discarded history, I realized that I had, so to speak, been, like him, involved as a toddler in "a bloody rough way", as Wittgenstein says. There perhaps lay the source—and the *resource* I think—of the dynamic that screamed in my dream and that linked the transference to his chaotic history. It seems to take a long time to reach these eradicated temporalities.

Conclusion

This long time, nevertheless, requires some precise tools. I think of the quixotic transference as a plural body, linking—with the help of books but also tales to be told—four elements that can be named: Don Quixote, Sancho, Rossinante and the donkey, and Dulcinea. I will now describe their qualities in order to approach trauma.

1. Sancho Pança is a kind of double for Don Quixote. Besides the famous disastrous adventures, most of the novel is occupied by a talking cure with Sancho. He is the "therapist" in the strict Greek etymological meaning. Nagy (1979) teaches us that in Homeric epics, *Therapon* means "the second in combat", the one who takes care of the soldier's body and psyche, and is in charge of the funeral duties. Sancho nourishes his master with food, but mainly with words. Often, we take care of the unburied dead brought by our patients. Sometimes, they take care of our ghosts. So, it is better to say that we and our patients are, by turns, Don Quixote and Sancho Pança, telling stories to each other. But this is not enough for a quixotic transference.

2. We need also, for this plural body, the corpus of a number of books. Even when analysts stay mute, their books and theories, their heroes of archaic times, speak for them. So, it does not take long for the patient to know how to corner the Sigmund, Melanie, Jacques, Anna, or Donald, whose adventures recorded in their books are as precious to the analyst as King Arthur's round table was for Don Quixote, all in order to help him go through this hellish work. By the way, our errant knight is said in Spanish to be *andante*, ongoing.

3. But, in order to go on, we need above all an engine and some fuel. Although our psychotherapy is not really fast, it is puttering about, scampering off, trotting along, and stumbling. We need a Rossinante as well as Sancho's donkey, who love each other, says Cervantes, the way that Patrocles and Achilles do. So, these two animals remind us that, in spite of our necessary and vain interpretations, the course of the transference depends on the humble loyalty of a gentle and stubborn "dynamic", which, willy-nilly, carries analyst and patient. Fortunately, the dynamic of the transference is slow enough for the two carriers to keep pace sometimes together.

4.   Last but not least, the fourth element of this transference is the star, Dulcinea. The Far-Away Lady of the Thoughts, she is also the Lady of the primary process, where the name of the father, standing for all guarantees of faith and of law, for the social link, crumbles. This feminine agency is at work since the oldest of times as a warrant for thought. She is perhaps a mother, who gives life and death, but much more. This feminine agency is not limited to the binary distinction of gender. She can eventually be a man, a river, or a cloud, an animal or a song, but mostly she is the beloved fiancée or the godmother whose address is written on the letters found in the pockets of dying soldiers, never to reach destination. That is to say, Dulcinea is an empty place. Beautiful or ugly, maternal or indifferent, gentle or cruel, abstract or concrete, she is the necessary addressee of the words, the condition for thoughts to emerge, a surviving form—"Nachleben", says Aby Warburg—in the loneliness and despair of hell.

We analysts, too, work in the name of a Dulcinea, on behalf of whom we sometimes meet together. Not for long, as Dulcinea is double-faced. The Lady of the Thoughts, the Dame of courtly love, is also the cruel, distant lady, who sends her knights on impossible missions, like those children, old and young, loaded with the task of healing their ancestors' traumas and of going to the hell of their place. In return, they are never rewarded publicly. Neither are we, when we go on with our patients' *andante*, between knowing and not knowing, trying to get out of the empty circle. But who cares? Sometimes, we receive fruitful feedback during a session. As for this patient, when he came out of his living death condition, he told me that the little bits and pieces of dreams and coincidences that I had disclosed to him had been more useful for him than all my Lacanian theories. These are delicate, quixotic matters, for which I advise taking Don Quixote as a supervisor.

References

Arendt, H. (1948). *The Origins of Totalitarianism*. New York: Harcourt, 1951.
Barker, P. (1992). *Regeneration*. New York: Dutton.
Barrois, C. (1990). *Psychanalyse du Guerrier*. Paris: Hachette.

Canavaggio, J. (1986). *Cervantès*. Paris: Mazarine.

Caruth, C. (Ed.) (1995). *Trauma: Explorations in Memory*. Baltimore, MD: Johns Hopkins University Press.

Cervantes, M. de (1605). *Don Quixote, Part I*. Madrid: Juan de la Cuesta.

Cervantes, M. de (1615). *Don Quixote, Part II*. Madrid: Juan de la Cuesta.

Chernow, R. (1993). *The Warburgs*. New York: Vintage Books.

de Sade, Marquis (1797). *Justine*. Paris: J. V. Girouard.

Felman, S., & Laub, D. (1992). *Testimony*. New York: Routledge.

Kerouac, J. (1991). *On the Road*. New York: Penguin Classics.

Marshall, S. (1944). *Island Victory*. Washington, DC: Zenger, 1982.

Nagy, G. (1979). *The Best of the Acheans*. Baltimore, MD: Johns Hopkins University Press.

Shay, J. (1995). *Achilles in Viet Nam: Combat Trauma and the Undoing of Character*. New York: Touchstone Books.

Warburg, A. (2003). *Le Rituel du serpent*. Paris: Macula.

PART III
CONTEMPORARY AMERICA

Introduction

Trauma is no stranger to America. Shay's book, *Achilles in Viet Nam* (1995), among other works about that era, makes that very clear, as does Drew Gilpin Faust's *This Republic of Suffering* (2008), documenting America's civil war trauma a century earlier. Coates, Rosenthal, and Schecter's book, *September 11: Trauma and Human Bonds* (2003), is an exceptional study of the trauma of 9/11, and Penner and Ferdinand's *Overcoming Katrina* (2009) shows us, in the most moving and, at times, horrifying oral histories, how a natural disaster linked with historical racism and political weakness to create an entire population of traumatized Americans. This concluding section of the book examines trauma and its transmission in various contemporary American contexts.

Howard Stein draws on his vast experience working with organizations—his experience of what he calls "disaster anthropology"—to offer us a *tour de force* on traumatic transmission of all sorts, not only vertically, from parents to children, but also horizontally, among people sharing the same horrific experience, vicariously, and potentially even from below to above. Drawing on examples ranging from the Oklahoma City bombing to ordinary leadership transition to corporate "downsizing" to the Worcester fire, Stein emphasizes that trauma is not only about the initial terrible experience, it is also about what happens to that experience in the social world. He argues that culture shapes, and economics is used to shape, the narrative of trauma, very often leading to enforced silence about its causes, dimensions, and consequences, the "cut-out" unconscious Françoise Davoine describes. Most important for Stein is the tragedy of disenfranchised grief, the negation of a healing process that guarantees continued suffering and leads to the kinds of enactments that transmit trauma to others.

Kevin Kelly's chapter on his work with New York City firefighters after 9/11 is also an illuminating analysis of transmission. He embeds his understanding in a moving description of this group's culture, which includes, very basically, its group identity, not only as a group of current comrades but a group with powerful generational links as well. He adds to our understanding of trauma the dimension of exposure to horror and explores a triad of PTSD symptoms, insomnia, irritability, and withdrawal, describing their cascading effects on those around the traumatized firefighter. He also raises the hopeful possibility that it is precisely the awareness of potential transmission to one's children that motivates firefighters to seek help, including, in one example, the help of a young daughter. Kelly's loving chapter thus ends with a more textured sense of the ebb and flow of emotional life between the generations and invites us to consider the families of trauma victims as not only potential victims themselves, but also as resources for healing.

My brief closing chapter functions as a coda to the book's main theme. I draw on Jane Fonda's autobiography to tell a tragic family story, a story launched amid the ambitions, fantasies and grave disappointments of Hollywood and played out, among other places, in psychiatric hospitals. Fonda reports the details of transmission in an uncanny way and movingly depicts a daughter's struggles to free herself from her mother's trauma by coming to know it. Fonda's psychic work is palpable and poignant, and its legacy is not only the narrative she offers us but, among many other contributions, the charitable organization she founded, even before she knew why she was doing it.

References

Coates, S., Rosenthal, J., & Schecter, D. (Eds.) (2003). *September 11: Trauma and Human Bonds*. Hillsdale, NJ: Analytic Press.

Faust, D. G. (2008). *This Republic of Suffering*. New York: Knopf.

Fonda, J. (2005). *My Life So Far*. New York: Random House.

Penner, D., & Ferdinand, K. (2009). *Overcoming Katrina*. New York: Palgrave Macmillan.

Shay, J. (1995). *Achilles in Viet Nam: Combat Trauma and the Undoing of Character*. New York: Touchstone Books.

CHAPTER TEN

A mosaic of transmissions after trauma

Howard F. Stein

Introduction

This chapter is a study of the *transmission of trauma in virtually any direction*. It is a mosaic or montage of vignettes that cumulatively illustrate the horrifying ease by which this transmission can take place. Studies to date focus on the intergenerational transmission of trauma, specifically in families from parents to children. What cannot be contained, mourned, and worked through in one generation is transmitted, for the most part unconsciously, as affect, mission, and task to the next generation. It is an amalgam of "deposited representation" (Volkan, Ast, & Greer, 2002) and identification. The fate of repression and dissociation is enactment. Among the most exemplary studies of this process are Volkan's *Bloodlines* (1997); Volkan, Ast, and Greer's *The Third Reich in the Unconscious* (2002); Brenner's *Dissociation of Trauma* (2001) and "On genocidal persecution and resistance" (2005); a series of papers by Apprey on intergenerational transmission of trauma among African Americans ("The African-American experience: forced immigration and transgenerational trauma (1993), "Broken lines, public memory, absent memory: Jewish and African Americans coming to terms with racism" (1996), "Reinventing the self in the face of received transgenerational hatred in the African American Community" (1998), and "From the horizon of evil to an ethic of responsibility" (2000)); an important paper by Hollander (1999) on the experience of totalitarianism during the Argentine "Dirty Wars" of the 1980s; and a moving essay by Katz (2003) on intergenerational transmission of trauma due to war and state terror.

In this chapter, I broaden the horizon of trauma transmission, and through a mosaic of portraits, suggest that trauma can be transmitted both "vertically" (and over non-generational time in organizations) and laterally or "horizontally". I draw my examples from the 19 April 1995 Oklahoma City bombing; the 3 May 1999 tornadoes in Central Oklahoma; the 3 December 1999 fire in Worcester, Massachusetts, in which six firefighters died; the terrorist attacks on the USA on September 11 2001; and the relentless waves of downsizings, RIFings, restructurings, re-engineerings, de-skillings, outsourcings, mergers, and hostile corporate takeovers that have characterized American workplaces since the mid-1980s. My data come more from "peripheral vision" than from intentional observation or planned study. I have learnt about the transmission of trauma from my various roles as psychoanalytic anthropologist, organizational anthropologist, organizational consultant, and clinical behavioural scientist and teacher in family medicine.

I have come by experience to the practice of what has come to be called "disaster anthropology", that is, by living with and through it with others. As observer, consultant, and counsellor, I have not had the luxury of living and working "outside the fray" of the patient's or client's or group's world, as psychoanalysts and other therapists typically have been able to do historically. Increasingly, however, in dealing with large group trauma, both helpers and those being helped share much of the same culture and the same event, which poses yet new challenges to the "disciplined subjectivity" (Erikson, 1964, p. 53) of observer and therapist alike.

In the sections that follow, I shall explore disenfranchised grief and trauma transmission, trauma transmission in political succession, lateral trauma transmission (and its prevention), recognizing trauma transmission in oneself, concurrent "vertical" and "horizontal" transmission, and the possibility of "reverse" vertical trauma transmission (that is, from younger to older, whether intergenerationally or within the same multi-generational cohort).

Disenfranchised grief and trauma transmission

In this section, I discuss the role of *unacknowledged and unacknowledge-able grief* in the transmission of trauma. In any disaster or catastrophe and its accounts, there are categories of people, categories of time, categories or types of timetables. Certain categories of people are publicly recognized, acknowledged; certain other categories of people are publicly unacknowledged, overlooked, ignored. Some categories of people court publicity, while others shy away from it. Some are discountable, whether in heroism, suffering, or even memory (Doka, 1989; Javors, 2000).

Who counts? Who is treated as though they do not matter? Who is remembered? Who is forgotten? Who is, or becomes, a social symbol, even a "social cynosure" (La Barre, 1946), that is, a category of persons to whom much public attention is devoted? What are the costs to each? When the armies of Montgomery and Rommel fought in North Africa during the Second World War, who gave much thought to the Bedouins who were caught in the clash of worlds? In disasters, who gets left out and forgotten, and what becomes of them?

These questions are all crucial (1) to the understanding of profound loss and grief that cannot, even must not, be recognized, and (2) to the consequences over time for such an emotional black hole in one's consciousness. Doka (1989) coined the term "disenfranchised grief" for the types of loss and grief individuals, families, organizations, and whole societies refuse to recognize as legitimate, and for whom they refuse to give space or time. Likewise, Davoine and Gaudillière (2004) describe how the experience of trauma becomes "cut out" of the social discourse. What is consciously banished from existence returns as a ghost, usually in the form of enactment. Those who must not acknowledge their grief find that the loss has come to "possess" them.

A disaster or catastrophe is an *event* in outside reality, and a disaster is also a *language, which is used to recreate that reality anew*. In their outward contours, some disasters are brief, acute, while others are long-lived, chronic. Over time, a disaster can become a language that hijacks an event. A disaster is a story, a set of stories, an evolving story, about an event, *after* an event. A disaster is also a kind or type of storyline about an event, one that *precedes* an event. The storyline is replete with characters, plot, sequence, structure, when things should unfold, and the "right" kind of ending. A storyline or "narrative" is a form we use to say how a story—and its event—*should* go. There are storylines for how a "good fire" or a "good bombing" goes, and for how heroes, healers, and the public respond. Often these storylines are obligatory, which is to say imposed, both from without and within.

There are public stories of heroism. There are private, secret stories, often at odds with those that are told and retold. There are many kinds of suffering: speakable, unspoken, and unspeakable. Many people get left behind. Many stories are only partially told, if even partially. Many stories are undiscussable. When we—as professionals, as lay people, as ordinary citizens—read and write stories of catastrophes, we are often more faithful to the way "things *should* go" (which is always someone's or some group's view) and to our methodologies than to the phenomena we are trying to understand and the people we are trying to help (Ritzer, 2000). We even have expectations about how disasters themselves *should go*: for example, what a good fire and what a bad fire are. Part of the terror is when "the perfect fire" goes bad (Flynn, 2000).

Individuals, organizations (fire and police departments, hospitals, clinics), and whole communities often take pride in their response to a catastrophe. Community pride can rest on a simple, fundamental sense of goodness of place. Sense of place can also rest on feelings of inadequacy and shame that can never be expunged, a badness that cannot be erased. There often lingers a secret shame and guilt that the calamity happened at all, that it happened in this place, as if to say that "we should have done differently or better in order to prevent it from happening". Some people have asked, directly or indirectly, how dare the 1995 bombing take place in the "Bible Belt"—and by someone who is not even identifiably "foreign"?

A disaster, and the response to it, might feel, for a while, redeeming, as if it suddenly put a place "back on the map" as a good place rather than as a backward or deficient place. The generosity of Oklahomans to fellow Oklahomans after the bombing at least temporarily improved the image of Oklahomans to the rest of the USA. The disaster can become a part of redefining a person and community's sense of place (see Feld & Basso, 1996; Fullilove, 1996). Conversely, *where* something happens is part of the "happening", the eventfulness itself. Sense of place is part of "place".

The sense of place where a trauma occurred can have both a positive and negative valence. For instance, almost as soon as Timothy

McVeigh was caught shortly after the Oklahoma City bombing, and some information about him provided to the news media, a medical colleague told me how grateful she was that McVeigh had been from New York and not Oklahoma. If he could not be the stereotyped Middle Eastern terrorist that had been expected, at least he was from outside Oklahoma, and a Northern state, "Back East," to boot! "Goodness" was preserved inside, in the "Bible Belt", as "badness" was ejected and located outside, on the East Coast. It was bad enough that the bombing took place in Oklahoma; it was virtually intolerable that the terrorist had himself been from Oklahoma. Part of the legacy of the trauma of the Oklahoma City bombing is to restore the sense of goodness and pride to the city and state.

In trauma, time does not merely "flow" in some steady fashion; it is punctuated. That is to say, there is a sense of how long mourning should last, and a language to describe its conclusion. On 4 July 1995, the governor of Oklahoma ordered the American flags to be hoisted to full mast, and declared that the 19 April 1995 bombing in Oklahoma City now had "closure" and "healing". In addition to official pronouncements, there were prevailing cultural understandings among European-Americans on the prairie that affected how long grieving was acceptable as well. When someone's home or barn burns down, or when someone's combine breaks down during wheat harvest season, neighbours and community quickly rally to "get people back on their feet". Neighbours will voluntarily rush in, unbidden, to cut what wheat remains, and to rebuild what has been destroyed. After the task is completed, the event is considered over, and "You go on down the road" and "get a life". Put in a formula, the purpose of community mutuality is to restore individual and family autonomy. The timetable for recovery from trauma is very short-term, measured in days, weeks, at most months. There is no place for lingering grief. This widespread cultural attitude toward time heavily influenced the response to the Oklahoma City bombing. It enforced silence and isolation upon those who remained traumatized and entombed in grief.

Here is where "disenfranchised grief" enters the picture: when the grief that is supposed to be over is not, and when categories of people who were officially "not directly affected by the bombing" (or other trauma) are, none the less, deeply affected emotionally, even physically. They are expected to be back to normal in function and in relationship. Here is where culture harms as well as helps to heal. About five years after the Oklahoma City bombing, I was invited to give a guest lecture to a class on organizational culture and organizational change. I was discussing the widespread sense of trauma, vulnerability, and loss among many "ordinary" Oklahomans I knew as well as by people who had physically been in the Murrah Federal Building and neighbouring office buildings during the bombing. Likewise, I described the cultural values and rules that shut out many people and their experiences from being acknowledged and addressed.

After class, a man approached me, in tears, and told me the story of how, at the time of the bombing, his wife had been an emergency room nurse who had left the hospital and rushed to the scene of the bombing to offer medical help. Upon arrival, she had seen wave upon wave of unspeakable injury and mutilation. She functioned; she did her job. Many of the injured—some of whom eventually died—were also brought to her hospital. In the months that followed, as the hospital returned to "normal" (or what is officially called "the new normal"), she found herself excluded from her usual social relationships in the hospital. No one wanted to hear what she had been through. The effect of the bombing was supposed to be over. She was stuck alone with her feelings and memories. Her husband, my student, became virtually the only person who would listen to her. Fortunately, here the marriage could *contain* the nurse's trauma. Other Oklahoma City marriages were not so fortunate, because the other party could not bear to listen to the trauma. This was "disenfranchised grief". This was a story that could not be told because no one could suffer the empathy needed to hear it. This searingly illustrates the process of trauma transmission.

This example does not exist in isolation. Although I do not have a large "sample size" to substantiate it, I have heard stories like this many times. They each are distinct, yet they have the common denominator of unrecognizable grief and trauma that would not be heard. There are certain patterns that play themselves out "like clockwork". Each year, in the month or so preceding 19 April, a policeman or fireman or emergency medical vehicle operator will come into a family medicine clinic. This person will come in with physical complaints for which no organic basis can be found. This person typically "hates to go to the doctor because only weak people go to doctors". But he or she is here, none the less. After reviewing the patient's physical history, the astute family doctor asks himself or herself "Why now?" and asks the patient whether there is anything about this time of year that is especially "stressful". Even more specifically, the physician might ask of the patient whether he or she was at all involved in the massive response to the 19 April 1995 bombing. No sooner is the question posed than the thick wall of the dam breaks, and the patient breaks down in tears.

Consider the following example, a variant on the earlier one. Around two and a half years after the bombing of the federal building in Oklahoma City, a University of Oklahoma Health Sciences Center faculty physician colleague was taking family medicine residents on a community medicine rotation at a local clinic for indigent patients. In a getting-acquainted fashion, the faculty physician was talking with the clinic nurse about her work and experience. At one point, she asked her whether she had been involved in the medical community's response immediately after the bombing. The nurse burst into tears, and a geyser of feelings and memories erupted. My colleague said that the nurse talked and talked, as if for the first time. The nurse said that two and a half years earlier, no one had "debriefed" her and asked what *she* had gone through. After volunteering some time at the site of the bombing, she returned to her work at the clinic, which everyone treated as "business as usual". Because she had not been in or around the buildings *immediately* after the bombing, she did not occupy the mental and linguistic categories of "victim" or "survivor" or "hero". Only certain kinds or categories of people were regarded as having been as "traumatized". Others simply pitched in to help; the work they were doing was regarded as ordinary rather than extraordinary. They were not regarded as being at risk for "secondary traumatization", that is, indirect exposure to trauma.

The occasion that unleashed the nurse's memory and emotion was my colleague's simple expression of interest in her possible role in the bombing recovery effort. My colleague had been one of the early responders to the bombing site and had learnt to enquire in this manner. The occasion was not a conventional "anniversary"-style reaction, but a crucial ingredient was similar: an event in the present strongly resembled a catastrophic event in the past and provided the environmental "stimulus" for the release of unconscious memory and affect.

Examples such as these have made me think of a third form of traumatization in addition to "primary" (or direct) and "secondary" traumatization. It is the trauma of enforced silence, isolation, and indifference, to be treated as if nothing terrible had happened, as if there was nothing to be upset about. One was expected to "tough it out" and not "act like a wimp" (weakling). "Get over it, and get a life" is a common cultural admonition to someone whose grief and hurt are taking "too long". Added to the tendency to use dissociation as an individual defence is the *dissociation induced by the group to sustain their own tenuous denial, dissociation, and repression in order to ward off intolerable anxiety and grief*. The challenge, I believe, is to *listen to the people whom we are trying to help* better than we listen to our theories and methods. We need to ask, to wonder, "What is it like to be you?" rather than *disassociate* (radically distance) ourselves from their experience, thereby abandoning them to their trauma.

Lest the reader think that the withdrawal of empathy is limited to those "indirectly" affected by a calamity (e.g., through identification with a unit of traumatization, such as a nation, ethnic group, religion, community, organization, or building), I wish to emphasize that even those immediately or "directly" involved incur the impatience and incredulity of those around them. Further, even these categories and distinctions are not self-evident, but are socially constructed, if not *imposed*.

Let me offer an example from my local newspaper, an article by Jay F. Marks in *The Oklahoman*, dated 10 April 2006 (nine days prior to the eleventh anniversary of the bombing of the Murrah Federal Building). The story is about eleven people in the US Department of Housing and Urban Development who refused to be relocated to the new Federal Building in Oklahoma City. They had worked in the Murrah Federal Building that was bombed, and, following the bombing, had been moved to an alternative work site. On 23 March, they received a letter "denying their bid to stay at the alternate work site" (2006, p. 1A). They had been unwilling "to relocate to offices adjacent to the site of a terror attack that killed many coworkers" (*ibid.*). They are "the last holdouts" (*ibid.*). Thirty-five of the 168 people killed in the bombing were from HUD.

The article then focuses on the experiences of Teresa Cook, a grant specialist, who was not injured because she had been working offsite that day. She could not remember driving home that day. Only after nine days did she find out that her best friend had been killed. She said that she "never has been able to return to the bombing site. Panic attacks and heart palpitations set in if she even gets close to that part of downtown" (2006, p. 3A). Her physician diagnosed her with PTSD. If Ms Cook is not allowed to continue working away from the federal building, "she may have to opt for disability retirement", which would be considerably less than her current salary (*ibid.*). "She said she felt obligated to keep working for the agency after the bombing on behalf of those who died" (*ibid.*). Marks concludes by quoting Ms Cook: "They make me feel like I'm of no value to them whatsoever" (*ibid.*).

Interpretatively, should we say that Ms Cook was "indirectly" rather than "directly" affected by the bombing? In the light of her experience, I think that the distinction itself damages many of those who suffered from the trauma of the bombing by denying the psychological reality of their experience. It would seem that Ms Cook might be *consciously* fearful of returning to the original area, but that she *unconsciously* might also feel guilty. Her experience is analogous to that of the World Trade Center employee who had exchanged shifts with his friend on September 11, 2001. Her anxiety may be not only about "going back" to the place of the trauma, but also about "going on" with life, that is, continuing to live when so many of her friends and work associates had perished. Unconscious survivor guilt might help account for the grip of her terror (e.g., "What right do I have to be alive when they are dead?").

She and her group of co-workers may be reluctant to return to work—a sentiment probably shared with many others—because it would feel more like a crude burial of their friends and colleagues than a carrying on of work on their behalf. Rather than categorize Ms Cook's behaviour (directly/indirectly affected, PTSD), attention to her meanings and affects, conscious and unconscious, would most probably take us to the heart of the matter of the experience of traumatization. Ms Cook's story made it to the newspaper: it is very likely that it was tacitly regarded as newsworthy at least in part because it resonated so strongly with the experience of others whose stories are shunned. Ms Cook is but the veritable "tip of the iceberg" of culturally disenfranchised grief. Shortly after the Oklahoma City bombing, I was visiting with a mental health professional in Allentown, Pennsylvania, which is over 1,300 miles from Oklahoma City. She was shaken by the bombing. She asked me, with great urgency, "What are we to tell our children? How are we going to protect our children anywhere in America?" *She spoke to me as if the bombing had happened to her.*

I wish to add a historical footnote to this discussion of the long and broad shadow cast by the 1995 Oklahoma City bombing. In the decade since the bombing, the downtown and adjacent "Bricktown" warehouse districts have undergone a massive and ongoing redevelopment and renewal. In part as response to the once prevalent view (and associated feelings of shame) that "There is nothing to do in Oklahoma City", the Bricktown area has seen the emergence of a baseball stadium, warehouses refurbished into restaurants, retail shops, hotels, clubs, cinemas, and a canal that some have said is meant to rival the Riverwalk in San Antonio. In the downtown proper, the Oklahoma City Memorial, a new Federal Building, the Cox Convention Center, and the Ford Center (a sports arena and convention centre) have been built. All of this is a source of local pride and of lucrative business.

Certainly, there are abundant valid economic and political explanations and reasons for this rebirth. But what is missing from this account is the emotional backdrop of the bombing. What is missing is as important as what is present in the picture. In every "revival" there is the unspoken reality and dread of death. Whatever else the urban renewal represents, I believe that it also serves as a thick emotional scab over the still-festering wound of the trauma of the bombing. It is as if to say, there is the official story, and there is "the rest of the story", as editorialist Paul Harvey might say. In the light of the discussion above, I believe that, despite the presence of the National Memorial and the adjacent Museum, the unfinished trauma and mourning over the 1995 bombing remains a widely shared secret that festers because it is not supposed to be. If anything, the urban revival is supposed to say to all the world that Oklahoma City is resilient and recovered, that "closure" has been followed by resurrection. Still, the spirited urban downtown renaissance is a close neighbour of the death it ignores at a high social cost.

I end this vignette with a speculation: might the rush to quickly "move on" from the Oklahoma City bombing be part of the legacy of the Dust Bowl of the 1930s? Could the memory of the Depression Dust Bowl (drought), as a long-lived symbol of collective trauma predispose Oklahomans to respond to a later traumatic loss, and thus to the course of grief? As I have discussed elsewhere in *The Culture of Oklahoma* (Stein & Hill, 1993), the two affective poles of many Oklahomans' self-representation and of the national image of Oklahoma are Oklahomans as seen in John Steinbeck's novel (1939) and the subsequent film (1940), *The Grapes of Wrath*, and in Richard Rodgers and Oscar Hammerstein II's musical *Oklahoma!* (1943). The former is a largely negative image, rooted in Depression Dust Bowl survivalism and flight to California. The latter is a celebration of the people, the land, and the sky.

In my experience, the Dust Bowl was both a source of pride in one's having persevered and survived it, and a source of shame to be lived down. Subsequent to the drought of the 1930s, Oklahoma undertook a vast programme of building man-made lakes and turning the state green. Similarly, much as Oklahomans took pride in their overwhelmingly generous response to the 1995 bombing, many were also embarrassed that the bombing took place in the Heartland, in the Bible Belt. It was as if to say: "How dare *that* happen *here!*" I speculate that at least part of the motivation behind the massive restoration and building programme in Bricktown and downtown Oklahoma City lay in a wish to reverse the emotional valence of the city from negative to positive, to burnish Oklahoma City's image and self-image in the face of the recent bombing and the long shadow cast by the Dust Bowl.

Trauma transmission in political succession

Political succession—understood in the broadest sense of all leadership transition—is a region rife with the possibility of trauma transmission. The passage of power and authority from one leader to the next, whether violent or peaceful, can also entail the passage of unfinished emotional business from one "generation" or cohort of leadership to the next. No type of group is immune from its reach: from large groups such as nations, ethnic groups, and world religions, to smaller scale groups such as workplace organizations (for instance, corporations, universities, government agencies, and religious institutions). Such transmission of trauma becomes the "mechanism" through which group "history repeats itself", or threatens to do so, and through which groups become "stuck" in time and are, thus, unable to change.

To cite an obvious historical example: the post-Stalin era of the Soviet Union, and now Russia (1953, the year of Stalin's death, to the present), has long been haunted by the memory of twenty years of unrelenting brutality which Josef Stalin and his agents perpetrated on vast populations under his rule. It was far easier for the people under his rule to rally against the common external Nazi enemy in the "Great Patriotic War" than to acknowledge how their own leaders, upon whom they were dependent, ruthlessly slaughtered millions of their own people. Mourning and letting go of the Stalin era was and remains complicated by the ongoing trauma from the middle 1930s until his death. Official repudiation is undermined by unrecognized identifications. It is difficult to live in the present, and to solve present problems, when the horror-ridden past is injected into everything present.

To show how absolutely mundane and insidious this process can be, I turn to a vignette from an Evangelical Protestant American church in the late 1990s, and how a church-wide trauma persisted long after the traumatic event was over. I once consulted with a "church in transition", which is how the problem was initially presented to me. Its once-beloved and affectionate long-time senior pastor had resigned four years earlier amid allegations of sexually molesting several children in his parish.

The once "normal" parish that had been church home to hundreds was suddenly immersed in scandal. The fact that it happened at all was a source of intense shame. Many congregants were incredulous: "How could this have happened to *us*, in *our* church? We are good Christians. Our minister was a pillar of the community." The shame quickly went underground and was transmuted into secrecy and intense church activity. A new, youthful and vigorous pastor was soon hired. He was full of ideas and energy. It was as if, through a frenzy of renewal, building remodelling and social programmes, the memory of the humiliation and feelings of betrayal could be erased.

The minister who succeeded the older pastor seemed aloof, emotionally distant, even haughty, despite his many successful initiatives. As I interviewed the current minister, the church deacons (lay leaders), and many members of the congregation, a picture began to emerge of short-circuited mourning over the previous pastor, and of the transmission of trauma to the next "generation" of pastor. In one deacons' meeting, several participants bitterly complained how emotionally unavailable their still-new pastor proved to be. One deacon then wryly observed, "The previous pastor was warm and fuzzy, and *that* didn't work out so well!" The room erupted in an anxious laughter of recognition. Now and then there were hints that the group was beginning to recognize its role in projecting the image and memory of the minister who had betrayed them on to the current pastor. Unwittingly, they had transferred their feelings towards their former minister on to their present one. They had inverted their withdrawal from him and a hesitation to get close into an accusation that he had withdrawn from them. They began to recognize that at least some part of "his" distance lay in "their" own distancing.

The group dialogue deepened. Some participants began to make connections between the two ministers. Someone said openly, "I *loved* Reverend Jones. His resignation is a big loss, even though he did some bad things." Another deacon added shortly thereafter, "You don't feel close to the new pastor because you can't *let* yourself get close to the pastor." Their accusation that he had "burned bridges" with the congregation gave way to a realization that they had refused to build some bridges with him as well.

One emergent task of the consultation was to help "decontaminate" the relationship between the minister and his congregation, and free it of the ghost of the previous pastor and his relationship with them. As the congregation began to mourn the loss of their former minister and of their devoted relationship to him, they likewise began to separate him mentally from their current pastor. They were a little less critical of the "lack of warm feelings from the pastor", and of his "people skill problems", and more accepting of him on his own terms—and perhaps also accepting of the fact that they might have unconsciously *chosen* a leader who would be emotionally distant so that they would not be hurt again as they had been by their previous pastor.

To summarize: this vignette, I think, poignantly illustrates how the *transmission of trauma can be played out in the leadership succession in a quite ordinary organization or institution.* Here the "generations" are obviously symbolic. Still, the transition was, none the less, one in "vertical" time, from one organizational era to the next.

"Lateral" trauma transmission (and its prevention)

In addition to being transmitted "vertically" (over generational time and over group time), trauma can be transmitted "laterally" or "horizontally" to members of the same group that shared the trauma. This, in fact, is what is so new and vexing for American (United States) therapists and counsellors who are working with victims of the Oklahoma City bombing and of September 11, 2001. Even though the therapists and counsellors were not literally in the buildings that were so brutally attacked, none the less they share the group trauma of those they are trying to understand and to help. Therefore they do not, and cannot, possess the same degree of emotional distance from the patient's or client's trauma as occurs in psychoanalysis or psychotherapy under more "normal" cultural conditions. Both transference and countertransference are coloured by these shared realities. The situation both allows greater empathy and fosters over-identification.

I would like to illustrate the process of the "lateral" transmission of trauma, and its prevention, through an event in which I was participant. The group was a planning committee for the first conference held by the Worcester (Massachusetts) Institute on Loss and Trauma, to be held on 20 October 2000. The 3 December 2000 would be the first anniversary of a fire that consumed the Worcester Cold Storage and Warehouse Company and took the lives of six firefighters. The fire was started by two homeless people who had been living in the building. Accidentally, they knocked over a candle, could not put out the fire themselves, and left the building without reporting the fire. The firefighters valiantly entered the building in search of people whom they did not know were already gone. Historically, the Worcester Cold Storage, though long vacant, was a massive monument-like structure in the downtown, one that virtually everyone knew of and had passed in their motor vehicles. Other buildings, other deaths, and other survivors are often far less symbolized and are, thus, far less noticed. In a sense, the story of the fire was about a *double abandonment*: first, the obviously abandoned warehouse building, and second, the homeless people, abandoned by society but whom the firefighters tried to rescue.

The 20 October 2002 conference was to be devoted to understanding the 3 December 1999 fire; thus, whatever else it was, it was part of the disaster and the response to it. Moreover, the conference speakers and attendees were writing and rewriting the story of the disaster, asking, how long does a fire burn, symbolically speaking? How do we deal with a fire we have already been burned by—some literally, some symbolically? How do we deal with the twin temptations of "becoming" the fire ourselves, and insisting that we were not even emotionally "singed" by its far-reaching flames?

With this as the context of the meeting, I turn to the process of the meeting itself. It turns out that this planning committee was not only a decision-making body, but also a microcosm of group processes ranging from Worcester to the USA generally. (President Clinton attended the funeral.) About ten of us had a weekly, and later, monthly, lunch meeting or visit, one of which occurred on 25 May 2000, for about an hour and fifteen minutes. I was "present" long-distance via a telephone placed on the conference table, between the chicken salad and yogurt, specifically, as committee member Marjorie Cahn later told me in an e-mail message. We discussed speakers, topics, workshops, and sequence. Nearly an hour into the meeting, someone noticed that in the entire planning thus far, *the fire itself* had not been explicitly, directly mentioned—a pattern that occurred in earlier meetings as well. Another person wondered where we should bring it up, how we should bring it up at the conference: "The fire, NOT the fire, where do we put it?" It was emotionally safer for us to attend diligently to logistical details of conference arranging than to the "hot" subject that was the very reason for having the conference.

From my distant office in Oklahoma City, I said that I had the fantasy, similar to that in families of alcoholics or drug addicts, that there is this giant elephant in the middle of the table. Everyone knows it is there, yet it is too emotionally enormous, taboo, to talk about, *even among us*. It is a secret that everyone "knows", if only unconsciously. Now, here, in Worcester, what is in the middle of the table is the fire, far more dangerous and consuming than a mere elephant. Someone brought up the issue of communication at the conference: how do we talk about bad events? On the one hand, we try to avoid them, speaking, for example, only about the firefighters' courage and the wish to get the fire behind us; on the other hand, we hyperbolize about the fire. I said that my fantasy, and perhaps our fear, is of being consumed by the fire. It is very hard to *put* a fire anywhere, even the subject of fire. Maybe we were identifying with it as a way of trying to control it, so as to not be burned by it.

As we were approaching the end of our meeting, someone brought up the issue of a "wrap-up" of the conference at its conclusion, on the subject of communication and synthesis. Another person then mentioned coffee and tea, evaluations, and continuing education presentations, and said that the wrap-up is "not a nuclear melt-down", an even more violent image of the fire. I said something to the effect that it was important for us, the planners, to track our own imagery and feelings, because they are mirrors of the kinds of metaphors and emotions that are, and will be, percolating throughout Worcester and far beyond. As the planning committee, we not only must deal with our resistance to the event that prompted the confer-ence, but with our planning committee's group process that is itself part of the conference.

In simple English: this is how people, including professional people, including people of very good will, deal with the fire and with its equivalents in other places. We struggle to understand; the strug-gle is part of the understanding. Helpers of all professions can be deeply and unconsciously affected by a disaster, and, thus, not even recognize its presence until it is *enacted* in some way. As Fromm writes (personal communication, 13 March 2006), "anyone who takes up the subject [of the Worcester fire] has to cope with being 'heated up' by it". Further, this planning committee underwent a kind of traumati-zation that echoes Winnicott's point about the experience of emptiness as the result of "nothing happening when something . . . might have happened" (1974, p. 106). The group had unconsciously expected the fire that had occurred in the recent past to recur in the group's very midst, but it did not.

I cannot help but speculate further that the attempt to place "me" (via the telephone) on the conference table was symbolic as well as practical: a kind of condensation of the wish to have me present (person, nutrient) against the backdrop of enormous loss and grief. When we talk about gathering data about the fire, some of the most crucial data we can "gather" is not only from "them", but also from "us". Ultimately, fidelity to genuine healing begins with fidelity to the catastrophe itself and to people's experiences and accounts. Part of that fidelity is to the observer, clinician, or consultant's own emotional response, that is, to one's countertransference. Attention to what is present, and to what is missing, in a group can help prevent the unconscious transmission of trauma. I believe that this episode in the life of the conference planning committee illustrates how "easy" this lateral transmission is to do in order to avoid feelings of anxiety and even deeper fantasies of annihilation.

Recognizing trauma transmission in oneself

In all forms of therapy and research informed by psychoanalysis, the self of the therapist, researcher, or scholar is recognized to be the central instrument of understanding and helping others. In this section, I address the process of recognizing trauma transmission in oneself as a crucial component of studying and healing trauma. I recognize that self-analysis has severe limits, and that it is in the psychoanalytic dyad that trauma is first transferentially enacted and then recognized. None the less, discovering it in oneself—and its harrowing ordinariness—is a step in realizing its ubiquity in families, cultures, and history.

In an earlier paper (Stein, 2000), I have documented in detail how I discovered the emotional effect on me of working with and studying organizational downsizing, reduction in force, rightsizing, restructuring, re-engineering, deskilling, outsourcing, and other widespread corporate forms of what is euphemistically called "managed social change". At the methodological level, following Bion (1959, p. 134), I take the observer's emotional response—his or her countertransference—to be at times the only reliable measure of social reality. At the abstract level, countertransference consists of nothing less than thinking about how we think, an approach taken by such writers as Bion (1959, 1962), Boyer (1999), Laub and Podell (1997), Stern (1997), Tansey and Burke (1989), and Lawrence (1997, 1999). What one knows is inseparable from what one can emotionally *bear* to know—what one can first embody, then examine—about oneself, about others, about the world.

By extension, a study of workplace trauma that begins with my own inner darkness becomes a vehicle for a journey into organizational darkness—a place of secrecy and dread often expressed in the idiom of the Holocaust. In the mid-to-late 1990s and early 2000s, I had been participant observer, consultant, employee, and scholar in understanding the experience of massive, often ongoing, organizational change in the USA. At one point, for several years I was the longitudinal internal consultant to the process of downsizing of The University Hospitals in Oklahoma City.

In the midst of these official and informal roles, a personal experience seared into me the nature of the trauma of downsizing and its related terms. In turn, it taught me far more than I had bargained for about the transmission of trauma within workplace organizations. From Freud (1936a) to Ogden (1989, 1997a,b), many psychoanalysts have examined their pathologies as conduits to insight. *The pathology of the self-observant observer becomes as much a "royal road" to the unconscious as is the dream of the patient* (see Erikson, 1964). In this section, I offer an incident from my own pathography as a signifier of cultural and historical, not merely personal, psychodynamics. I describe the experience of my own derealization (the making of reality unreal). Here, the interior experience of a culture (organization) on the part of worker, consultant, and observer alike provides a crucial guide to that organization or culture "itself". My own traumatic reliving offers vital information about group trauma, its transmission, and its embodiment in me.

In March 1998, I was typing a reference list for the bibliography of a manuscript I was completing. An early entry in the alphabet was *The HUMAN Cost of a Management Failure: Organizational Downsizing at General Hospital* (1996). It was co-authored by four people; I could only remember three: Seth Allcorn, Howell Baum, and Michael Diamond. As I typed, I felt a dreadful panic. I was flooded with terror. I felt as if I were going to die immediately. The feeling was dire. "Emotional" was entirely "physical". I turned quickly from my computer, and, without consciously thinking, I picked up the telephone and called Michael Diamond, a fellow organizational consultant, a psychoanalytically orientated theorist and dear friend. He quickly completed the reference. I was the "missing" fourth author whom I could not remember. I had disappeared to myself. Out of breath, I asked him to help me to understand what was happening.

I felt confused, "crazy". What Michael Diamond and I pieced together was that my temporary lapse of memory (a parapraxis of derealization) coincided with the intolerable realization (1) that I was already, in fact, dead, at least symbolically; (2) that my experiences with several near-firings and constant job self-reinventions and justifications of my own in recent years did indeed feel like constant death-in-life; and (3) that I felt that at some level, or in some part of myself, I had already disappeared. I was already dead, missing—even to myself. Up to now, I had "successfully" dissociated all of this.

At another level, in response to living and working at the brink of being dead, I made myself dead, killed myself off, first. At least I would be in control of the fatal moment and of the final deed. At least, in that last act, I would destroy myself. I would perform the execution. I would master the terror of passive victimization by actively becoming the aggressor against myself (see Freud, 1920g). I would turn years of workplace harassment and private Jew-baiting upon myself.

In my own symbolic action, I fulfilled—embodied—an organizational wish: to make disappear, to kill off, an entire way of thinking and working, and to replace it with one that negated it (see Erikson, 1968). My individual, personal symptom consisted also of *the institution-in-me*. I was its container, the embodiment of intolerable wishes, fantasies, and defences. I became the battleground of metaphorical Nazi and Jew. My symbolic death would kill off intolerable organizational thought about the experience of workplace life. My personal experience was a living illustration of traumatic transmission. I was able to "use" myself and information gained from my self to supplement and give emotional depth to other more direct and conventional ways of learning about workplace organizations undergoing massive change.

I want to briefly add a more recent personal example of how this *in vivo* recognition of traumatic transmission occurs. This time, the context is the tenth anniversary of the 1995 Oklahoma City bombing. Mid-morning on 19 April 2005, I was driving to the University of Oklahoma Health Sciences Center from home about twelve miles away. I knew that it was the tenth anniversary of the bombing, and that there were many memorial ceremonies being held this day. As I was about to exit from the interstate, I discovered that the interstate was blocked off, quite reasonably to keep traffic from congesting the crowded downtown area where so many people had gathered. My reaction, however, was far from "reasonable".

I suddenly felt a terrible panic, palpitations, sudden sweating. I felt imminent danger. I had to consciously concentrate on driving; I wended my way to work via several side streets. "What was happening?" I asked myself. Via a series of associations, I realized that I had taken the identical route, and had encountered many roadblocks, on 19 April 1995, about an hour after the explosion at the Murrah Federal Building had taken place. Although I had no "reason" to be afraid, in fact I was undergoing traumatic reliving. Unconsciously, I was experiencing trauma transmission at the cultural level. It would have been normal for me to experience frustration, but not terror, at encountering the roadblock ten years to the day after the bombing. The feeling of enormous danger "told" me that something else emotionally was going on. After I came to understand my emotional reaction, I was able to calm down and proceed to work. Clearly, I had been reliving— re-enacting—the feelings of terror that I had felt a decade earlier in response to the act of terrorism. I came to realize how insidious and how utterly out-of-awareness trauma transmission can be.

Concurrent "vertical" and "horizontal" trauma transmission

In this section, I discuss the possibility of group trauma being trans- mitted both vertically and horizontally at the same time, or at least during the same time period. My example comes from the ubiquitous presence in American life of what has come to be grouped together as forms of "managed social change". Since the middle 1980s, they have become all too familiar as virtually obligatory ways of "solving" corporate declines in profit. They go by the names of downsizing, rightsizing, reductions in force (and the acronym RIF), redundancy (as mass firings are called in the UK), restructuring, re-engineering, outsourcing, deskilling, and managed health care. I have discussed at length elsewhere the cultural psychology of these acute and chronic traumas (Allcorn, Baum, Diamond, & Stein 1996; Stein, 1998, 2001, 2004; see also Uchitelle, 2006).

Here, my focus is on the experience of having been treated as disposable waste and the expectation of imminent disposability. Far from these widespread organizational forms being based on rational and reality-orientated decision-making, they are rife with narcissistic rage and sadism. They are workplace brutality in the guise of the economic "bottom line". Since the mid-1980s, our cultural vocabulary has become saturated with business euphemisms, the main purpose of which is to disguise the brutality that has become pervasive in American workplaces. Through the sleight of words, psychological violence to people appears instead in the form of linguistic smoke- screens that make individual and group forms of bullying look both rational and necessary. It is as if to say, "Through the magic of euphemism, violence directed against people is transmuted into look- ing like good business. Therefore, we need not feel guilt or shame."

We all know the terms, but it is likely that we have become lulled into uncritical acceptance of what they are supposed to mean, as opposed to what they actually mean: for example, downsizing, reduction in force (and its acronym, RIF, which is both noun and verb), rightsizing, re-engineering, restructuring, deskilling, outsourcing, managed health care, and the like. We rarely speak directly of "firing" people from their jobs, or of "terminating" people; to do so would make the violence too close to the surface of recognition. The British often use the term "redundancy" for the process of rendering people superfluous. In all these cases, people come to be regarded and manipulated as disposable things, inanimate objects, mere "numbers".

Aggression appears in the guise and language of pure necessity. For instance, we often speak of "getting rid of dead wood", of "trimming fat", even of "cutting down to the bone" in order to make a "lean, mean, fighting machine" that is at once more productive, more efficient, and less costly. Fewer and fewer people are expected to do more and more work, to be more productive, and, thereby, make the company more profitable. "Don't be a whiner," the supervisor warns, "Just be glad you still have a job." Managers and workers are treated as disposable objects rather than sentient human beings. The only "constituency" upper management considers is the shareholders, and they often fire (or promise to fire) large numbers of people, which immediately raises the stock value—though only temporarily. The trouble is that such people-cutting becomes the first, and often the only, solution that corporate executives and managers consider. No one is safe; even uppermost management can be "axed" at the wish and whim of the shareholders.

The result is often an "anorexic organization" that consists of a demoralized, uninspired, uncommitted workforce. Individual and institutionalized bullying ultimately is self-defeating. Yet, personal and official intimidation persists. After over two decades of evidence that "managed social change" wrecks organizations, the choice to eliminate many jobs or to endlessly reorganize them remains uppermost in the minds of decision-makers. Feelings of persecution, disorientation, and futurelessness simply do not count. The need to sacrifice in order to "save" the company remains paramount. Yet, the practice of constant sacrifice eats away at the very organization it is supposed to save.

In this workplace atmosphere, "vertical" and "horizontal" trauma transmission are rampant. New leaders, new recruits to middle management and the work force—many of whom were RIFed from their previous jobs—soon hear the stories, worries, and anger of those they join in the company. While certainly not in the official tour, corporate video, and operations manual, these are the affective life-blood of the organization: "what it feels like to work here". They traumatize both old and new employees alike. Old work-teams that had worked together for years, "hand in glove" both functionally and emotionally, are cavalierly dismembered and, in the name of greater efficiency, many of their members are fired.

Product of re-engineering and restructuring, work-teams of people with no history whatsoever are expected to produce as if they were a "well-oiled machine". No time is left to mourn what they had lost; the only time that counts is meeting the next deadline. Nor do relationships matter. In an earlier time, a secretary or administrator was worth gold to the organization because he or she possessed a Rolodex or computer address book of contacts and "knew how to get things done" informally. With repeated firings and restructurings, relationships atrophy into narrow "job descriptions". The "time and motion" vision of Frederick Winslow Taylor ("Taylorism") a century ago triumphs in this corporate world of "Neutron Jack" (Welch of General Electric) and "Chainsaw Al" (Dunlap of Scott Paper and Sunbeam). People become reduced to mechanical functions in the corporate machine. (No wonder the cultural allure of "re-engineering" and "restructuring" the workplace and workforce!)

Not only are workers traumatized themselves, they tend to withdraw into the world of their narrow task, hoping magically "that if they [management] see me working hard, they'll value me, and they'll pass me over during the next RIF". These people no longer recognize themselves to be members of an organization; they are virtually wage slaves in an oppressive regime, praying to be passed over, as in the Jewish Passover, when, according to tradition, God's Angel of Death spared the firstborn in the Hebrew households, but killed the firstborn in every Egyptian home. Many employees start to develop survivors' narratives, such as "The ones that got RIFed must have done something wrong. They must have been bad workers." Short-circuiting mourning, they detach themselves emotionally from the ones who are gone, and develop shallow relationships with the workers who remain or who are recruited in the future. Feeling that the "psychological contract" (Levinson, 1962) between employer and employee has been cancelled and betrayed, employees have far less of a sense of emotional attachment and loyalty to each other, to management, and to the company. Work ceases to have the earlier overtones of meaning, and becomes more "just a job". One often works with one foot already out the door—keeping a curriculum vitae circulating—so one might leave before he or she is left (abandoned). The transmission of trauma in vertical and horizontal directions lies both in what is said and done, and in what is not said and done. Bullying and indifference are close emotional relatives.

Here, I offer two brief vignettes that illustrate the ordinariness of this process. The first one comes from a discussion I had with a participant at a conference after I had made a presentation on downsizing. She came up to affirm from her own experience what I had said. She then described a harrowing experience she had had at a new job she took in the late 1990s. A corporate executive had gathered all the new employees in one place and proceeded to orientate them to the company. He said to them approximately as follows: "Don't think for one minute that you're indispensable to the company. There are a lot of people out there hungry for your job. Imagine sticking your finger in a bowl of water and then removing it. And imagine that our company is that bowl of water. If you leave, that's how much you'll be remembered. So do your work as though your job depended on it." She went on to say that she shuddered at what he had said and at the menacing imagery he had used. "This was not a welcome," she added, "but a threat even before you started your job. It made me feel like a nobody from day one." It does not require much imagination to sense the induction of abandonment and annihilation anxiety precisely in the place that one had hoped to be made secure.

The second example comes from notes I took during a middle-management hospital post-downsizing meeting about seven months after 500 people had been laid off from a workforce of 3,500. Here, a veteran nurse, now in nursing administration, speaks about the atmosphere in personnel (the unit where we were meeting). She had had to walk through the department to get to our conference room:

> Personnel used to be upbeat, where you could go in the hospital to feel good. Not upbeat now. It is worse in personnel than in other hospital departments. There is a feeling of helplessness, hopelessness, power-lessness. You want to scream and say: "I'm affected, too! Not only the people who are no longer here . . ." There were no raises in personnel

except the *internal auditor* who showed [to the upper hospital management council in charge of the layoffs] what could be done on the
computer. *He* got a raise. "Just get them out [the ones being laid off]"
was the message we got. "And we don't want to hear about it." No
one got any pay or even a compliment for the kind of work we did
[two-week-long "work fairs" in which they provided support and
information for each group whose jobs had been eliminated].

This second vignette vividly shows the process of trauma transmission in action and in memory. The space is filled with the absence
of those who had been laid off, and with the enforced silence among
those who are "survivors". The experience of what had happened
becomes a corporate secret that everyone knows.

These two vignettes can, perhaps, shed some light on the dynamics of the Columbine High School shootings by Dylan Klebold and
Eric Harris in Littleton, Colorado, on 20 April 1999. Over two years
before the September 11 attacks on America, we were already terrorizing our own. Here, the fact that Eric Harris's father had been RIFed
from an oil and gas company might be a part of the intergenerational
("vertical") transmission of trauma that set his son up to avenge the
father. The family, after all, is where one first glimpses the meaning of,
and the need for, redemption and revenge. Almost as a silent pact, one
generation takes upon itself the sacred duty of filling the parental
generation's voids—even if it is not specifically bound to loyalty. One
can imagine how patterns of "deposited representation" (Volkan,
1997) and identification in the Harris and Klebold households "prepared" Eric and Dylan to aspire to redeem their parents' losses and
unfulfilled ambitions, if not their shattered dreams.

It does not take "monsters" to produce "monsters". The monstros-
ity comes from the (intergenerational) obligation to redeem the past in
the future. And—to continue my speculation—when the child who
bears the torch of redemption is not permitted by his peers to redeem
his parents, but is instead ridiculed as an outcast, he is confronted by
his parents' (and parents' generation) rage and despair. Perhaps an
identity deeper than of success is that of failure (despite initial
success). The battle in Columbine High School resulted, after all, not
only in defeat, but also humiliating self-defeat after an initial glee-
filled triumph.

Perhaps Eric Harris was prepared for this role by his family atmosphere, and beyond it, by the workplace world of downsizing. Let me

first link Eric's father with the far wider American workplace. Those who are being fired feel they are being terrorized, not merely dismissed from a job. As with re-engineering, if downsizing were a purely rational (as opposed to rationalized) process, it would not be so heavily ritualized. The sadism and brutalization that cannot be openly spoken are overwhelmingly felt. RIFing and re-engineering are rituals of degradation and of dehumanization in the guise of reality-based and, thereby, necessary business practices. Bloodless massacres are experienced as massacres, none the less.

Millions of American workers are the symbolic *desaparacidos*, the disappeared ones, like those of the Argentine "dirty wars" of the 1980s and the Nazi "transports" to death camps. Everyone knows and no one knows. The brutality is superseded by, and enshrouded in, euphemism and denial (Suarez-Orozco, 1990). Knowing becomes not-knowing, un-knowing. Workers and leaders expect themselves and others to proceed with redoubled effort *as if nothing had happened, as if no loss had occurred*, to work harder and longer in order to keep their jobs and make the company productive and profitable. People become things rather than persons and turn one another into inanimate, functioning objects.

Now, if these workplace scenarios are played out throughout the USA, as they have been for over a decade, they are likely to have powerful emotional "residues" and resonances. I would speculate that among the most vulnerable types of communities and families are those of socially mobile professionals, members of the upper middle to upper class, such as those who live in Jonesboro, Arkansas, and Littleton, Colorado. Harris's father, a geologist, had entered the oil exploration industry at the time of the boom (1978) and was a casualty of the subsequent "bust".

My argument-from-culture here is not one of cause and effect (for instance, the popular argument that families in which there has been traumatic downsizing and re-engineering are most "at risk" for violent enactment). Instead, it is an argument about vulnerability, dread of futurelessness, anxiety over loss, that comes from a shared social predicament and from mutual identification (see Faludi, 1999). These day-to-day realities might not even be spoken about at the dinner table or around the television set. They are more inferable from a raised voice, a sullen glance, heavy silence, or an unaccountable car accident. Yet, they are at least as palpable a presence as the violence in films, on television, and in popular video games. They are less a matter of directive "child-rearing" than they are emotion-laden communication about hope, dread, meaning—and both the *loss of meaning and the destruction of meaning*.

The Columbine High School experience is not without a horrific irony, which I am grateful to Fromm for pointing out to me (personal communication, 13 March 2006). The school had become polarized between the "jocks" and the "Trenchcoat Warriors" (to which faction both Eric Harris and Dylan Klebold belonged); each side dehumanized the other and, in the process, dehumanized themselves. Not unlike the resolution in Shakespeare's tragedy, *Romeo and Juliet*, the eruption of violence re-humanized the entire social situation by inflicting loss and grief upon everyone.

The possibility of "reverse" vertical trauma transmission

In this final section, I consider the counterintuitive idea that vertical transmission might *also* occur in the reverse of the usual direction, that is, from younger to older, or from younger to older members of the same cohort, such as in organizational workplaces. The phenomenon of "elder abuse" of parents by adult children immediately comes to mind. Just as returning American soldiers from the Second World War brought new and liberating ideas and irreversible change to their families, communities, and workplaces, likewise returning soldiers from Germany returning from the First World War brought tales of heroism and despair to their homes, families, communities, and workplaces.

More recently, the terrorism that Eric Harris and Dylan Klebold wrought had effects far wider than the students and teachers in Columbine High School. I contend that, in order to understand trauma in that situation, one must think of it spreading in all directions, including to the *ascending* generations of parents and grandparents. Certainly, in the wake of relentless downsizing, deskilling, and outsourcing, those who have been "terminated" bring their trauma-born bitterness, despair, rage, and grief to the next employer and job they take. Their darkness (mistrust, hypervigilance, attenuated relationships) spreads in all "directions", including upward. At least, one ought to consider the possibility of reverse vertical transmission of trauma when working with people psychopolitically, organizationally, and clinically.

Conclusions

In this chapter I have not painted a single picture of the process and experience of the transmission of trauma. Instead, through many vignettes, I have painted a mosaic or collage of the many ways in which social trauma might be transferred between people. Specifically, I have explored the directions in which trauma might go. The examples further validate the intimate relationship between trauma, loss, and mourning—or the inability to mourn. They also attest to the *ordinariness* of transmission of trauma in contrast to the much more publicized and analysed experiences, such as the Nazi Holocaust. The transmission of trauma can be reduced only when its presence is first recognized and authorized. Trauma can be grieved, and its transmission halted, only if it can be acknowledged and accepted that, in fact, it happened and deserves to be mourned.

References

Allcorn, S., Baum, H., Diamond, M. A., & Stein, H. F. (1996). *The HUMAN Cost of a Management Failure: Organizational Downsizing at General Hospital.* Westport, CT: Quorum Books.

Apprey, M. (1993). The African-American experience: forced immigration and transgenerational trauma. *Mind and Human Interaction,* 4: 70–75.

Apprey, M. (1996). Broken lines, public memory, absent memory: Jewish and African Americans coming to terms with racism. *Mind and Human Interaction,* 7: 139–149.

Apprey, M. (1998). Reinventing the self in the face of received transgenerational hatred in the African American community. *Mind and Human Interaction,* 9: 30–37.

Apprey, M. (2000). From the horizon of evil to an ethic of responsibility. *Mind and Human Interaction,* 11: 119–126.

Bion, W. R. (1959). *Experiences in Groups.* New York: Basic Books.

Bion, W. R. (1962). *Learning from Experience.* New York: Basic Books.

Boyer, L. B. (1999). *Countertransference and regression.* Northvale, NJ: Jason Aronson.

Brenner, I. (2001). *Dissociation of Trauma: Theory, Phenomenology, and Technique*. Madison, CT: International Universities Press.

Brenner, I. (2005). On genocidal persecution and resistance. *Mind and Human Interaction, 14*: 18–34.

Davoine, F., & Gaudilliere, J-M. (2004). *History Beyond Trauma*. New York: Other Press.

Doka, K. J. (1989). *Disenfranchised Grief: Recognizing Hidden Sorrow*. Lanham, MD: Lexington Books.

Erikson, E. H. (1964). *Insight and Responsibility*. New York: Norton.

Erikson, E. H. (1968). *Identity: Youth and Crisis*. New York: Norton.

Faludi, S. (1999). *Stiffed: The Betrayal of the American Man*. New York: William Morrow.

Feld, S., & Basso, K. (Eds.) (1996). *Senses of Place*. Santa Fe: School of American Research.

Flynn, S. (2000). The perfect fire. *Esquire, 134*(1): 64–79, 129, 131–133.

Freud, S. (1920g). *Beyond the Pleasure Principle*. *S.E., 18*: 7–64. London: Hogarth.

Freud, S. (1936a). A disturbance of memory on the Acropolis. *S.E., 22*: 239–248. London: Hogarth.

Fromm, M. G. (2006). Personal communication.

Fullilove, M. T. (1996). Psychiatric implications of displacement: contributions from the psychology of place. *American Journal of Psychiatry, 153*: 1516–1523.

Hollander, N. (1999). The individual and the transitional space of authoritarian society. *Mind and Human Interaction, 10*: 98–109.

Javors, I. (2000). Grief that dares not speak its name. *Clio's Psyche, 7*: 88–89.

Katz, M. (2003). Prisoners of Azkaban: understanding intergenerational transmission of trauma due to war and state terror. *Journal for the Psychoanalysis of Culture and Society, 8*: 200–207.

La Barre, W. (1946). Social cynosure and social structure. *Journal of Personality, 14*: 169–183.

Laub, D., & Podell, D. (1997). Psychoanalytic listening to historical trauma: the conflict of knowing and the imperative to act. *Mind and Human Interaction, 8*: 245–260.

Lawrence, W. G. (1997). Centering of the Sphinx. Symposium: International Society for the Psychoanalytic Study of Organizations, Philadelphia, June.

Lawrence, W. G. (1999). Thinking as refracted in organizations—the finite and the infinite/the conscious and the unconscious. Symposium: International Society for the Psychoanalytic Study of Organizations, Toronto, Canada, June.

Levinson, H. (1962). *Men, Management, and Mental Health.* Cambridge, MA: Harvard University Press.

Marks, J. (2006). Federal workers face date to move. *The Oklahoman,* 10 April.

Ogden, T. (1989). *The Primitive Edge of Experience.* Northvale, NJ: Jason Aronson.

Ogden, T. (1997a). Reverie and interpretation. *Psychoanalytic Quarterly, 66:* 567–595.

Ogden, T. (1997b). Reverie and metaphor: some thoughts on how I work as a psychoanalyst. *International Journal of Psychoanalysis, 78:* 719–732.

Ritzer, G. (2000). *The McDonaldization of Society.* Thousand Oaks, CA: Sage.

Stein, H. (1998). *Euphemism, Spin, and the Crisis in Organizational Life.* Westport, CT: Quorum Books.

Stein, H. (2000). From countertransference to social theory: a study of Holocaust thinking in U.S. business disguise. *Ethos, 28:* 346–378.

Stein, H. (2001). *Nothing Personal, Just Business: A Guided Journey into Organizational Darkness.* Westport, CT: Quorum Books.

Stein, H. (2004). *Beneath the Crust of Culture.* New York: Rodopi.

Stein, H. F., & Hill, R. F. (Eds.) (1993). *The Culture of Oklahoma.* Norman: University of Oklahoma Press.

Steinbeck, J. (1939). *The Grapes of Wrath.* New York: Penguin, 2002.

Stern, D. (1997). *Unformulated Experience: From Dissociation to Imagination in Psychoanalysis.* Mahwah, NJ: Analytic Press.

Suarez-Orozco, M. (1990). Speaking of the unspeakable: toward a psychosocial understanding of responses to terror. *Ethos, 18:* 353–383.

Tansey, M., & Burke, W. (1989). *Understanding Countertransference: From Countertransference to Empathy.* Hillsdale, NJ: Analytic Press.

Uchitelle, L. (2006). *The Disposable American: Layoffs and Their Consequences.* New York: Knopf.

Volkan, V. (1997). *Bloodlines: From Ethnic Pride to Ethnic Terrorism.* New York: Farrar, Straus and Giroux.

Volkan, V., Ast, G., & Greer, W. (2002). *The Third Reich in the Unconscious: Transgenerational Transmission and its Consequences.* New York: Brunner-Routledge.

Winnicott, D. W. (1974). Fear of breakdown. *International Review of Psycho-Analysis, 1:* 103–107.

CHAPTER ELEVEN

Heroes at home: the transmission of trauma in firefighters' families

Kevin V. Kelly

In the spring of 2002, firefighter Mike and I were both new to our roles; I had just become the consulting psychiatrist to the Counseling Services Unit of the New York City Fire Department, and Mike was just becoming a psychiatric patient. He recognized that, like everyone else in the FDNY, he was suffering from the psychological effects of the World Trade Center collapse, but he made his ambivalence explicit: "I know I need to be here, but that's not why I'm here—if it was just for myself, I'd tough it out." He went on to explain that, as the senior man in his firehouse, he saw how traumatized the younger men were. "They need to be here, and they're not going to come unless they see me doing it, so that's why I'm here."

In the time since then, I have had the opportunity to learn a great deal from Mike and his brethren about trauma, and to make some observations about how it might be transmitted. This chapter will present those observations, with the understanding that they are derived from a rather homogeneous and unique population, in the aftermath of an extraordinary series of events.

The FDNY, the CSU, and the WTC

The New York City Fire Department (FDNY) includes about 11,400 uniformed firefighters and 2,800 Emergency Medical Service personnel. The Counseling Services Unit (CSU) provides mental health services to Department members; before 9/11 it had one office, in lower Manhattan, and a staff of about a dozen non-medical psychotherapists and substance abuse counsellors. Those professionals saw roughly fifty cases per month, often members whose supervisors required them to come for evaluation, and most commonly for alcohol problems.

When the planes hit the World Trade Center, all FDNY personnel were summoned to duty. Many of those on duty were sent to the site, and many others made their own way there. The best available estimate is that, by the time the second tower collapsed, 500 FDNY members had arrived on the scene. Of those, 343 died that day. Much larger numbers arrived shortly after the collapse, and all FDNY members took part in the rescue and recovery operations, which continued until May 2002.

The terrorist attack, the multiple deaths, and the horrific recovery work all had profound psychological effects on the survivors. In a matter of days, the CSU began to expand its services to meet the mushrooming need. Within a few months, the system included six offices around the metropolitan area, with a staff of twenty-nine civilian mental health professionals, plus extensive networks of Peer Counsellors (injured or retired firefighters who received mental health training) and volunteer psychiatrists and therapists, who saw FDNY personnel either in the firehouses or in their own offices. Anticipating the transmission of trauma, the CSU extended its services to the families and loved ones of FDNY members. In the years since 9/11, the CSU has seen an average of 330 new cases each month.

I first came into contact with the FDNY as one of the volunteer psychiatrists, though I had no previous experience with firefighters, and no special expertise in trauma. A few months later, I was hired by the CSU to provide ongoing clinical services to CSU clients and supervision, consultation, and education to the CSU staff. This paper is based on my experiences in that setting, including direct contact with about 600 patients to date, and on discussions with other FDNY and CSU personnel. Most of my clinical contacts have been brief, involving consultation, referral and/or pharmacologic management. I have seen a few dozen family members and significant others directly, but most of my information about the transmitted effects of trauma comes from the firefighters' own reports. (For a more extensive discussion of the material in this and in the following section, see Greene, Kane, Christ, Lynch, & Corrigan, 2006, especially Chapters Two and Three.)

Firehouse culture

Some generalizations about the firefighters and their social world are necessary as a background to understanding how they experience and communicate trauma; like all such statements about large groups, these will be oversimplified and will admit of exceptions, but in my experience the following observations generally hold true.

Despite years of efforts to promote diversity, the FDNY remains demographically and ethnically homogeneous. Only a few hundred firefighters are African-American, and only forty-three are women (since all of the firefighters I have seen clinically are male, I will try to minimize semantic awkwardness by referring to them in the masculine form). The vast majority are first- and second-generation Irish and Italian Catholic young men, raised in the working-class areas of the boroughs surrounding Manhattan. Many of them come from FDNY families, with fathers, grandfathers, uncles, and brothers also "on the job". Firemen often address each other as "brother", and in many cases this is literally true; almost a quarter of the firefighters who died at the WTC had fathers, sons, or brothers who were active or retired Department members.

Perhaps not surprisingly, the tribal mentality in this population runs strong and deep. Loyalty to the brethren is a core feature of most firefighters' psychology, and rivals even loyalty to the family. Like soldiers in combat, firefighters at a fire literally depend on each other for their lives. They take great pride in their role as professional rescuers, and the culture frowns on any expression of neediness or weakness.

This set of attitudes leads to a curious paradox in the firefighters' relationship to their families, illustrated by the cherished icon of a burly firefighter carrying a small child to safety. On the one hand, they are often deeply involved in their children's lives; part of the appeal of their job lies in the fact that the schedule permits them to spend more time than most fathers do with their children. They tend to have preserved their enjoyment of latency-age pleasures, especially sports, and many serve as coaches for their children's teams. Paradoxically, their well-established identity as paragons of manliness gives them freedom to indulge in stereotypically maternal activities, and they often take pride in describing themselves as "Mr Mom".

On the other hand, the attitude of protectiveness often produces some distance between the firefighter and his family. His daily work exposes him to both danger and horror, and this experience is shared with the "brothers" but not with the family at home. Firefighters are loath to discuss the gruesome details and the emotional impact of their work with wives, girlfriends, or children, believing that their proper role is to protect the family from these fears and horrors. Of course, their significant others are aware of what they do, of the danger and, to some extent, of the horrors, and the father's silence can aggravate the sense of fear and isolation the mother and children might feel.

Several of these themes are illustrated in one firefighter's description of his firehouse as "The Land of the Lost Boys". The reference to Peter Pan and his comrades depicts a group of latency-age males who battle danger bravely, and who defiantly refuse to submit to conventional norms of adult behaviour, but whose bravado also defends against the gnawing fear of, at any moment, being permanently cut off from home and family.

Post 9/11 stress and its disorders

The collapse of the WTC produced trauma for the firefighters in any number of ways. The diagnosis of post traumatic stress disorder, which grew out of military psychiatry, has historically been understood as the consequence of personal danger, in the form of assault, abuse, or a near-death experience in combat, but the FDNY's 9/11 experience provides an experiment of nature that could challenge this understanding. The devastation there was so complete that only about 150 of the firefighters present at the collapse survived the near-death experience. Many of these survivors had extensive physical injuries, and all of them had serious psychological trauma, but the number of

PTSD cases among FDNY members is many times the number who were in the collapse, so the precipitating trauma for most must involve something other than immediate personal danger.

Of course, the large number of sudden deaths, mostly among healthy young adults, contributed to the traumatic effect. Everyone who was in the FDNY at that time knew some of the victims personally, and some members knew dozens of them well. This widespread traumatic grief was accompanied by an expectable prevalence of intense survivor guilt. Anyone who had been a firefighter at that time asked himself "Why did I survive?" The true answer, of course, was usually "pure chance", but to accept this reality would entail accepting the individual's utter helplessness in the face of random death and destruction. For many, the omnipotent fantasy that they could have done something to change the result, even with this fantasy's attendant guilt, seemed preferable. One man explained his reluctance to accept help for his psychic distress succinctly: "I'm s'posed to feel like shit—I'm alive."

In addition to personal danger, traumatic grief, and survivor guilt, conversations with traumatized firefighters suggest another important source of psychic stress—one that has perhaps been underestimated in previous trauma studies. (An important exception to this generalization is the work of McCarroll and colleagues (McCarroll et al., 1995).) In the months following 9/11, all the members of the FDNY worked on "The Pile" of debris, hoping at first to rescue survivors and later to recover bodies or parts. In the early phase of the work, it was often necessary to dismember bodies in order to extricate them, while later the work involved removing bodies or parts in states of advanced decomposition. The firefighters' sense of duty and loyalty compelled them to pursue this work, often with fanatic devotion, until the last scrap of material was examined and removed, but the toll on their own health and well being, psychologically as well as medically, was enormous. When they can be persuaded to discuss their traumatic dreams and flashbacks, they most often describe horrific images of the recovery work, so that *horror* appears as a primary source of traumatic stress, at least as powerfully pathogenic as danger, grief, and guilt.

The term "horror", as used here, refers to the individual's spontaneous subjective reaction to direct contact with mutilated human remains, an event that happened all too commonly to the firefighters at the WTC site. This experience is, of course, familiar to firefighters, but the situation at the WTC was extraordinary because of the magnitude of death and mutilation, the length of time required to complete the work, and the fact that so many of the dead were known personally to the rescuers. Although the rescue and recovery workers were consciously looking for human remains, aware that they would probably be in advanced states of dismemberment and decay, and nevertheless fervently hoping to find them, they could still not prepare themselves psychologically for the infinite variety of mutilation and decomposition, so each episode of finding new remains had the traumatic impact of an unexpected event.

The experience of face-to-face contact with a human body that has been burned, disfigured, or dismembered resonates with the most primitive and disturbing of primary process fantasies. Because of the close neural connection between affective centres and the sense of smell, it is expectable that the olfactory dimension of the experience would have an even more disturbing effect than the visual, and, indeed, many firefighters report, even years later, that anything which reminds them of "that smell" can summon up the entire WTC experience in an instant. But beyond simply seeing and smelling the remains, the firefighters had to handle them, no matter how burned or decomposed, and thus their efforts to treat the remains respectfully required violating the primitive prohibition against disturbing the dead.

Such an intensely disturbing experience, often repeated many times over the course of months, can cause the individual to feel fundamentally changed, no longer able to communicate freely, either with his former self or with others who have not had the same experience. Aware of how disturbing these traumatic images are, the firefighter cannot imagine inflicting them on his family by talking about them at home. At the same time, he is most reluctant to discuss them with his colleagues, for fear of appearing weak and/or reactivating the trauma, so he finds himself alone with the impossible task of trying either to metabolize the experience or to forget it.

The symptoms of post traumatic stress disorder in this population are strikingly similar across the hundreds of cases I have seen, perhaps because of the similarities in the patients' background and experience. I have learned to recognize and to anticipate a clinical triad of very specific symptoms, involving insomnia, irritability, and withdrawal.

The patients regularly describe *middle insomnia*; the typical complaint is that "I fall asleep fine, but I wake up suddenly two or three hours later, and then I'm tossing and turning for the rest of the night." The awakening is always abrupt, and sometimes caused by a remembered nightmare with manifest content recognizably referring to the WTC experience. They also report a very typical *ego-dystonic hostility*, characterized by sudden outbursts of rage that the patient himself experiences even at the time as irrational and out of character, but which he feels powerless to control. Finally, these once gregarious fellows now show a marked *withdrawal* from contact with friends and family. They prefer not to go out socially, and to stay alone even at home. They retreat from athletic activities, family events, and social gatherings. (One unexpected consequence of this pattern is a decrease in the prevalence of alcohol abuse; for most firefighters, drinking is a social activity, and is given up along with the rest of social life.) These symptoms, particularly the hostility and withdrawal, play a central role in the transmission of trauma from the firefighter to his family.

How trauma is transmitted to the family

The children and significant others of those firefighters who were not killed on 9/11, but who have felt the traumatic effects of this event and its aftermath, have experienced transmitted trauma in a variety of ways. Most obviously, fear for the life of the firefighter going about his daily work, which the family has always felt even if the prevailing ethos has forbidden them to name it, is now even more urgent and palpable. Children who have seen the ubiquitous televised images of the collapse, and who know how many of their parents' brethren died there, find it even harder than they did before to comply with the unspoken demand that the fear be denied. In many cases, wives have been unwilling or unable to collude with this silence, and have urged their husbands to retire from firefighting. This openness might be less pathogenic than the denial of fear, but it creates another form of stress, as the men feel torn between loyalty to the job and the brethren and duty to the family. This conflict is often the precipitating factor in their presentation to the CSU.

Besides trying to cope with the risk that forms a chronic and inescapable fact of firefighting life, the families have suffered from the firefighters' physical and psychological absence. For many months after 9/11, the firefighters were so absorbed with the recovery work that they were hardly ever home, and when at home they were either asleep or preoccupied with getting back to "The Pile". A firefighter whose daughter was born shortly after 9/11 had a profound reaction to the birth of a son three years later, when he realized for the first time that he had missed the first year of his daughter's life.

For many firefighters, the work of recovery and the fantasy of achieving "closure" by finding bodies or parts sustained them through many months. When that work came to an end, with remains found for only a third of the victims, another phase of the reaction began. It was then that the full syndrome of PTSD became wide-spread, and the firefighters who were physically reunited with their families became psychologically withdrawn from them. The ethos of protectiveness combined with the symptomatic tendency toward withdrawal, leading the firefighters to avoid contact with their fami-lies even as they stayed at home. The families often experienced this absence as if the husband/father had died along with his brethren on 9/11, and indeed the firefighter's unconscious identification with the dead might well lie behind his withdrawal.

The full clinical picture of PTSD includes, paradoxically, symptoms both of "arousal" and of "avoidance", the latter resulting from the patient's efforts to escape the distress that accompanies the former. In this population, the "avoidance" appears as social withdrawal, and the "arousal" as irritability. The traumatized firefighters regularly report a vulnerability to sudden outbursts of rage, both at strangers and at loved ones. Anger at strangers might be more dangerous (epi-sodes of road rage with potentially life-threatening consequences are not uncommon), but anger at loved ones causes the patients more dis-tress. The symptom most often responsible for overcoming their reluc-tance to seek treatment is usually described as "taking it out on the kids" or "biting everyone's heads off"; one firefighter captured the ego-dystonic nature of this behaviour by describing himself as "being a total asshole at home".

In other situations, the firefighters' reactions take the form of hyper-vigilant and counterproductive worry about the family's welfare. A firefighter involved in disaster preparedness became con-vinced that another attack on New York was inevitable, and decided to move his family to a rural area in the Northwest. His children opposed moving away from their schools and friends, and he became so paralysed by the conflict between their wishes and his fears for their safety that he sold their house, but failed to buy a new one, and the family had to move in with relatives for several months. A dispatcher, whose radio contacts with the firefighters in the WTC were the last conversations many of them had, became preoccupied with a fear of intruders, and had an extensive system of bright lights and security cameras installed in the back yard where his children played. At first the children enjoyed the novelty, but soon they internalized his fears and stopped playing outside. The children's behaviour in this situation could be interpreted as an unconscious identification with the traumatized parent, but a more direct and compelling understanding would focus on the traumatic effect of the parent's bizarre behaviour on the child.

Thus, in these families, the child experiences the father as insecure and unpredictable. The man who was once busily and happily involved in his children's activities might have disappeared from the home for many months, and when he returns he is likely to withdraw in solitude. If he does emerge, he might be over-solicitous and worried about the child, then fly into a fit of rage minutes later. When he leaves for work, the child's gnawing but impermissible fear that he might not return alive is even more pressing.

In addition to feeling the direct effects of the father's erratic behaviour, the child might be further traumatized by a disruption of the parents' relationship. The husbands' irritability and withdrawal have often proved intolerable to their wives; many of the wives have presented to the CSU with depression, or have withdrawn psychologically from their husbands. Some firefighters reacted to their trauma by having affairs, perhaps trying to counteract their own distress or to cope with their wives' inability to respond constructively. In some cases these conflicts have led to divorce and in others to acrimonious cohabitation, but in either case the children are likely to suffer as a result.

How the rescuers are rescued by the next generation

Despite the extensive trauma they have suffered, the firefighters are generally a hardy and resilient lot. They are highly resistant to entering treatment, but once they take that step, they generally do well. In many ways, the next generation provides the motivation necessary for overcoming resistance to treatment and for making adaptive life changes.

Perhaps surprisingly, suicidal ideas are not a prominent feature in this population, even when they are suffering intensely. This might be partly the result of their religious convictions and partly a paradoxical result of survivor guilt—those who did not die at the WTC feel consciously that they do not deserve to join the dead heroes, but deserve instead to continue living and suffering. But the reason they give most commonly for not considering suicide is that "I would never do that to my kids." Indeed, many of the men found a fulfilling response to their bereavement and guilt by becoming surrogate fathers to the children of their dead brethren.

Thus, their own children, and those whose fathers died, give the men a reason to go on living and a chance to fashion an adaptive response to their trauma. Furthermore, as described above, the realization that their symptoms are causing distress to their children is often the factor that finally overcomes their considerable resistance to seeking treatment. An additional layer of resistance is encountered in those cases where psychotropic medication is recommended, and here, too, the firefighters' attachment to their children can be used to therapeutic advantage. The idea of accepting prescribed medication for a psychological condition is usually abhorrent to these men, whose self-image is built on being the strong one who rescues others. They can often, however, be persuaded by a benevolently manipulative appeal to parental responsibility: "I'm sure you're right that you don't need it yourself, and if you were only thinking of yourself you'd just tough it out, but you have other people to think of; you know how your kids are affected by your irritability and withdrawal, and *they* need you to be big enough to tolerate taking meds."

This formulation echoes Firefighter Mike's comments about setting an example for the younger men in his firehouse, and the parallel is important. Many of the more senior firefighters have been forced to retire since 9/11, primarily because of lung disease resulting from exposure to the toxic dust at the WTC site, and some of these men have found a rewarding second career as peer counsellors, modelling for the next generation in their profession the acceptability and value of mental health treatment.

Other retirees have found satisfaction in the role of "Mr Mom". Most of the men are happy being firefighters, and involuntary retirement, even when accompanied by disability compensation, requires a major psychological adjustment. But when family circumstances permit them to become full-time parents, the transition can become tolerable and even welcome.

Finally, when the men eventually achieve some mastery of the trauma, the resulting change in their attitudes often leads to a different and more constructive approach to parenting. Firefighter Mike was one of those who were buried in the rubble of the collapse, and he spent some months at home recovering from his injuries. He recalled that, when he was leaving home for his first day back at work, his five-year-old daughter was obviously worried, and asked him whether she could do anything to help. His first impulse was to adopt the protective stance, as he would have in the past, reassuring her that she need not worry and that the firemen would take care of everything.

"But," he explained, "something told me that wasn't the right response. So instead I said, 'You know, there *is* something you could do; you could give me a big hug, and then I could take your hug down to the firehouse and pass it around to all the other guys, and that way everyone would feel better.'" This affirmation of his little girl's efficacy in helping her father and his brothers seems likely to serve her better than the protective denial that prevailed before 9/11.

References

Greene, P., Kane, D., Christ, G., Lynch, S., & Corrigan, M. (2006). *FDNY Crisis Counseling: Innovative Responses to 911 Firefighters, Families and Communities*. Hoboken, NJ: John Wiley.

McCarroll, J., Ursano, R., Fullerton, C., Oates, G., Ventis, W., Friedman, H., Shean, G., & Wright, K. (1995). Gruesomeness, emotional attachment, and personal threat: dimensions of the anticipated stress of body recovery. *Journal of Trauma Stress, 8*: 343–349.

CHAPTER TWELVE

Afterword: lost and found

M. Gerard Fromm

"And yet they, who passed away long ago, still exist in us, as predisposition, as burden upon our fate, as murmuring blood, as gesture that rises up from the depths of time"

(Rilke, 1945)

With this epigraph from the poet, Rilke, Jane Fonda (2005) begins a critical chapter of her autobiography, a chapter in which she tells the story of her having become emotionally lost in what she eventually realizes is the trauma of her mother's life. Against the backdrop of Hollywood and Broadway, it is the story of two troubled people forging a terribly troubled marriage in an impossibly heady context. Henry Fonda is adored by his feisty tomboy daughter, despite his morose disposition and proclivity for rage and for the devastating silences he had suffered from his own father.

Frances Fonda is regarded by her daughter with more mixed emotions, primarily in response to how the child Jane perceived her mother's femininity: sometimes sweet and lovely, often long-suffering, inadequate as a source of pleasure for her husband, pathetic in her attempts, ultimately broken, as, her marriage deteriorating, she descended into depression and became lost to both herself and her children. Psychiatric hospitalizations followed, without evident benefit, and Frances Fonda became increasingly suicidal. Accompanied by a nurse on a visit to the family's northwestern Connecticut home, Frances retrieved a hidden razor blade from her bathroom and, back at the hospital a month later, on her birthday, cut her throat.

When her mother arrived home for that last visit, Jane, who had been playing upstairs with her brother, was called to greet her. Enacting the kind of anger we would now recognize as avoidant attachment, Jane refused to acknowledge her mother's presence at all. Later, when the other call came, she fought it as well:

> In the middle of my lesson the phone in the stable rang. It was Dad telling whoever answered to make me come home immediately. But I took my time. There were so many dead bugs . . . in the dirt driveway . . . to stop and examine. [p. 17]

Her preoccupation with dead bugs already speaks to an unconscious knowledge: "In some deep part of me that wasn't my mind, some part that could keep secrets from the rest of me, I knew what was coming" (p. 17).

In the year before her suicide, Jane Fonda's mother had developed a new hobby, one involving dead bugs. The opening story of the book describes how Frances Fonda would cautiously unscrew the lid of the jar in which she had placed the butterfly she had caught in the meadow, delicately etherize it and then use tweezers to carefully pin the body to its white backing. She had quietly taken up this activity in the midst of her mysterious hospitalizations. Jane, too, quite out of character, had found herself frequently in the hospital around this time, for ear infections and broken bones.

In that same year, Frances had shown her eleven-year-old daughter her botched breast implant, hacked off her hair with nail scissors, and wandered the neighbourhood outside her friend's New York apartment in her nightgown. Jane, too, was walking in her nightgown,

> propelled by the same nightmare: I was in the wrong room and desperately needed to get out, to get back to where I was supposed to be. It was dark and cold and I never could find the door. In my sleep, I would actually move large pieces of furniture around my bedroom trying to find the way out . . . [p. 15]

There is more than one way to understand this dream. At some level, it is perhaps the dream of a first daughter, in love with her father, competitive and hateful toward her demeaned mother, frightened of, and guilty about, the Oedipal victory she also desires. But it may also represent the acute experience of being lost in transmission, of feeling locked into the wrong place, alone and terrified. That the child Jane dreamed her mother's desperation for an exit as her own might speak, not only of the pain a child feels in response to a parent's pain, but also to the child's strong identification with both the parent's pain and their task—in this case, the desperate task of getting out—as deeply hers to accomplish, perhaps for both parties. Jane Fonda came to feel that "trying to find the way out" was her task for a lifetime, and an unlikely moment in that process involved one of the psychiatric hospitals in which her mother had been treated.

Many years after her mother's death, the adult Fonda petitioned for and received her mother's psychiatric record. "I was alone in a hotel room . . . when I opened the thick envelope. When I saw the title, 'Medical Records of Frances Ford Seymour Fonda,' I couldn't breathe. I . . . crawled into bed . . . my body started shaking" (p. 25). How sweetly evocative it is that Fonda crawled into a bed—with her mother, so to speak—after so many dreams that had led her to bolt from her bed and from the terrifying identification with her mother's plight. With the good fortune of good enough early development, a child's bed is one of their first holding environments (Winnicott, 1965), the legacy of maternally derived security, into which one can safely relax and from which one can dream the stories one needs to tell oneself. Jane returns to a bed in the hope that its holding will give her the strength to face a very different kind of bedtime story—a real life story that functions like one of those terrifying children's fairy tales and says to Jane, now after the fact, "Learn about this potential you so it doesn't become the actual you."

In these records, Fonda learnt for the first time things she had not known but had "caught the doomed scent of" (p. 30) as a child and had, she thought, lived out in some way in her own life: that, for example, her mother had been sexually molested as a little girl, that she had quite literally been imprisoned as a child by a disturbed father, and that she had lost her own mother to a younger, illness-prone sister named Jane. So, in her own life, the little girl Jane loses her mother to an illness and seems to call her back through illnesses of her own. She dreams of being imprisoned in the wrong room.

Perhaps most profoundly, the adult Jane realized that she knew in her body, though not in her consciousness, something about her mother's molestation, and that it had shown itself in her own relationship to sexuality, not only in a virtual imprisonment as the sex object of powerful men in the movie industry but, to her astonishment, in a puzzling preoccupation: "For the last decade—not knowing why until now—I have been drawn to studying the effects of sexual abuse on children" (p. 29). Jane Fonda went on to found the Georgia Campaign for Adolescent Pregnancy Protection in 1995, illuminating in the process the link between childhood sexual abuse and teenage pregnancy.

Gould (2002), reporting his experience as consultant to the United States Holocaust Museum, relates a frequent occurrence. An aged man, in a rumpled jacket, goes to the information desk, hands the receptionist a box, and says, "Will you hold this for me?" The box turns out to contain, in the example Dr Gould cited, the tattooed skin that this man had cut from his arm when he was freed from the concentration camp and which he had kept hidden for fifty years. "I'm going to die soon; I haven't told my family about this and I don't want them to find it," he says; "Will you hold it for me?"

This is a most unusual definition of a "holding environment", but a critical one. Because, to the degree that the traumatized person cannot contain his experience, it is lived out in one way or another in his or her family, and to the degree that it cannot be contained or metabolized there, it relies on—it absolutely needs—institutions to hold its objects, its affects, and the evolving societal narrative into which traumatized people may bring their experience. The Holocaust Museum serves that purpose for an aging generation of survivors and their families; the medical records department of a psychiatric hospital served that purpose for Jane Fonda, as she attempted to come to terms with the private holocaust of her mother's life.

As a child, Fonda's intuitions, even premonitions, about her mother "scared me, and I moved away from it. Now as an adult, I can see it as *her* story, not mine" (p. 30). "I have spent far too much energy obliterating all in my life that represented my mother. This has taken a profound toll." "I moved out of myself—my body—early on and have spent much of my life searching to come home." "Dedicating this book to her marks another turning point . . ." (p. x).

Jane Fonda's account of someone who "passed away long ago" but whose "murmuring blood" leads to a "burden upon (her) fate" and to "gesture(s) that rise up from the depths of time" in her own life is a compelling illustration of becoming lost in the transmission of trauma. Her autobiography is also a story of having found herself, with the help of family, friends, therapists, and the stories preserved and yet so often buried in psychiatric records—another reminder to the mental health profession that clinical work is close kin to journalism, indeed that it records the very personal and thus sacred histories cut out of accepted social discourse (Davoine & Gaudilliere, 2004).

Becoming found in transmission means, inevitably, separation—"her story, not mine"—but not repudiation. Instead, it opens a space for grief, for pity in its more honourable sense, and for genuine understanding of the other on whom one's own sense of self has depended and from whom an essential transmission has taken place. As Fonda learnt, obliteration of the other obliterates the self as well; in her case, it obliterated her capacity to inhabit her body. For the former child dreaming of being locked in the wrong room and desperate to find the way out, Fonda's words are striking: in her dread of the transmission, she "moved out" of her body and now she can "come home". And she can do so because she has realized that the moving out of her body *was* the transmission, conveyed, for example, in her mother's showing her the botched breast implant, one of the many marks of her having left her own body to dissociatively survive her childhood and to put it in the desperate service of holding on to a man as an adult.

Jane Fonda, too, has made marks—marks on a page, which became a book, the dedication of which to her mother "marks" a turning point, she says. She has found herself in the process of finding her mother. Thus, the process of transmission of trauma finds its most profound endpoint—the inscription of emotional truth into the narrative of the generations, honouring one and liberating the other.

References

Davoine, F., & Gaudilliere, J-M. (2004). *History Beyond Trauma*. New York: Other Press.

Fonda, J. (2005). *My Life So Far*. New York: Random House.

Gould, L. (2002). Managing depressive anxieties: consulting to the United States Holocaust Memorial Museum. Presentation given at the Austen Riggs Center, 11 January.

Rilke, R. M. (1945). *Letters to a Young Poet*. Mineola, New York: Dover, 2002.

Winnicott, D. W. (1965). The theory of the parent–infant relationship. In: *The Maturational Processes and the Facilitating Environment* (pp. 37–55). New York: International Universities Press.

INDEX